CASSELL STUDIES IN PASTORAL CARE AND
PERSONAL AND SOCIAL EDUCATION

TAKING CHILDREN SERIOUSLY

Other books in this series:

R. Best (ed.): *Education, Spirituality and the Whole Child*

R. Best, P. Lang, C. Lodge and C. Watkins (eds): *Pastoral Care and Personal-Social Education: Entitlement and Provision*

M. Calvert and J. Henderson (eds): *Managing Pastoral Care*

G. Haydon: *Teaching about Values: A New Approach*

P. Lang, R. Best and A. Lichtenberg (eds): *Caring for Children: International Perspectives on Pastoral Care and PSE*

P. Lang with Y. Katz and I. Menezes (eds): *Affective Education: A Comparative View*

O. Leaman: *Death and Loss: Compassionate Approaches in the Classroom*

J. McGuiness: *Counselling in Schools: New Perspectives*

J. McGuiness: *Teachers, Pupils and Behaviour: A Managerial Approach*

L. O'Connor, D. O'Connor and Rachel Best (eds): *Drugs: Partnerships for Policy, Prevention and Education*

S. Power: *The Pastoral and the Academic: Conflict and Contradiction in the Curriculum*

J. Ungoed-Thomas: *Vision of a School: The Good School in the Good Society*

P. Whitaker: *Managing to Learn: Aspects of Reflective and Experiential Learning in Schools*

CASSELL STUDIES IN PASTORAL CARE AND
PERSONAL AND SOCIAL EDUCATION

TAKING CHILDREN SERIOUSLY

Applications of Counselling and Therapy in Education

Edited by

Steve Decker, Sandy Kirby,
Angela Greenwood and Dudley Moore

CASSELL
London and New York

Cassell
Wellington House
125 Strand
London WC2R 0BB

370 Lexington Avenue
New York, NY 10017-6550

www.cassell.co.uk

First published 1999

British Library Cataloguing-in-Publication Data
A catalogue record for this book is available from the British Library.

ISBN   0-304-70518-7 (hardback)
       0-304-70519-5 (paperback)

Typeset by Kenneth Burnley, Wirral, Cheshire
Printed and bound in Great Britain by Biddles Ltd, Guildford and King's Lynn

Contents

Series Editors' foreword

There is a great deal of feeling attached to schooling. Anyone who has read, watched or listened to the 'work' which children and teenagers produce as the result of a well-planned learning experience – we eschew the words 'well-taught lesson' intentionally – will know that the emotions are a significant factor. Learning is by no means exclusively cognitive. Indeed, our response as observers is itself not purely intellectual. Those of us whose task it is to assess teachers and students against supposedly objective criteria, know on reflection that our judgements are influenced by our feelings: we 'warm' (or not) to the teacher or find ourselves inspired, moved or touched by elements of beauty or pathos he or she introduces to the topic. The inclusion of the words 'school phobic' in our educational vocabulary indicate the extent to which just one emotion – fear – might thwart the aims of institutionalized learning completely.

The relationships between emotions and intellect, between feeling and thinking, and between all these and behaviour are clearly complex. When we respond to an experience with, say, fear, do we do so because we apprehend danger at some subconscious level, or is our (cognitive) understanding of the situation an essential prerequisite for the danger to be recognized? None of the interactions which make up our daily existence are without emotional content, that is for certain. Yet the school curriculum seems at times to have been conceived as though they were. Neither the potential of feelings for enriched learning experiences, nor the capacity of emotional factors to disrupt, block or destroy the child's ability to learn are given the importance they deserve. Moreover, if we accept that there are depths of feeling beneath the surface – feelings of rage, terror, betrayal, longing and so on – against which the more rational ego defends (McGuiness 1998, pp. 66–8), we must acknowledge that most of the teacher's work is with the superficialities of personality and that our claims to develop the 'whole child' are hardly justified.

The merit of this particular book is not just that it takes children as emotional beings seriously, but that it takes seriously the implications for the caring professions – notably teachers but clearly also those involved in counselling and therapy in educational contexts – of the fundamental importance of the emotions. In the age of the 'literacy hour' and the 'numeracy strategy', a proper consideration of *emotional* literacy by those who determine the curriculum is still a long way off. If they read this excellent volume it will be brought a good deal closer.

RON BEST AND PETER LANG

REFERENCE

McGuiness, J. (1998) *Counselling in Schools: New Perspectives.* London: Cassell.

Preface

The idea for this book emerged after we had collaborated on counselling and therapy projects in education for several years. We each had very different backgrounds and experience in education but had developed a common conviction that generally there was a clear need for a more focused approach to emotional issues in schools. We tested this conviction with some research, reported elsewhere (Moore et al. 1993, 1996), which confirmed that there are a significant number of pupils whose learning is affected by emotional disturbance and whose needs are not met with the resources normally available to schools. We then decided to establish our own Counselling and Therapy Service for Schools in order to put into practice some of the recommendations we developed from the results of our research.

Through our various contacts we were aware that although there were many other examples of good practice in this field, provision for the emotional needs of children in schools remained patchy and overall woefully inadequate. We wanted to try to do something more to gain wider recognition of this issue. This book was then born from the desire to promote the cause in which we believe so firmly: children have the right to have their emotional needs taken seriously.

STEVE DECKER, SANDY KIRBY
ANGELA GREENWOOD AND DUDLEY MOORE
March 1999

REFERENCES

Moore, D., Decker, S., Greenwood, A. and Kirby, S. (1993) Research into demand for counselling/therapeutic provision in a group of primary schools. *Educational Research,* 35(3), 276–81.

Moore, D., Decker, S., Greenwood, A. and Kirby, S. (1996) Research into demand for counselling/therapeutic provision in a group of secondary schools. *Pastoral Care in Education,* 14(1), 3–6.

Notes on contributors

Kate Ashby trained at the Froebel Educational Institute and has had fifteen years' experience as a classteacher in London primary schools. She has worked with both able/talented children and those with special needs. She has a particular interest in emotional literacy and has attended circle-time courses and the Antidote conference. She has now left the state sector in order to join a small school where she hopes a more holistic approach will put the child, not the paper, back at the centre.

Steve Decker is Head of the Counselling Division at Anglia Polytechnic University. He is a chartered psychologist, having practised as a local authority educational psychologist. He is also the co-founder and co-director of the Benfleet Open Door Service, a voluntary counselling agency which was started in 1979. He currently offers counselling to adults and young people.

Heather Geddes is a teacher interested in children whose social and emotional experiences interfere with their capacities to learn. As a result of the experience of working in an Intermediate Treatment Unit for young people at risk she trained as an educational therapist and subsequently worked in child guidance. Here she appreciated the value of collaborative work between disciplines and has since promoted joint work and training with teachers working with children with emotional and behavioural difficulties in the classroom. She is currently involved in research with a particular focus on Attachment Theory and working with children 'out of school' and in private practice.

Michael Green is in the final year of training as a child psychotherapist with the Society of Analytical Psychology in London. He is currently working at a child and family centre in east London. Prior to training as a psychotherapist he taught English in mainstream secondary schools and an off-site unit, then was the specialist teacher in a child guidance unit where he developed his interest in therapeutic work with children in their own schools.

Angela Greenwood returned to primary teaching in 1982 following pre-school development work in Zambia and a break when her children were small. Experiences with children whose difficulties were severely affected by emotional factors prompted her to train as an educational therapist in 1989. Educational therapy thinking and practice has been invaluable in her work with children and with teachers and families in her position as a Special Educational Needs Co-ordinator at a primary school, and in clinical work with individual children and groups. As a member of Antidote she believes in the importance of emotional literacy and emotional health for the development of a healthy society. Angela Greenwood is a Quaker.

Dr Peter Hindley is a Consultant and Senior Lecturer in Child and Adolescent Psychiatry at St George's Hospital Medical School and with the Deaf Child and Family Services, Pathfinder Mental Health Trust, at Springfield Hospital, London.

Gill Ingall worked for many years as a teacher both in the north of England and in London. For much of that time, she specialized in working with children with emotional and learning difficulties, both within a school setting and in off-site units. Her work as groups teacher in an inner city primary school took place in parallel to her starting the Observational Studies course at the Tavistock Clinic. Since 1994 she has trained as a child psychotherapist there. During the training, she continued her interest in schools by working as a school counsellor in a secondary school for a year.

Sandy Kirby is head of personal and social education and staff development manager in a comprehensive school in London. Both aspects of her work require her to be involved in the emotional development of both students and beginning teachers whilst also supporting the training needs of the whole staff. She is a trained counsellor and is actively working with young people.

Stuart Livingstone has been a headteacher in a state primary school for the past decade. As a secondary special needs teacher he was introduced to using therapeutic disciplines in schools by Steve Decker. He has developed these ideas over the past fifteen years and has now created a model which is systemic in structure following and adapting ideas from the Tavistock Centre, London. Recently appointed to another primary school, Stuart is working with a senior lecturer at Homerton College, Cambridge in order to undertake research into the potency of systemics within a school which is new to this way of working.

Jean Lloyd works part-time as Senior Lecturer in Education (English) at Anglia Polytechnic University, School of Education and has twenty years' teaching experience, predominantly in early years mainstream education. Since qualifying as a counsellor and undertaking further training in working with children with emotional difficulties, she combines the above post with work as a child therapist in school and agency settings. She has recently begun work at the Little Haven Children's Hospice in Essex.

Margaret Lush trained as a musician and started her working life as a peripatetic instrumental teacher. Her interest in understanding children led her to complete an MA in the psychoanalytical observation of infants and young children as well as a foundation course in group therapy, both at the Tavistock Clinic. In January 1995, jointly with Gill Ingall, she addressed the conference of the Forum for the Advancement of Educational Therapy and Therapeutic Teaching on their group work in a primary school. Margaret Lush is currently looking after her own small child, and hopes in the future to train as a child psychotherapist.

Paul McKeever has lived and worked with young people in south London for thirty years, following his work in the early years of the Cotswold Community. He has been involved variously at adventure playgrounds, as a detached youth worker, at a centre for drug users, with residential initiatives for the young homeless, and at various group projects for distressed and delinquent young people. He has studiously avoided any type of qualification and most forms of training, other than British Sign Language, which he recommends as the key to direct and unambiguous communication.

Dudley Moore has more than thirty-five years' experience of working in a wide variety of settings in mainstream and special education. His interest in language acquisition led to a PhD on phonological development in deaf children and the publication of several articles in this field. As a trained counsellor he works in a private capacity for Open Door (a voluntary service). After early retirement from the headship of Hawkswood School and Service for deaf children he now works part-time for the National Deaf Children's Society.

Jenny Mosley is Director of Quality Circle Time, a consultancy that promotes circle time for adults and children nationally and internationally. She also is a lecturer on an MEd for Creative Arts in Therapy, Education/Positive Relationships/ 'Counselling' and group work at the School of Education, Bristol University. She is the author of *Turn Your School Round, Quality Circle Time in the Primary Classroom* and, with Eileen Gillibrand, *She Who Dares Wins*.

Ruth Musgrave is employed by Newham Conflict and Change Project in east London. She works with schools interested in developing an ethos of mutual respect based on nurturing healthy relationships. Her input includes running workshops on creative ways of working with conflict with teachers, lunchtime supervisors, students and sometimes parents. She also helps schools to set up peer mediation schemes. She has spent the last twenty-five years working as a teacher, adult educator and trainer in Britain and in Bangladesh.

Helen Reed is the Personal and Social Development Co-ordinator for the National Deaf Children's Society (NDCS), a voluntary organization for parents and families of deaf children. She is a culturally deaf person and uses both her personal and professional experiences in all aspects of her work with deaf children, their families and professionals in the field of deafness. She has worked as a research psychologist with deaf adults who have mental health needs at the Pathfinder Mental Health Services NHS Trust in London and was educated at the Universities of Liverpool and Bristol. She is a member of the Deaf Family Therapy Team and also represents NDCS on the British Society of Mental Health and Deafness.

Gillian Salmon trained as a teacher and worked in a range of educational settings. As a mature student, she took a psychology degree at Birkbeck College and then trained as an educational therapist at the Tavistock Clinic. She is Programme Convener of the Diploma in Educational Therapy, organized by the Forum for the Advancement of Educational Therapy and Therapeutic Teaching and validated by the Roehampton Institute. In 1987 she went to Edinburgh University to train as an educational psychologist and she currently works with Thurrock Educational Psychology Service in a post which incorporates work in the Child and Family Consultation Service.

Introduction

Dudley Moore

Taking children seriously? What do we mean?

Firstly, we mean the whole child: the breathing, thinking, feeling, talking, unique individual, who perceives, interacts, responds with all of her being. Secondly, we mean trying to understand what is being communicated by the child and responding with care and respect by listening and observing attentively, thinking carefully about her behaviour and its meaning and avoiding a knee-jerk response to difficult, challenging behaviour. We also assert that the child has a fundamental need for significant adults in her life to take her seriously, and we believe that a school potentially provides an environment in which this could be done to the greater benefit of child, adult and, ultimately, society. At the present time this notion appears to be pie in the sky. However, the following chapters contain evidence of some encouraging work being done in this area, and suggestions about how schools can move towards becoming healthier environments for emotional growth.

In putting this book together, we have tried to provide some practical answers to what we see as being extremely important, if somewhat neglected, questions about the emotional world of children within the British education system. Any sensitive teacher faces these questions every day of the working week:

- What can be done about the feelings which erupt in the classroom and disrupt learning?
- Learning is clearly being blocked by some emotional trauma – how can we deal with it, and help the child become free to learn?
- The National Curriculum is all very well, but . . . aren't we forgetting something important?
- Can I cope with the feelings this child is arousing in me? Can I respond more helpfully, not just react to her demands?
- How can I deal with the needs of the curriculum plus the needs of the child?

When these questions are not taken seriously at the appropriate time children's education suffers, teachers' efforts are undermined, and the government produces some worrying statistics.

For those with ears to hear and eyes to see there is enough evidence around to demonstrate that it makes good sense to focus some attention on the emotional wellbeing of our children, for example the work of Goleman (1996) referred to in Chapter 5 by Jean Lloyd, or Wilson (1996). Concern about this issue has prompted the formation of Antidote, a group of professionals whose aim is 'to create an emotionally literate culture, where the facility to handle the complexities of emotional life is as widespread as the capacity to read, write and do arithmetic' (Antidote 1997). The fact that there is a significant problem to be dealt with is beyond dispute. The Mental Health Foundation in 1993 calculated that nearly two million children under the age of 16 (1 in 5 schoolchildren) suffer from mental health (or emotional/behavioural) problems, Hayden (1997) found that primary school exclusions tripled over a two-year period, and our own research (Moore et al. 1993, 1996) has indicated that in primary schools at least 8 per cent and in secondary schools at least 5 per cent of pupils suffer some emotional disturbance which badly affects their learning. (We also found that generally schools do not have the resources to meet the needs of these pupils, although they do recognize the value of counselling/therapeutic work, and place it at the top of their list of preferred resources.) In its Green Paper 'Excellence for all Children' (DfEE 1997) the Labour government recognizes the problems posed by children with 'emotional and behavioural difficulties', realizes the need for an emphasis on preventive measures and acknowledges the high cost to society of failure to tackle the problem. For many pupils any preventive measures will come too late, so both preventive and remedial action is needed. We support the view of Morrisroe and Millward (1998) that a strong emphasis should be placed on a preventive approach, and a rationale can be provided for school-based work on emotional literacy which empowers and enables individuals. Among the elements in the government's proposed overall strategy are 'a range of specialist support to meet the varied needs of pupils within this broad group', 'wider dissemination of existing best practice' and 'early identification and intervention'. We feel that this book has something to contribute to these areas in a very practical way.

There is also an important point to make about the imbalance we perceive in the current approach to education. Over the past few years there has been an enormous emphasis on the curriculum – the content of education has been more and more closely examined and defined, while its delivery has been rigorously inspected. There is a danger that, in the current gloss of highly efficient, precisely defined content and systems, the needs of the individual child, particularly the emotional ones, remain totally in the shade. This could well have undesirable consequences for our future society (Goleman 1996). The tension between the child and the curriculum, the process and the content have been the subject of debate for many years, and no doubt getting the balance right will exercise educational minds for many years to come. There is a place for the efficient and rigorous work on the curriculum, but there must also be a prominent place for the needs of the individual, including emotional needs (Bennathan 1997, Collarbone 1997).

We feel that in the current climate this latter place has been lost: the balance has tilted steeply away from the child with a focus concentrated on quantitative assessment at the expense of those qualitative aspects of education which cannot be easily measured. The work described in this book shows some of the ways in which this imbalance might be corrected.

One of the reasons why the work featured here achieved results is that the professionals involved, despite considerable constraints, made the time to think seriously about the children they were trying to help. We are very conscious that the demands made on most teachers allow little or no time for them to think about the emotional development of their pupils, or deal with the emotional factors in teaching and learning (Saltzberger-Wittenburg, Henry and Osborne 1983); this is reflected in the fact that most teacher training has now become entirely curriculum focused, as child development and psychology have been eroded from course content. If teachers do not have the time to think about their pupils as individuals, then certainly children are not going to learn to think about their own feelings and how they affect their behaviour. It is our view that time can be found without compromising curriculum work, for emotional issues arise throughout the curriculum; indeed it can be argued that if time is not found then curriculum work will be compromised anyway, since intellectual and emotional processes do not function separately because they are inextricably interwoven. Hence time must be found!

Some time could be found in the personal-social area of the curriculum, but in general this opportunity has been neglected, as the subject is often given low status, presented in tutorial time by teachers without any specific training to deal with socio-emotional competence. Schools have also been under increasing pressure to avoid investment in those areas where it is difficult to find a measurable outcome to be expressed as an impressive statistic.

In the first part of this book Paul McKeever and Steve Decker look at some of the issues underlying pupils' failure in the education system. They pose some difficult questions about how we can make learning relevant, how we can provide motivation, how we can salvage some dignity for such pupils. Paul McKeever vividly describes the extreme disaffection which can result from failing to address individual emotional needs and Steve Decker discusses the same issue from a more general point of view. This opening part, emphasizing what can go wrong, shows the clear need for the kind of therapeutic approaches described in the following parts, and points to the need for us all to take emotional issues seriously.

In Part II, Michael Green and Angela Greenwood explore ways in which imaginative and creative work can be used as a vehicle for helping children deal with difficult emotions. Jean Lloyd gives examples of counselling/play therapy at work in a primary school and Sandy Kirby discusses two ways of counselling secondary students, contrasting a short, focused approach with a long-term open approach. Peter Hindley and Helen Reed describe their experience of working on emotional literacy with deaf children and suggest that their package of materials could be used profitably with mainstream pupils too. Inevitably some of these authors are making similar points in different ways. They all illustrate the value of therapeutic opportunities for children and show how this practice can be taken seriously.

Part III deals with group work, with reports on introducing therapeutic groups into primary schools by Michael Green and Heather Geddes and by Gill Ingall and Margaret Lush and with accounts of the use of circle time by Jenny Mosley and Kate Ashby. Here there is a wealth of material, which demonstrates the value of taking groups seriously.

In Part IV the focus shifts to the whole school. Ruth Musgrave describes a project which helped young people deal with conflict, including some examples of peer mediation; Stuart Livingstone applies therapeutic principles to the management of a school; Angela Greenwood shows how the work of an educational therapist can bring significant benefits to a school; and Gillian Salmon looks at how teachers can be helped to think about the emotional responses of themselves and their pupils. This part illustrates the value of taking schools seriously.

All the authors are practitioners who have applied themselves to the task of taking the emotional development of children seriously, and we hope that their experience as reported here will be of some help and encouragement to those readers who wish to find a better way. To adapt the quotation from Miller (1983) cited in Chapter 2, 'every child has a legitimate, narcissistic need to be noticed, understood, taken seriously by the adults in his life'.

REFERENCES

Antidote (1997) *Realising the Potential. Emotional Education for All.* Report on Antidote Conference, London Voluntary Sector Resource Centre, January 1997.

Bennathan, M. (1997) Every child a valued child. In Proceedings of Antidote Conference. London Voluntary Sector Resource Centre, January 1997.

Collarbone, P. (1997) A community of learners. In Proceedings of Antidote Conference, London Voluntary Sector Resource Centre, January 1997.

DfEE (1997) *Excellence for All Children. Meeting Special Educational Needs.* Norwich: The Stationery Office.

Goleman, D. (1996) *Emotional Intelligence.* London: Bloomsbury.

Hayden, C. (1997) *Children Excluded from Primary School.* Milton Keynes: Open University Press.

Miller, A. (1983) *The Drama of the Gifted Child: The Search for the True Self.* New York: Basic Books.

Moore, D., Decker, S., Greenwood, A. and Kirby, S. (1993) Research into demand for counselling/therapeutic provision in a group of primary schools. *Educational Research,* 35(3), 276–81.

Moore, D., Decker, S., Greenwood, A. and Kirby, S. (1996) Research into demand for counselling/therapeutic provision in a group of secondary schools. *Pastoral Care in Education,* 14(1), 3–6.

Morrisroe, J. and Millward, L. (1998) School-based prevention and counselling psychology. *Counselling Psychology Review,* 13(1), 18–25.

Saltzberger-Wittenburg, I., Henry, G. and Osborne, E. (1983) *The Emotional Experience of Learning and Teaching.* London: Routledge and Kegan Paul.

Wilson, P. (1996) *Mental Health in Your School.* London: Jessica Kingsley.

Taking Issues Seriously

'To live a creative life we must lose our fear of being wrong.'
Joseph Chilton Pearse

Part I: Issues

The education system fails some pupils because emotional issues are ignored.

- What are these issues?
- How do they challenge us?

CHAPTER 1

When learning is a dangerous thing

Paul McKeever

One afternoon at the unit where I work, a group of 15/16-year-olds were having a discussion. The topic for debate was supposed to be a consideration of the ways rules and expectations affect our daily lives. As usual, most of the young people were determined to show that nothing existed that could hold sway over them. In their opinion nearly everyone in the world – except themselves – was a fool. Teachers and social workers headed the list. The police were in there too, but at least they merited a certain esteem, given that they could be capable of a certain low cunning mixed with unyielding malice.

Then – almost out of nowhere, as if he were speaking to himself – one of the young men put his hands behind his head and announced with satisfaction: 'I know I'm arrogant, and I know I'm ignorant – but I'm ignorant for all the right reasons.' Taken aback by this declaration, my immediate response had been to check out with the young man what he understood by the word 'ignorant'. Knowing him as I did, I couldn't believe he would ever tolerate anyone using that word against him. It became clear, however, that in his mind 'Ignorant' described a condition of partial knowledge: that you might know some things, but you didn't know everything. Reflecting on it, he remembered a whole list of teachers in secondary school who had told him he was 'ignorant'. Sometimes he had been bothered, other times not. The thing that had made the difference was the tone of the voice – the attitude he perceived behind the words. Indeed, in his short secondary school life, he had been expelled from two schools because he had assaulted teachers who he thought had been 'looking at him'. In effect, his problems with learning stemmed not from intellectual considerations but from the attitudes which he suspected lay behind certain teachers and the educational process that they upheld – and which in his case he felt as judgemental, dismissive and personally abusive.

This particular young man was the son of drug-dependent parents. He was large, white, untidy and dirty, with little sense of routine. He struggled to maintain an ordinary school existence but he was usually tired and disorganized, and he was likely to deal with any criticism – real or imagined – with his fists.

By the time I met this young man at 15, he had been out of school completely for over a year. No alternatives had been offered him. The authorities worked on the assumption that because he had been unco-operative and violent in two schools, he would behave similarly in others. They saw clear evidence that he had no particular appetite for education, and I even suspect that they may have thought they were doing him and themselves a favour by allowing him to 'pass out' of the school system two years early. The secret acknowledgement was that education wasn't for the likes of him.

The thing that had changed the situation was the prospect of both his parents being sentenced to prison. Suddenly the young man might need to be accommodated by Social Services and so some sort of action had to be taken.

The Wayside Centre where I work is a small unit for up to 12 young people who are usually between 15 and 16 years of age. It attempts to offer both group work and education. The project is funded primarily by Social Services, with Education funding the salary of one teacher. The criteria for referral have grown ever tighter over the years and now allow only for children accommodated by the local authority, children on the Child Protection Register, those who are persistent offenders in danger of custody, or offenders who have just been released from custody. In each case the young person must have no other possible educational placement. Essentially we are the social and educational equivalent of the Last Gulch Saloon.

The centre is non-residential so the young people live in a variety of situations – foster homes, children's homes, a few with their parents. It is not rare for some of the young people effectively to be homeless.

The young people who attend Wayside cannot be regarded as typical. It sometimes feels as if we function as a bizarre distillate formed from the whole haphazard range of personal and social malfunctioning: disordered, inconsistent and abusive homes; poor social skills; predatory and superficial peer relationships; manipulatory and hostile relationships with adults; serious exploitation; lack of feeling for others; profound depression and worthlessness.

Hoghughi (1992) aptly describes such catch-all labelling as 'the ragbag or dustbin category of characteristics'. From the psychiatric and counselling points of view, such a 'dustbin category' holds little allure. These young people have always defied assistance. They disregard appointments and when you finally meet them they tell you to 'fuck off'. No remarkable insight will change their lives, nor will a resonant title like Attention Deficit Disorder combined with a Ritalin-type drug give a certain medical respectability to their behaviour. Instead they are consigned to a no man's land of neglect and rejection.

They are among us but not a part of us. Politically they are disowned.

Yet one experience is common to all these young people: for the major part of their lives they have been involved with schools. At age 4 or 5 they entered primary school and set off on their educational careers.

Within that school experience there is another common trait. All will have failed to last the course. Some will have stopped attending school, others will have been expelled. Most of them will have been identified as having 'special educational needs'. Some will have been to specialist schools, including boarding schools, Educational and Behavioural Difficulties schools and Community Homes with Education. Various solutions will have been attempted and most will have failed. All of them by age 15 will have ended up with nothing.

Such was the case with the young man in my group. Expelled from two schools, he had had his chance and had blown it. He could regard this as a just reward for his misbehaviour and hostile attitudes, or he could deal with it another way.

He chose another way. Essentially he turned the system on its head. Instead of allowing the school to diminish and reject him as a fool and a failure, he reversed the process and dismissed them. In this way he managed to hold on to some measure of self-respect and a belief in his own functioning.

It is my contention that a number of our most disaffected young people – including some who may still attend school – have developed strategies for emotional survival that are based on a denial of the very validity of learning. I would go further: it is my experience that certain young people in their middle adolescence set about dismantling what they may have learnt earlier in their school lives. In order to survive intact, they are compelled to reject not only school and teachers but more fundamentally the intellectual apparatus that allows them to think logically, assess evidence, learn from experience and pursue conclusions.

In contrast to the many young people who experience education in a fairly neutral way, accepting information with perhaps a slight query, these young people resist information as if their lives depended upon it. One plus one equals two may seem the most trite piece of learning. Why is it then, that so many of these young people have such tremendous difficulty with such fundamental mathematics?

It is never lack of ability. Rather it is what these sums represent. Namely, an ordered, predictable world where the same safe things happen reliably over and over again. A place which is fair and just. A world which is secure and under control. A world which bears no resemblance to the world these youngsters inhabit, where there is little security, little predictability – other than that the worst will inevitably happen – and precious little safety. Why should $1 + 1 = 2$ when you've been abandoned by your mother, abused by your father and humiliated by the system?

My understanding of what these particular young people are doing is that they are trying to hold on to what is real and valuable within themselves. They know that it isn't much. They fear that it may be nothing at all. They feel under constant threat and attack. And if they subscribe to $1 + 1 = 2$ they understand in the deepest way that this step requires them to let go of their past lives and betray the little bit that makes sense to them. They will become traitors to themselves and thereby guarantee their own nothingness. That is why they are so intransigent, and so ferocious in their antagonism.

These youngsters arrive at our centre with the most threadbare of educational records. Perhaps there will be a statement of educational needs from their primary school, but whatever may have been tried will have been given up in defeat long ago. Written evidence may even extend into their first year of secondary school claiming that certain academic standards have been reached, but by age 15 these accomplishments are profoundly absent. I have regularly witnessed 16-year-olds staring at basic arithmetical questions as if they were hieroglyphic representations from another planet, and I have become accustomed to the same young people regarding a pen or pencil as an object which might have unearthly powers and do them some terrible harm.

I used to think this was the result of lack of practice, of mental rustiness, of unmitigated sloth even. Perhaps these remain part of the story. Much more to the point, though, is what Claude Steele (1991), Amos Wilson (1992) and many others have described in relation to the schooling of black children in the USA as 'the need to dis-identify with achievements'. Although he is writing specifically about black students on another continent, the picture Steele paints is one I recognize daily in my workplace among youngsters both black and white, male and female.

What I see in these young people is not an indifference or carelessness towards education but a profound hostility. Sometimes this can be displayed as defiance, as in the child who refuses to do anything and challenges you to force her compliance. This child will draw some satisfaction at least from the group mayhem and adult indignity she will have generated.

On the other hand the compliant child may well bury his head in a sheet of paper and repeatedly – day after day after day – go over a particular piece of work which he probably accomplished successfully in primary school. Often this young person will tear up the sheet at the end of the session, distraught at the sight of some minuscule imperfection. Consequently he ends up with nothing, and so is able once again to start from scratch the next time.

Neither the defiant nor the compliant young person will have submitted to the purpose of education as defined by those in authority. Such young people will have learnt not one thing laid out for them in the curriculum. By taking up a position of 'psychic alienation' as Steele (1991) describes 'the act of not caring', by 'de-emphasising achievement as a basis for self-esteem', they are endeavouring to protect themselves against 'the spectre of devaluation' that they perceive as the true purpose of the educational system. In such circumstances – as the young man asserted – there are indeed good reasons to be ignorant.

Schools are dominated by adult perceptions and demands. Adults have always arranged the curriculum and organized the system in which teaching takes place. At the present time the adults within schools are in their own turn dominated by ever more prescriptive requirements imposed by politicians and the market economy and the need to demonstrate achievement in terms of examination results and standards of attendance and behaviour.

However, within the process of 'delivering education to its consumers', a school has to engage in a range of dynamic exchanges with its children. If there is to be a productive outcome, it helps if there is a maximum of common beliefs and aspirations between the school, its students, the students' families and the wider social fabric. There is a conviction that both the aims and the process of education are inherently and universally beneficial.

Yet if one looks at the history of education in England no such universal beneficence is apparent. In the decades before the 1960s it was usual for children of the unskilled working class to be relegated as a matter of course to secondary modern schools to be prepared for a future of low-paid employment. During the 1960s and 1970s it was clear that an extraordinary percentage of black boys were designated as 'maladjusted' and were moved into establishments whose priority was behavioural control rather than learning. In the days of comprehensive education a strange conglomeration of truancy centres, sanctuaries, support units, off-site units, sin-bins and Intermediate Treatment Centres were used to soak up a varied assortment of disaffected youths. At the present time, clearly identifiable groups of young people – ranging from black children to children in the Social Services Care system – are notoriously over-represented in expulsions, special schools, referral units and psychiatric treatment programmes – or are supposed to function without any education at all.

This process of selective exclusion from mainstream education has therefore been happening for a long time. The jargon may change, the nomenclature of disguise may vary, but the reality of discarded groups of children stays the same.

In effect, the unspoken consensus is that these children have no apparent educational motivation (either on account of their dysfunctioning families or perhaps – as Hans Eysenck declared – as a result of their genetically inferior IQ). They are held to serve no particular function in the future beyond a kind of pariah existence as single mothers, drug takers, petty criminals, prisoners and psychiatric patients.

In his book *Palm Sunday* the novelist Kurt Vonnegut (1981) uses the term 'Triage' to describe a system common to all human endeavour. Triage is the allocation of limited treatment facilities for battleground casualties. Vonnegut argues that one group (the elite) is favoured and significantly rewarded. The second group (the journeymen) have access to limited resources as long as they perform adequately certain tasks and do not challenge the status quo. As far as the third group is concerned, it is ignored, faceless and invisible – indeed, Vonnegut observes, they 'might as well be corpses'.

It is my experience in over twenty years of work with disaffected young people in London that the overwhelming majority of them belong to this third group. They have no presence beyond being objects of fear and disapproval. Essentially they are poor and/or black. In this light, issues of individual pathology or educational impairment seem minor matters, contributory rather than fundamental.

As things stand, these young people experience education not as an enrichment of their lives which may lead to their own advancement but as something which may destroy the precarious foundations upon which they base their existence and which must therefore be resisted at all cost.

It is common to view individual young people as 'the problem'. Evidence is gathered to illustrate areas of dysfunctioning. Statements concerning a child's inability to concentrate, disruptive behaviour, serious intellectual underfunctioning, short attention span, volatility, aggression and rudeness are standard. The recommendations put forward to improve matters are equally predictable: firm boundaries, clear structure, individual attention, small groups, consistent teachers and behaviour programmes. It remains a wonder why anyone bothers with assessments at all since the outcomes are so banal.

Indeed the function of assessments is largely for the benefit of the adults. To the hard-pressed teacher an assessment offers the benefit of help or (better) a way out, to the educational psychologist it offers an opportunity to practise her formal skills; to any other adults involved it offers the chimera of a 'solution'. Instead of the daily experience of an exhausting, wearing, confusing and often unlikeable child, the adult is temporarily reassured by words of reason and explanation. Briefly there is relief from powerlessness. As Klaus Theweleit (1987) asserts in his exploration of the potency of fascist urgings in Nazi Germany in his book *Male Fantasies*, 'To the bourgeois ego, the world appears manipulable, controllable, knowable', and its horror is of 'the dark continent' of chaotic disorder that lurks beneath. Franz Kafka (1964), too, wrote that 'The real fear is fear of what lies beneath the surface of things, and this fear will not be dispelled.' In the same way, educational assessments attempt to superimpose 'order' on to members of those groups society most fears and is least prepared to understand.

It is a strange experience to be in the company of young men and women who may be highly knowledgeable about the internal combustion engine, the legal system, drug use and the intricacies of respect and esteem within peer groups but who apparently can't multiply six times two, don't recognize a fraction, are nonplussed by percentages, can't spell their own address, don't know the name of the Prime Minister, locate Jamaica next to Australia, think the North Pole is probably hot, imagine the Thames is the sea and have never heard of Jesus Christ.

It is possible to try to deal with this lack of knowledge by means of an educational onslaught. In this way, there is an assumption that in the past there have been great gaps in learning and there needs to be a reconstruction of limited areas of knowledge. It is as if the individual blocks of information have been somehow mislaid and they need to be collected together again and the cobwebs brushed off. Enthusiasm, good relationships and thoughtful encouragement will raise self-esteem in the student and improve her intellectual functioning. I believe such an effort is misguided and futile, and that there is abundant evidence that working in this way is demoralizing for the teacher and painful for the child. In extreme cases such work is both mentally and physically dangerous, risking violence and abuse.

Years ago a colleague praised the efforts of a 15-year-old boy as he struggled with some maths. It had taken weeks of coaxing to get him ready to attempt any sort of schoolwork. Probably my colleague felt an understandable thrill of achievement as she watched the boy knuckling down and her praise became more fulsome. Suddenly the boy leapt to his feet and slapped my colleague around the face with a ferocious blow. I had to drag him away from her. I felt his body shake with tears. He kept repeating: 'A fuckin' baby should be doing this – a fuckin' baby.'

As a result of this incident it was no surprise that my colleague left her job. The boy's life careered from one such event to another, and within a year he was dead from an overdose of heroin. The problems of addition and subtraction were hardly central to his existence, though a knowledge of volume and quantity might have helped.

This may be an extreme example but I think it illustrates the great tide of powerful emotions that seethes beneath the apparent carelessness and disinterest displayed by certain young people towards school. No one should be fooled by dismissive remarks and cool apathy, as if nothing matters. There is rage here, and passion, and great danger for those who don't recognize it as such and fail to work with it.

Anger and injustice rather than intellectual malfunctioning are at the heart of our work. Stereotypically boys aim their anger outwards while girls aim at themselves. Today young men still threaten to punch my head in as they did twenty years ago, while girls arrive from hospital casualty departments after failed overdoses as they seem to have been doing for ever.

Don DeLillo asked about Jack Ruby, the killer of Lee Harvey Oswald,

Does anyone understand the full measure of his despair, the long slow torment of a life in chaos, going back in time to the earliest incomprehension he can remember, a truant, a ward of court, living in foster homes, going back to the first blow, the shock of what it means to be nothing, to know you are nothing, to be fed the message of your nothingness every day for all your days, down and down the years? (DeLillo 1998)

Listen to the word 'chaos' in that passage. He's not describing a boy who forgets his homework and PE kit, although such a child is often termed 'chaotic'. An untidy bedroom is 'chaotic' too, as if the word were a synonym for 'disorganized'. Chaotic lifestyles suggest poor timekeeping, unreliability, lack of routine, a haphazard attitude to the 'important' things in life, doing everything in a rush and thereby leaving things annoyingly undone.

This is not the chaos DeLillo means, nor is it the chaos that accompanies the young people who attend our centre. Their chaos is that of 'the formless void – the condition of total disorder or confusion'. In our work we have to recognize the profundity of that disorder and confusion, we have to unravel its particular manifestation in each individual child, and we also have to try to understand the different strategies each child has developed in order to function within that chaos and keep herself physically and psychically alive.

SOME YOUNG PEOPLE

B is a 15-year-old white girl. She is the second of 5 children, fathered by 4 different men. She doesn't know her own father. Her mother is a wispy, fragile woman who seems to pay more attention to her dog than to her children. Her mother finds it difficult to talk about B because she gets upset and is reminded of the disastrous way she has managed her life. In effect, she can't properly see B at all because her own preoccupations get in the way.

B is strikingly pale, almost a ghost, and usually wears her hair tied back tightly off her forehead. She has been on the Child Protection Register for many years under the category of emotional abuse and there are considerable suspicions that sexual abuse has also occurred. Sometimes she gives hints but she is never clear. She has been accommodated by Social Services for a year and lives in a local home for adolescents.

The majority of her time she spends in her room, and much of that in bed. Her room is immaculate. Posters of the pop group Take That cover the walls. She forms intense, exclusive relationships with other young people in the home which subsequently fall apart and from that moment there is no sign that any relationship existed. It is wiped out. The board is blank once more.

Fairly regularly, she takes overdoses of paracetamol. Normally she does this outside the home and she phones to say what's happening. She tends not to overdose on her own but with her latest female friend.

She has been interviewed by two psychiatrists who are both deeply concerned. They feel she is very likely to kill herself. One of the doctors has offered appointments for her but she's not interested.

As for her schooling, her attendance at secondary school was always poor and finished in Year 11. School served no purpose for her.

She now attends the Wayside Centre. She is as often absent as present. Sometimes she is prepared to sit down and open a book – but that's as far as it goes. She stares at the page for a while and then starts to complain about feeling ill and wanting to go home. She collapses into a heap or lies across some chairs, hiding her face. She makes no response.

C is a 16-year-old black boy we have been working with for 15 months. When he was less than 6 months old he was left at a police station by his mother. His mother then went into psychiatric hospital. He spent his early years in care before going to live with his maternal grandparents in the Caribbean. At age 12, his mother requested his return to England but the reunion didn't work and he went back into care. In London his father got into contact and was rehoused with the help of Social Services so that C could live with him. This arrangement lasted no more than a few weeks and

C was again back in care – convinced that his father had exploited him to improve his accommodation.

C is well over 6 feet tall and is keenly interested in bodybuilding – as if he is constructing his own personal body-armour. He currently lives with experienced black foster parents. Since returning to England he has hardly been to school. According to C, he has to live life on his own terms and trust nobody. Whatever he considers important, he works out for himself. Any other way is foolishness.

At Wayside, everything we try to do is contested by C. He interrogates us about everything we suggest. If he agrees one time, it doesn't mean he will agree over the same thing again. He is like a giant immoveable stone that can only be shifted a minuscule distance by the continual exertion of every muscle in one's body. It's his contention that as he can read he doesn't need English, as he can add he doesn't need maths, and as for the rest – what he doesn't know doesn't count, and anything more he needs to know he'll work out his own way without interference from fools like us. He is contemptuous of adults and masterfully abusive. He will tolerate nobody else's point of view – particularly a black person's.

A typical session with C will involve 50 minutes of argument and manoeuvres followed by 10 minutes of work. The next session will be the same. And the next. More or less unbroken, for 15 long months.

D is a small, timid-looking white boy of 15 years who always wears a cap pulled down over his eyes. He lives with his mother and elder brother since his alcoholic father finally left home a couple of years ago. In a recent 12-month period he went on a spectacular criminal spree as a lone burglar and conman, for which he received a hefty non-custodial sentence.

His secondary school barely noticed him when he was there and equally didn't notice when he stopped going. The school was surprised when the court brought to their attention the fact that D hadn't attended for 2 years.

At Wayside, D's routine is to arrive late and almost in secret. Faced with work, he will look momentarily eager and then instantly panic. He will bleat for reassurance and stop whenever it's not forthcoming. It is as if he seizes up. If something is explained to him he will nod vigorously and promptly forget. He will not retain information. He always starts from scratch, as if he has wandered panic-stricken into an unknown land. He avoids contact, as if other human beings are poisonous.

E is a 15-year-old girl of mixed race. When she was age 2, one night there was a fire in her home in which her sister died and she herself was terribly burnt. The following years were spent in hospital undergoing a series of complicated and painful operations to rebuild her face, arms and hands.

She has been raped and now lives in a home for adolescents. She has desperate dependent relationships with a variety of young male staff and is prone to bouts of great exhilaration followed by awful immobilizing depressions. Her bedroom is filled to overflowing with soft fluffy toys which she names after members of staff. She is perceptive and articulate with an unnerving instinct for fairness – which makes her a considerable management problem. At night, she can't bear to go to sleep. She too has taken overdoses and talks matter-of-factly about the benefits of death.

She now attends Wayside regularly. She absolutely refuses to co-operate with any part of the programme unless she happens to feel in the mood. As for education, she will have none of it, though she loves discussion and play, and has contracted a sudden enthusiasm for photographic development. Often the only way to communicate with her is through an intricate system of quizzes.

G is black and 16 years old and insists on being called a 'child' rather than a 'young man'. When G was 12, his father died after a tragic illness and the family has never recovered. Mother is often overwhelmed with hopelessness, but she places her faith in the wellbeing of her children. At 14, G became increasingly awkward at school and started staying away from home. Despite his mother's wishes, he repeatedly refused to go home and now lives in a private home for black children.

He is able to generate the most intense passions and antagonisms. Every adult who has dealings with him is at some time completely at the end of his tether and dangerously close to being out of control. G seems to have the number of every adult and has his finger on everyone's self-destruct button.

He is capable of the most acute perception of inequality when practised by others yet remains entirely free of any such clarity with regard to his own behaviour. He can detect sophisticated racism and examples of unfairness but can be personally bigoted and obscene to an extreme. The responsibility for injustice always lies with others.

In the classroom he professes to be a model student with model aspirations. However, if a piece of work proves difficult he will promptly blame others for their inadequate explanations. If he gets anything wrong he will declare that Wayside is a 'shit heap' fit only for no-hopers and isn't sufficiently challenging to his abilities. He refuses to attend any session that smacks of reflection and discussion because such matters are 'beneath' him and useful only to 'those misfits who have got problems' – which obviously doesn't include him. He basks in his own accomplishments but can become hysterical with the sense of his own failings.

'I am the devil,' he admitted miserably when we first met him.

WHAT IS TO BE DONE?

If ever there was a bad time for youth to be complicated in its unhappiness it is now. Current therapeutic systems (the few that exist) are set up to work with people who acknowledge their problems and are 'ready to be worked'. Contract-based counselling and Brief Therapy aim at quick solutions. Cost-effectiveness and through-put reign supreme, and the numbers game is the only one that counts. The majority culture demands conclusions and is suspicious of reflection and experience. We behave as if we have forgotten that healing can be tortuous and can take an awfully long time. We cannot admit that some healing will never happen and yet remain prepared to go on trying.

All the young people I have described can survive and may even do well. It is usually to their credit that they have kept functioning for so long. When we first meet them, invariably we are aware that they are burdened human beings. They have scarcely ever been children. They may come with a history of vile behaviour but there remains, always, the ghost of a hurt child.

Our prime function is to face that hurt and work with their sense of aggrieved fury at the injustice that has been done them. In an adolescent, this is rarely a pretty sight. But it has to be done, because without that recognition nothing else can be achieved.

In the main, people prefer to keep pain manageable. They allude to it, skirt around it, control it, minimize it. They fear the consequences. Many of the young people with whom we work are contemptuous of well-intentioned adults because these adults have failed them when it came to the point of containing their anger. Their lives have become a history of exclusions and expulsions so that emotional expression becomes linked with punishment.

This need not be so. A place can be 'safe' and can get on with its business. But it has to be truthful – and truthful in ways that the young people can associate with their own lives. This is not necessarily the truth of 'real life' as seen by adults.

Janusz Korczak, the Polish pedagogue who chose to accompany the children from his orphanage to extermination in Auschwitz, was of the opinion that 'Grownups and children cannot understand each other. It is as if they are a different species' (Lifton 1998). This may be so. But we need to see with the eyes of a child if we want to make any sense to them – like the nursery teacher who spends her days crouched to the ground so that she can experience her classroom at her pupils' level.

All this takes persistence and time. Workers have to 'discover' each child, have relentlessly to find a way through the abuse, the accusations, the projections and the violence. Workers have to create an environment that is evidently fair and have to learn that the fairness is never adequate and know that they will continually fail in their efforts to be fair but must remain prepared to acknowledge to the young person that they have indeed failed (yet again!) but will continue trying.

Lies, prevarications, jargon, obfuscation are daily things. As Winnicott (1957) maintained, 'It is a prime characteristic of adolescents that they do not accept false solutions.' Korczak, too, warned of the capacity of children to detect 'the ring of a counterfeit coin'.

Instead of behaving as if we adults are honourable people who deserve respect and who know what's best, we have to recognize that we have to earn these children's attention. Indeed, to some degree, we have to earn their forgiveness. As Winnicott observed, 'The anti-social child is searching in some way or other to get the world to acknowledge its debt.' It is only when a young person feels good enough about herself to be able to forgive some of the pain that adults have caused that she can at last begin to move intellectually and start to trust in education.

As Claude Steele (1991) bluntly puts it, 'The only reason something is meaningful and worth learning is because a meaningful other wants you to learn and remember it.' If we wish these young people to have a life different from the one prepared for them we must first enable them to leave that life with their dignity intact.

REFERENCES

DeLillo, D. (1988) *Libra*. London: Jonathan Cape.
Hoghughi, M. (1992) *Assessing Child and Adolescent Disorders*. London: Sage.
Kafka, F. (1964) *Diaries 1910–1923*, ed. M. Brod. Harmondsworth: Penguin.
Lifton, B. J. (1988) *Janusz Korczak: King of Children*. London: Chatto and Windus.
Steele, C. (1991) Race and the schooling of black Americans. *Atlantic* (magazine, Boston).
Theweleit, K. (1987) *Male Fantasies*. Cambridge: Polity Press.
Vonnegut, K. (1981) *Palm Sunday*. London: Jonathan Cape.
Wilson, A. N. (1992) *Understanding Black Male Violence*. New York: Afrikan World Infosystems.
Winnicott, D. W. (1957) *The Child and the Outside World*. London: Tavistock.

CHAPTER 2

Failing to learn or learning to fail?

Steve Decker

'Why do you think that the school has asked you to see me?' I asked a young man in a secondary school.

'Because I'm mental,' he replied.

'What makes you think that?'

'Well, I must be mental to have to come and see a psychologist,' he answered, with his head drooping.

Unfortunately, this was not an uncommon exchange between youngsters and me. Only the self-description varied between 'mental', 'dumb', 'nuts' and 'stupid'. This response worried me a great deal in my early days of practising as an educational psychologist. I felt that the very fact that I was meeting with some young people was reinforcing exceedingly negative views of themselves. I resolved to do something to combat these views.

I became aware, through talking with many of these young people, that they had devised quite elaborate methods of avoiding being placed in situations which revealed their difficulties. This process has been described as becoming invisible (Pye 1988). Although this response has self-destructive results, it has a certain 'intelligence' about it. I reasoned that as I had access to standardized Intelligence Tests I could show these pupils that they might have specific difficulties but that overall their intelligence was on a par with their peers.

I remember the first time I put my plan into operation. I gave the Wechsler Intelligence Scale for Children to an articulate 14-year-old boy with a reading age of 7.5 years. I was certain that his scores would reinforce my perception of him as a person of at least average intelligence. His overall score was in the 120s (the above average range), with some variability in sub-test scores, but none dropping below average. Having scored up the test when he was present, I drew up the test profile and explained the results to him:

'Now you can see from this line, which represents your scores, as compared to this line beneath it representing the average response, that you are obtaining results well above average. In other words you are not mental, or stupid at all,' I concluded, not without an air of self-gratification.

'But I must be,' he replied, 'because I can't read.'

Such exchanges taught me an important lesson about the nature of self-esteem.

The person who daily fails to do a common task required of all adolescents, i.e. to read, bases her self-assessment of intelligence on more pragmatic criteria than the psychologist with the esoteric compilation of 'pure measures' of intelligence. The child's self-perception is constantly reinforced and she soon begins to incorporate into her self-structure a piece of personal knowledge, 'I cannot read', which becomes extended into a more comprehensive assessment, 'I cannot read because I am mental/dumb/stupid, etc.'

The paradoxical statement 'I have a poor opinion of myself and I don't deserve it!', attributed to W. S. Gilbert, nicely exhibits the complexity of the process of self-assessment. This viewpoint was also held by the psychoanalytically inclined critic Hans Keller who in an early essay wrote,

> There would thus seem to be necessary a twofold preparation for the attainment of self-knowledge, viz. to admit to oneself
> (1) that one isn't so important as one hopes to be and
> (2) that one isn't so unimportant as one fears to be. (Keller 1995)

One can see how the youngster struggling to cope with tasks easily accomplished by her peers can become preoccupied with fears of unimportance and insignificance. Any successful therapy must help achieve the balance indicated by Keller.

MAKING SENSE OF SPECIAL NEEDS WORK

All professionals in the area of special needs have their own biases and assumptions. These are based on a variety of factors including personal experiences, personality and training. The influence of training, as well as the professional culture in which one practises, has an effect on what is considered the appropriate form of 'treatment' to offer the young person with the label 'special needs'. For example, the culture of educational psychology as represented by most training courses gives a strong regard to applied behavioural approaches, systems theory and curriculum-based assessment. Although an understanding of psychometrics is still an important aspect of educational psychologists' culture, it is not stressed as much as it was in the training which I experienced in the 1970s.

Within the psychometrically-biased training I received, there were two features of particular interest: what was seen as valuable to measure, and what was seen as unimportant. The Intelligence Test, as represented by the Wechsler and the Stanford-Binet, was considered the paragon of the psychometric test. Following on close behind were tests which purported to break down complex tasks into simpler sub-abilities in order to help the tester analyse the missing or deficient skills, e.g. tests of reading which looked at the supposed sub-skills making up the complex task of reading. Lower in reliability, validity and training time were tests of personality. I do not recall any lectures on self-esteem and only two briefly mentioned methods of assessment. I was never required to use these measures in training and rarely came across any educational psychologist who used these or other methods of assessing the young person's view of her self. The effect of training on my practice was to predispose me to respond in certain ways because of the expectations of the culture I had absorbed through training and the reinforcement of my peers. However, it did dawn on me that we seemed to be offering a very narrow range of options to young people. As I had always had an interest in the variety of therapies which were in existence, and were constantly developing, it appeared that educational psychology was behaving like the doctor who says, 'I always give these three medicines – they always work, and if they don't then the patient is incurable!'

Fortunately, the culture had those who were pointing to the deficiencies of a strictly psychometric regime. In particular, those psychologists influenced by Kelly's theories of Personal Constructs (e.g. Bannister, Salmon and Ravenette) acted as a useful counter-weight to the prevailing view. Tom Ravenette, especially, was an important influence on my developing practice and I found a framework of special educational needs presented in his book *Dimensions of Reading Difficulty* (Ravenette 1968) a useful aid in making sense of my own practice.

In this book, Ravenette, drawing on the ideas of Jerome Bruner, discusses a way of conceptualizing the difficulties encountered in special educational needs, and from this develops a rationale for the approaches we offer. For me, this had the effect of justifying eclecticism, or its latter-day equivalent of integrative practice, and helped to locate the place of addressing self-esteem within the helping regimes. The framework offers a tripartite division of difficulties encountered when working with children with special educational needs. (The divisions suggested come from the ideas of Ravenette but the development is my own.)

Children with 'coping difficulties'

The phrase 'coping difficulties' is used to indicate those children unable to complete tasks because they lack the necessary skills. For example, in a reception class within infant schools it is expected that there will be a range of self-help skills apparent when children first enter school. One of these skills might be the ability to tie shoelaces. Some children will be proficient at this, others may have a rudimentary ability which may result in a very loose knot likely to become undone, and another group may have no skill at all. The reception classteacher normally takes this in her stride. There is no assumption made about 'innate ability', rather the assumption is that such a skill depends on several factors including finger co-ordination and, most importantly, previous exposure to the skill. In a household where the child has not had to tie shoelaces, either because others perform the task or because there are no lace-up shoes, the skill will not be acquired. Infant teachers understand this and do not immediately classify the child without the skill as having 'special needs'. Instead, when necessary, the skill is introduced and in many infant classrooms will be found a cardboard cutout shoe, with laces, on which the child may practise.

School can be seen as the place where thousands of skills are learned which help the child cope with her present and future environment. When facing a situation requiring certain skills which one lacks, one struggles to cope. The challenges can be met when the appropriate skills are present.

Those familiar with the Special Educational Needs culture of the 1980s will recognize the enormous influence of skills-based approaches within educational psychology. The behaviourally trained educational psychologist will confront the child's problem as a 'coping difficulty' in which the rational approach is to perform an analysis of the task and the required skills. The skills' profile of the child will be obtained and from this a behavioural programme will be devised which offers a structured introduction to the necessary skills. The programme will build in a reward schedule and this acts as the short-term incentive to the child to continue building up the repertoire of skills (e.g. Ainscow and Tweddle 1979).

This approach offered teachers more specific advice than they had previously been used to receiving. Instead of a psychological report concluding 'she needs lots of individual attention', teachers now received more specific advice concerning tasks and programmes of work. In order to fulfil these programmes the child still required 'lots of individual attention' but at least the teacher was more aware of how the time should be used, provided it was available. The approach did offer a useful technology which yielded success with children. It also demonstrated its success through the establishment of a baseline score which enabled teachers to see that progress was being accomplished.

However, in practice it is not always so easy. Teachers are aware that it is possible to give a child a task which, in itself, is not too difficult and yet the child will meet it with an attitude of failure. I can recall on many occasions offering a child a task which was met immediately with a comment such as 'I can't do it' even before it had been examined. I sometimes get maths-phobic adults to experience the same effect in lectures by announcing that 'Before you can leave tonight you must solve the following' and immediately put on the overhead projector screen a mathematical-looking formula. In effect, the task is simple as the final part of the equation multiplies by 0 and thus the answer is 0. However, many adults admit an immediate inner panic which prevents them examining the task in detail. Advocates of the behavioural approach will argue that it is possible to desensitize oneself to this inner panic, but they may underestimate the number of occasions in school on which the panic feeling is repeatedly reinforced. The child in school with a reading difficulty will not only have an extensive history of reinforced failure, but also the reinforcements will continue to occur many times during a school day. Desensitization programmes are likely to have little effect in the face of constant daily reinforcement of failure.

In one sense, a problem with the behavioural approach is its rationality. Unfortunately, humans are often not rational when feelings of potential failure are evoked. The learner who is presented with a structured programme around an area in which she has experienced constant failure may well be propelled into an inner panic which prevents an engagement with the task rationally. I believe that this is why many teachers have struggled to help youngsters through behavioural programmes and yet have not met with success.

Children with 'relevance difficulties'

The second area Ravenette points to is that of motivation. In order to learn, we need to understand the point of learning. We may fail to have acquired the skills through a lack of good teaching or a failure to be exposed to them but we may be perfectly convinced of the need to acquire them (i.e. coping difficulties). However, it is a different matter to be exposed to the possibility of accessing the necessary skills but to see no point in doing so. Anyone who has struggled to achieve an examination in a topic in which they have little intrinsic interest will know how hard it is to learn the material.

I recall a 15-year-old being referred to me for non-attendance at school. She turned up with her school exercise books and presented her case to me in a very rational manner. 'Please look at my books and see if there is anything wrong with them,' she requested. I had to admit that they looked reasonable, if not outstanding. 'I can read, write and do maths at the level I wish.' she continued. 'I do not wish to take GCSEs. I have obtained a good full-time job by lying about my age. If I come back to school for the next eight months I will lose the job and probably, with unemployment the way it is, not be able to get employed when I leave school. Tell me why I should attend.'

I had to admit to being stumped. There was little point in arguing about exams and long-term prospects as the teachers had done this *ad infinitum*. In effect, she was arguing that her actions had more relevance to her than the thought of spending the next eight months in school. Looking at it from her perspective it was difficult to disagree. In the event the problem was not a psychological one, and I refused to work any further with her, which conformed with her wishes if not with the school's!

A further example of relevance difficulties occurred when I visited the home of a 13-year-old non-reader. I had a family discussion, which involved the boy and his parents, and his father soon announced to me, 'I don't know why you're bothering, as I can name you 10 people who can't read and who earn more than £20,000 each year.' It was little wonder that the boy might feel that reading was not a particularly important topic, exposed to this environment.

The behavioural technique attempts to address this problem through the provision of rewards. However, this only provides extrinsic motivation. Indeed the research of Lepper, Greene and Nisbett (1973) suggests that it can be counter-productive to control behaviour extrinsically, as it may lead to a situation where the task is only fulfilled if the reward is apparent. There are not many situations outside behavioural programmes where such contingent reinforcement will occur.

The education system has attempted to look at relevance issues by examining the curriculum on offer. At one time in British education this was the responsibility of the school, but over recent times, with the advent of the National Curriculum, the responsibility has become centralized. The intent is to ensure uniformity and 'relevance' on a general scale.

The special needs pupil is sometimes struggling with relevance at an individual level. If her culture does not value schooling and education such a pupil may be arriving at school with a view that what is on offer is irrelevant. At the personal level, in her daily life, the preoccupations of teachers may seem arcane. I recall a boy of 7 who had not made a start with reading, causing much concern to his infants' school. However, if you attempted to help him through some pre-reading activities he soon engaged you in a discussion about his personal life. In particular, he would want you to know that he was hoping soon to have his own parents. He had spent his life in a children's home and had been informed that he was a possibility for adoption. Not surprisingly this was of much more relevance to him than trying to do matching or copying tasks, which, although he would co-operate, clearly left him cold.

It is important to appreciate the personal nature of relevance. Unless we are aware of the specific and personal circumstances for a child experiencing special needs she is unlikely to be affected by the Secretary of States for Education's belief that the National Curriculum provides a curriculum which is relevant to the 1990s!

Children who 'defend against learning'

We have seen that when children are regarded as having coping difficulties, the limitation of this approach is that it may not give due attention to the emotions associated with failure. An attempt can be made to focus on these emotional aspects by regarding children as 'defending against learning'.

Prior to my formal training as an educational psychologist I had an experience which probably taught me more about the effects of long-term failure than the whole of my training. In order to practise as an educational psychologist I began to realize the need to pass the driving test, as the work would involve a considerable degree of travelling between schools, often with bulky test equipment. I began to take driving lessons. My first failure of the driving test I pinned firmly at the feet of my driving instructor. He was unsympathetic to the needs of an anxious learner, believing that the only motivational tactics possible were those associated with heavy criticism. On the day of the driving test he took me out for an hour before the test and criticized everything I did. As we drew up to the test centre I felt like cutting my losses and going home, and as he left the car he mumbled, 'You may pass.' Needless to say I did not.

On the second occasion of failure I could no longer blame it on the instructor, who I felt was sensitive to my needs as a learner. However, following this failure I found myself with a new set of thoughts. 'Perhaps,' I reasoned, 'I do not need to learn to drive a car. After all, I can ride a motorbike and I am sure you can get carriers which could take the tests.' I even extended this argument against learning to drive a car by reflecting that there might be occasions when I would only need to take a short journey during the day and I could use a bicycle which would be much healthier!

Those familiar with cognitive dissonance theory will see that my mental contortions were an attempt to reduce the discomfort associated with personal failure. Indeed, as the third test approached, I began to experience some even more dissonance-relieving, yet dangerously self-destructive, thoughts. 'Perhaps,' I thought, 'I am not a car driver. Could there be something about me and driving which makes it just impossible for me to function as the driver of a car? It could be that I am congenitally incapable of driving.'

Although with hindsight it is easy to laugh at such thoughts, at the time the reality of them was very strong. I did know about the theory of cognitive dissonance then, but the sense of failure was far stronger than any rational knowledge about the cognitive processes. Fortunately, I passed the driving test on the third occasion, but I do seriously wonder whether I would have proceeded to a fourth attempt.

This taught me a great deal about how children may feel in a situation in which they may be regularly exposed to the experience of public failure. If we take a child failing to read as an example, consider the number of cues each day experienced by such a child within school, even with the most sensitive of teachers. From the wall displays which are unreadable, to the work given to colleagues which they cannot access, to the letters home which they cannot read but their peers can and the many other indirect and direct cues all carrying the same message – 'You can't do something most others can.'

This message is exceedingly painful. The healthy response to pain is to avoid it and therefore this child becomes one who 'defends against learning'. In effect the child may take up a number of different cognitive positions to relieve the pain of failure. Perhaps the child may adopt the strategy of blaming the teacher, but this may be difficult if there are many children who have learned with the teacher. Another position is to downgrade the subject, to act as though it is not important to rectify the area of failure. However, it may be difficult to do this with an area such as literacy, where it is self-evidently the gateway to all learning, which school and parents may continually point out. Unfortunately, the most likely position to be adopted is the most dangerously self-destructive, that the explanation is: 'I am a non-reader.' In other words the continual experience of failure teaches the child a lesson which must become incorporated into the permanent self-image.

Teachers often talk about the shutters put up by children with whom they are attempting to work in an area of failure. It appears to be strange that a child should block attempts to give help. Yet from this perspective we can immediately see what is happening. If the child has experienced the pain of failure around reading she will be alert to any signs that reading is on the horizon, in the way that anyone who has experienced something painful is extra alert to cues of a repetition of the dangerous situation. Into play may come the mental set, 'I am a non-reader.' This may relieve some of the stress by, in effect, arguing that someone who is a permanent non-reader cannot become a reader. In other words, the self-image has fixed on a quality of 'non-readership' which relieves the person of the effort of attempting and the pain of failing.

I have found many instances of this attitude within children who are failing. It is not uncommon to discover a child within junior education who is several years adrift with her reading level. In tracing the history of the child I have discovered firm evidence of a sensory difficulty, often intermittent hearing problems, at the infant level. It is not difficult to hypothesize that the original cause of the child failing to access the early reading work in the infant school was because of the physical difficulty. However, once the child noticed the lack of progress when compared to that of her peers, feelings of failure will begin to take their effect. By the time the child has reached junior education, the physical difficulty may no longer be in existence but the secondary effects of failure may now be making their mark.

Many teachers will recognize this pattern. The problem is how to rectify it.

THE TRADITIONAL RESPONSE

As I have worked with children and considered my responses to their differing needs I have been aware of how 'the system' attempts to deal with the three areas of difficulty outlined above. Children with coping difficulties are now seen as requiring a structured introduction to the needed skills. Teachers and advisers have become adept in using applied behavioural techniques, sometimes linked to information technology, as a response to coping difficulties, often with success.

The area of relevance difficulties has also evoked important responses. At the national level the importance of relevance has been appreciated, although it is not always clearly apparent what values are being incorporated in the justifications of relevance within the National Curriculum. At the more individual level teachers have recognized the need to make what they offer more meaningful to youngsters and I have come across many good examples of individual reading programmes being tailored around the personal interests of the child.

In my view it is the area of 'defending against learning' which evokes far less satisfactory responses from the system. The traditional response is clear and unequivocal. To put it simply the advocates of applied behavioural approaches will argue the following:

> Children who fail do not access the necessary skills. This will affect their self-image and self-esteem. They need to experience success in the areas of failure in order to achieve a more positive view of themselves and to thus influence their self-image. The use of behavioural approaches will address both their lack of skills and their poor self-esteem. The programme is carefully structured to ensure success (not total, but on the majority of occasions). Thus through success we can build up the repertoire of skills alongside a more positive sense of self.

This sounds very persuasive but is built upon a premise, seldom questioned, which is that success leads to a more positive sense of self. Indeed, it may appear to be self-evidently true that if we are successful we feel more positive about ourselves. And yet a moment's reflection might begin to cast some doubts on this. Is it not the case that some very successful and striving people have a drive to keep on proving to themselves that they are worthwhile? Cannot the drive for continual success sometimes be as a compensation for deep inner feelings of a lack of worth?

I believe there may be a cultural matter at issue here. We live in a society where success is held up to all as something to aspire to, and children are well aware of this. The successful person is seen as being achievement orientated and there is an assumption that with this success will go personal fulfilment along with a sense of self-esteem. But is this assumption justified?

It is worth considering the origin of self-esteem in order to see whether success is an important ingredient. In her book *The Drama of the Gifted Child* Alice Miller (1983) considers the origin of self-esteem, drawing on the work of psychoanalysts concerned with early child development. She writes about healthy narcissism, a necessary aspect of healthy development, which provides the basis for a positive sense of self. Within this discussion she isolates the basic ingredients of this need within the infant to develop 'a healthy self-feeling': 'Every child has a legitimate narcissistic need to be *noticed, understood, taken seriously and respected* by his mother' (p. 49; my italics). Although Miller is only discussing early infant development at this point, it is clear that she believes that these ingredients are necessary whenever self-esteem is at risk.

In essence this point of view is arguing that self-esteem can only be enhanced in a relationship, as it is only with another person that one can feel noticed, understood, taken seriously and respected. If, for example, a child is working on a computer-aided structured learning programme then these needs will not be fulfilled. This viewpoint also correlates with another aspect of learning which is known by all teachers and yet is often not fully understood. We argue, as a piece of common sense, that failing does not have to be a disaster. Indeed, teachers may remind us that many scientific discoveries were made through investigating the causes of failure. In failing there may be important information to discover, which may be more important to us than being successful. Yet in spite of this piece of common sense it seems that it is rare in education for these positive effects to be felt. I would suggest that the reason is that the child who fails often feels that she loses some or all of the qualities of the relationship outlined by Miller's view. In other words at the point of failure the child no longer feels 'noticed, understood, taken seriously or respected', and remember that at this point of failure she is likely to be hypersensitive to this possibility.

I would argue that the child who is defending against learning has experienced damage at the level of self-esteem and that in order to gain access to the curriculum she urgently needs this damage to be addressed.

THE PLACE FOR THERAPEUTIC APPROACHES WITHIN EDUCATION

In the early 1970s research reported by the educational psychologist Dennis Lawrence set the cat among the pigeons in the world of 'remedial education' (Lawrence 1971). He showed how the provision of counselling to pupils with reading difficulties and low self-esteem seemed more effective at boosting reading scores than the traditional approach of remedial education. The research was disputed from a variety of quarters, but it did have the effect of raising the issues of the importance of self-esteem in learning and the role of the relationship in influencing feelings about the self.

Although some educational researchers felt that the research had not proved its point, many teachers felt that it confirmed their experience concerning the effect of the relationship on learning. Most sensitive teachers, interested in their pupil's self-esteem, will have had the experience of a child who had previously been a failure suddenly 'cuing in' to them and making a huge boost in learning within a short time.

I recall experiencing this effect as a fledgling educational psychologist. I decided in my first year of practice to offer some individual reading help to several children within a junior school. I felt that I needed the experience of tailoring reading programmes and that by working with several children it would enhance my credibility in offering advice to teachers. In one instance I recall that the child was extremely effective in sidetracking me from the tasks in hand, usually skills-based exercises. Instead, he would talk to me about his life and his interests. Before long the sessions became 'chats' with little or no reading content. I felt guilty about this as I was not fulfilling my strict brief with the school, and yet I was aware that he had a need to talk about issues in his life and that the weekly session was meeting this need. As we progressed, however, interesting reports came from his classteacher. He now seemed more relaxed in class and was making good progress in his reading. His parents reported that 'he seemed lighter'. (I have found this phrase recurring on many occasions from the parents of other children who have been worked with in this way.) All in all, the effect of providing this therapeutic space seemed very positive.

Lawrence's work may appear to be inconclusive to those who want to argue strictly from an educational research perspective, but the experience of those who offer counselling and other therapeutic approaches in schools does back up these results. It is important, though, to see what is being argued here, which is not just that some children would benefit from the effects of counselling or therapy in schools. The clear conclusion is that children's self-esteem can be damaged through failure and this may then affect their ability to access the skills they need. The reparative need in these children is for a relationship which notices, understands, takes seriously and respects them. In some cases it may be necessary to provide a therapeutic approach such as counselling or educational therapy for the individual child. However, positive self-esteem is a need of all children. Taking these arguments seriously would have an effect for all teachers and for their training. In the same way as all teachers need the skills of planning and implementing differentiated work, of relating what they offer through the curriculum in a relevant manner to the needs of young people, they also need the ability to relate to learners in a way which notices, understands, takes seriously and respects, even at points of failure. There is clear evidence from the much neglected yet crucially important research of Aspy and Roebuck that teachers who are able to offer such relationship qualities within their teaching are more effective not only in boosting self-esteem, but also in achieving better academic results as well as managing the classroom in more effective ways (Aspy and Roebuck 1983).

However, there will be youngsters who do need an individual consideration and to address the needs of damaged self-esteem is not a matter requiring apology. Lawrence provides useful ways of assessing self-esteem (Lawrence 1981, 1988), which can indicate the degree of difficulty. Counselling and other therapeutic approaches considered in this book have developed methods based on the premise of a relationship which notices, understands, takes seriously and respects the child. We have the means by which we can prevent many youngsters from developing into frustrated, unfulfilled adults. We now need the will to make use of these approaches.

REFERENCES

Ainscow, M. and Tweddle, D. (1979) *Preventing Learning Difficulties: An Objectives Approach.* Chichester: Wiley.

Aspy, D. and Roebuck, F. (1983) in *Freedom to Learn for the Eighties,* ed. C. Rogers. New York: Merrill.

Keller, H. (1995) *Three Psychoanalytic Notes on Peter Grimes,* ed. C. White. Institute of Advanced Musical Studies, King's College London.

Lawrence, D. (1971) The effects of counselling on retarded readers. *Educational Research,* 13(2).

Lawrence, D. (1981) The development of a self-esteem questionnaire. *British Journal of Educational Psychology,* 51(2).

Lawrence, D. (1988) *Enhancing Self-Esteem in the Classroom.* London: Paul Chapman.

Lepper, M. R., Greene, D. and Nisbett, R. E. (1973) Undermining children's intrinsic interest with extrinsic rewards: a test of the 'over-justification' hypothesis. *Journal of Personality and Social Psychology,* 28(2).

Miller, A. (1983) *The Drama of the Gifted Child: The Search for the True Self.* New York: Basic Books.

Pye, J. (1988) *Invisible Children.* Oxford: Oxford University Press.

Ravenette, A. T. (1968) *Dimensions of Reading Difficulty.* Oxford: Pergamon.

Taking Practice Seriously

'Imagination is more important than knowledge.'
Albert Einstein

Part II: Practice

The emotional wellbeing of children can be promoted within education.

- How can counselling and therapy be used in schools?
- How can we use therapeutic approaches in the classroom?
- How can children with special needs benefit by addressing emotional literacy in the classroom?

CHAPTER 3

Active imagination in schools: unlocking the self
Michael Green

> But active imagination, as the term denotes, means that the images have a life of their own and that the symbolic events develop according to their own logic – that is, of course, if your conscious reason does not interfere . . . when we are careful not to interrupt the natural flow of events, our unconscious will produce a series of images which make a complete story. (Jung 1935a)

> To the extent that I managed to translate the emotions into images . . . I was inwardly calmed and reassured . . . I learned how helpful it can be, from the therapeutic point of view, to find the particular images which lie behind emotions. (Jung 1963)

In this chapter I outline two techniques based on Jungian principles for working with children in schools. I describe a 'storymaking' method for small groups, and a 'drawing and talking' method of counselling for use with individual children. Both techniques are relatively simple to use, were enjoyable for me and the children I worked with, and proved to be successful in helping the children with their difficulties.

These techniques are adapted from methods developed for use by school counsellors in the Canadian school system (Allan 1988, Allan and Bertoia 1992). At the core of this way of working is a belief in the transforming power of imagination. Both methods I describe involve children in making up their own stories and drawing whatever they choose. They are encouraged to use their imaginations to the full. I have called this way of working 'active imagination', a term I have borrowed from Jungian analytic thinking.

JUNG AND IMAGINATION

Jung placed great importance on the power of imagination to transform and heal. He saw it as a dynamic process of 'active, purposeful creation' (Jung 1935a), a means by which the conscious mind could tap into the deeper energies of the self. For Jungians the self includes not just the conscious but also the unconscious psyche and has at its core an archetypal, organizing, creative power. This core self cannot be directly experienced. A scientific understanding of this core energy could relate it to DNA. A more mystical understanding might be to relate it to concepts of God.

With his adult patients Jung used a technique he called 'active imagination' which he described in one of a series of lectures he gave at the Tavistock Institute in London in 1935. The patient would be encouraged to focus on an image from a dream, a painting or on a particular strong feeling and permit a free flow of whatever images came into his mind. A modern analogy might be to think of this as consciously choosing to enter the virtual reality of your unconscious mind. In dreams we enter the same world, but without the element of conscious choice and without the possibility of actively participating in the events that unfold. Active imagination has been described as 'dreaming with open eyes' (Samuels, Shorter and Plaut 1986).

Through this imaginative work, unconscious material is brought into consciousness, triggering a process in the psyche through which the self seeks to resolve inner conflicts through a process of internal mediation, finding a way forward for us when we are stuck. Jung called this 'the transcendent function . . . a combined function of conscious and unconscious elements . . . of real and imaginary quantities [which] facilitates a transition from one attitude to another'. When we are in the grip of a powerful internal conflict, provided we can find a space to give the oppositional forces and ideas within us equal expression, this healing force within the psyche will find a symbolic solution to unite these warring elements.

> when there is full parity of the opposites, attested by the ego's absolute participation in both, this necessarily leads to a suspension of the will, for the will can no longer operate when every motive has an equally strong counter motive. Since life cannot tolerate a standstill, a damming up of vital energy results, and this would lead to an insupportable condition did not the tension of opposites produce a new, uniting function that transcends them . . . From the activity of the unconscious there now emerges a new content . . . that governs the whole attitude, putting an end to the division and forcing the energy of the opposites into a common channel. The standstill is overcome and life can flow on with renewed power towards new goals. (Jung 1923)

A 'living symbol' is created that incorporates the previously opposing forces in the psyche. Active imagination provides a means of setting this process going and of observing the self in action as it works to bring together parts of the psyche that are in conflict. With this internal conflict resolved, the previously blocked energies are now available for life's challenges. Children find it easier than adults to open themselves up and allow this fluid collaboration between their conscious and unconscious. Much of their play takes this form, and the importance of play for development is widely understood. Winnicott acknowledged its deep, healing power when he said that 'playing is itself a therapy' (Winnicott 1971). Children enter more freely into their imaginative worlds and, once they feel safe, give uninhibited expression to their visions.

Through the free play of imagination children are able to work at a deep level on those unresolved conflicts which can lead to problems with their behaviour and their learning. The drawings and stories produced by children in these activities have great importance: they are symbolic representations of work that has gone on deep in the psyche.

Jung did not work with children as he believed that psychological difficulties experienced by children were caused by unconscious conflicts in their parents, and therefore best worked on via the parents. He felt that the task of childhood was to develop ego strength, and that development of the self was a task for later in life. He was also concerned that the child's fragile ego might be overwhelmed by bringing into consciousness archetypal material from the collective unconscious. However, Michael Fordham, the pioneering Jungian analyst who founded the Society of Analytical Psychology in London, states in contrast that 'a child simply cannot help being in touch with archetypal forms and processes' (Fordham 1994).

Fordham, inspired by Melanie Klein's work, and seeing how compatible her theories were with Jung's ideas, took Jungian thinking back into childhood and constructed a developmental model, based on Jung's principles, in which the self is shown to be active from earliest infancy. He demonstrated that it was possible to work with children on early archetypal material, centred around bodily experiences, to facilitate the self-realization Jung called 'individuation', without children being damaged by the intense affect within the archetypes (Astor 1995).

Despite the fact that Jung did not envisage 'active imagination' as a technique to use with children, and did not, to my knowledge, use it as a method for group work, I use his term as it best describes the dynamic way in which imagination is first activated and then leads the way, in both the individual and the group methods of working which I describe. The work seems very similar to how Fordham (1994) described Jung's method:

> Jung supported tendencies in the patient to let his imagination work on its own with minimal interference from the ego. If the correct time has been chosen there follows an organized fantasy taking the form of a dream in which the patient then learns how to participate as one of the figures: in this way a dialectic can develop between the ego and the archetypal imagery called active imagination. The process is facilitated by dancing, painting, carving wood or modelling clay.

The creative activity of making stories and drawing pictures, either individually or in groups, in the safe, containing atmosphere created by the counsellor, also stimulates this innate healing process. The counsellor's job is to be a 'caretaker ego' who interferes as little as possible, so that, as in Jungian analysis, 'once the conditions are in place the process has its own momentum, guided by the archetypes' (Astor 1995).

Jung placed great importance on giving expression to the powerful images that come into consciousness at such times. This can be through any of the creative arts: writing, drawing, painting, sculpture, music or dance. He saw this as a way of freeing damned up forces in the psyche that hold back growth, and in severe cases can lead to mental breakdown. The driven quality, the need to create that is a feature of great artists' lives, points to the importance of such imaginative work for them. Working on the images facilitates resolution of the conflicts they symbolize by keeping open the channels between the conscious and the unconscious to allow the self to play its healing role.

The understanding which Jung had of these inner mechanisms came from his own personal experience. Shortly after he broke with Freud, as the world stumbled into the insane bloodbath of the First World War, he entered a period of personal crisis, his 'confrontation with the unconscious'. He allowed himself to let go, 'to be carried along by the current without a notion of where it would lead me', knowing as he did so the risk he was taking:

> In order to grasp the fantasies which were stirring in me 'underground' I knew I had to let myself plummet down into them, as it were. I felt not only violent resistance to this, but a distinct fear. For I was afraid of losing command of myself and becoming a prey to the fantasies – and as a psychiatrist I realized only too well what that meant. (Jung 1963)

As he struggled to hold on to his sanity, he wrote down the fantasies that came into his mind, and drew each day in a notebook. He found:

> To the extent that I managed to translate the emotions into images – that is to say, to find the images that were concealed in the emotions – I was inwardly calmed and reassured. Had I left those images hidden in the emotions, I might have been torn to pieces by them . . . As a result of my experiment I learned how helpful it can be, from the therapeutic point of view, to find the particular images which lie behind emotions. (Jung 1963)

Jung survived his 'confrontation with the unconscious' and came back from this perilous inner journey with a new understanding of the mind, central to which was a deep respect for the value of imaginative work in facilitating the psyche's inner healing powers.

There are parallels to Jung's thinking in the work of Melanie Klein. Her idea of the depressive position (Klein 1935) proposes that there is a crucial stage in development during which the infant reconciles the split between his fantasies of an all-good mother who feeds him and changes his nappy and cuddles him, and an all-bad witch mother who isn't there when he wants her. Unconscious aspects of the relationship with the mother are brought into consciousness so they can be compared to the conscious reality of the actual mother. This is a painful time for both of them as the child experiences conflicting flows of love and hatred and the mother has to be strong enough to bear the expression of both kinds of feelings in order to facilitate the child's development. Out of this struggle a new symbol forms in the psyche, a secure good internal object, from which further development can follow, including – most crucially for learning – the capacity to use symbols. The depressive position can be seen as a manifestation early in life of Jung's 'transcendent function', reconciling opposites through symbol formation. Michael Fordham's understanding of this common ground between Kleinian and Jungian thinking, in particular between ideas of unconscious fantasy and archetypal images, gave him a means of developing his own unique thinking (Astor 1995). Further similarities can be seen in the work of Hannah Segal, a post-Kleinian psychoanalyst. In writing of the links between unconscious fantasy, personality structure and thinking, she describes a process that sounds not unlike 'active imagination':

> we have access to these [unconscious] phantasies in the analytic situation, and through mobilizing them and helping the patient to relive and remodel them in the process of analytic treatment, we can affect the structure of the patient's personality. (Segal 1964)

I think the same principles concerning the value of imagination apply to all creative work. In every secondary school there are children who are disruptive and perform poorly in most areas, yet will take more interest in the creative areas of the curriculum: Art, Drama, Dance, English. I would suggest that they intuitively know they get something they need from such work. Teachers can see in such children a similar calming effect taking place to the one Jung found in himself.

In primary schools skilled classroom teachers are using these principles every day in encouraging creative work of all kinds with their classes. These activities are of immense value. When I have gone into primary schools, the classes in which children seem to be happiest, where there is a busy hum of focused activity and an excitement about learning, are those with the most imaginative, most carefully mounted work on the walls. The challenge for teachers is to create a safe environment for these energies to unfold, a task made more difficult by the increasing numbers of severely deprived and damaged children that are in British classrooms. For these children imagination can seem very dangerous. Their inner worlds are a war zone. They do not yet know that these feelings and ideas can be expressed without someone getting hurt.

DRAWING AND TALKING

Over time a relationship forms, problems are expressed symbolically in the drawings, and healing and resolution of inner conflicts can occur. (Allan 1988)

This is a simple counselling method that can be used in schools and is particularly suited for younger children for whom a standard, talking-based form of counselling can be difficult. All that is required is a room to work in where you won't be disturbed, a supply of A4 paper, some folders, a pencil, rubber and ruler, and felt pens or crayons available if asked for. I would, however, strongly recommend anybody planning to work like this to read Allan (1988) for a more detailed account of this method and the theory behind it.

The method

The counsellor (specialist teacher/therapist/education therapist/etc.) meets with a child for half an hour each week, and simply asks the child to draw a picture. The child is told in the first session that in this time they can draw and talk about anything they want, that drawing and talking can help when things are not going too well; each week's drawings will be kept in a folder which will be given to the child at the end of their work, when things are going better.

While the child is drawing the counsellor doesn't talk, but is attentive to the child and the drawing being produced. Once the drawing is finished the counsellor can encourage the child to describe what's happening in the picture, but does not push the child to talk if he or she seems reluctant. Any interpretation of drawings should be on the lines of how something in the drawing might be like the child's situation, (e.g. 'That mouse looks a bit scared to me, I wonder if you feel a bit like that when . . . ?') and not a direct statement that the child 'is' something in the picture. This distancing allows the child a freedom to continue experimenting with the symbol they have created and leaves open the possibility of change. The symbol is a bridge between the child's conscious and unconscious; its value can be lost if too reductive a meaning is placed on it. The symbol has come from deep in the self and part of it is of the self and as such it is numinous, to be treated with respect.

In fact, particularly early on in work with children, I feel it best to say little about what their drawings and the stories they make around them might mean to them personally. Instead I might try to explore with the child what is happening in the pictures, what the different figures might be feeling, etc. A relationship of trust needs to be developed. Premature interpretation can halt the integrative, healing work of the imaginative process by flooding the child with anxiety. A feeling of being able to play with imagination and develop their own symbols needs to be nurtured first. Jung's view was that 'the doctor should assiduously guard against clever feats of interpretation. For the important thing is not to interpret and understand the fantasies, but primarily to experience them' (Jung 1928).

More recently, Arietta Slade, an associate professor of clinical psychology at the City University of New York, has written about the need for a process of consolidation, of building a language of emotion, of giving the child time to develop a security in her own self-understanding before beginning to talk about her feelings. The vehicle for this is telling a story:

> Once a child can tell a story, emotions begin to emerge within the context of the narrative . . . The man is mad because his car is broken; Barbie is scared, Barbie is happy. The process of naming feelings is a first step in differentiating affect states: distinguishing one affect from another, distinguishing speaking about emotion from acting on it, and distinguishing the emotions of one character from another. It typically accompanies the emergence of narrative and is a vital stage in the child's learning how to speak about his or her own feelings, and it is perhaps the first step in discovering how the child feels. It is the beginning of finding sense in terrain that had most likely seemed frightening, overwhelming and unknowable. It is only after a child has developed the means to express such inner experiences that the therapist can address the child's own feelings. If we ask a child to listen to us talk about his or her own feelings before language has taken on an organizing function with respect to emotions, play will be interrupted, behaviour will become disorganized, and the child will most likely withdraw. (Slade 1994)

I usually suggest to a child that they draw a house, a tree and then a person in their first couple of sessions, as I find these drawings particularly helpful in my attempts to understand the child's inner difficulties. Valuable information is provided by the size of the drawing, its position on the page, the presence or absence of detail, the facial expression (on the house and person), broken windows, holes in the tree trunk (there is a strong correlation between such holes and traumatic events, their position on the trunk giving a rough indication of when they occurred in the child's life, with the ground as birth, the crown of the tree as the present), etc. Gentle questioning about how various features of the drawing occurred ('How did the windows get broken?' 'What would your guess be about how that happened?') provide further opportunities for a child to express, in a safe, symbolic form, the impact on him or her of real life events. For more about understanding the possible meanings in children's drawings, see again Allan (1988), also Wohl and Kaufman

(1985) and Koppitz (1968). When the work with a child is coming to a close I again ask them to draw a house, tree and person, and this provides a way of assessing how much real change has taken place internally.

The setting

It is important for the sessions to take place at the same time and in the same place each week, in a room that is private and free from interruption. I have found that protecting the child's space is one of the most difficult things about working in schools, but vital in establishing the trust and the feeling of security necessary for the work to succeed.

Confidentiality

As in most therapeutic work, the sessions are confidential, with the usual proviso that if the child is at risk in any way I would need to share this. This is made clear to parents beforehand, and to the child at the first meeting. However, I do say to parents that I will be sharing in general terms what I learn about their difficulties with their classteacher, so as to think about how best to help them, and that I can share this knowledge with them too. Negotiating this aspect of the work with both teachers and parents requires sensitivity, but having their own private space to think is of tremendous value for children, making it well worth the effort. This unusual situation for the children highlights the 'special' aspect of the work for them, adding to its potential power.

Working in a school

For almost two years I worked in this way for one morning a week, in a primary school close to the child guidance unit where I was based. The headteacher had requested my involvement and was very supportive of my work in the school. I made it clear that this method of counselling was new to me, and that this would be a bit of an experiment. During my time in the school I worked with five children, all of whom at the start of work were having difficulty in controlling their behaviour and were underachieving. By the end of treatment all had shown distinct improvements in their behaviour and in their ability to concentrate on their work. A significant factor in this was their ability to begin to form a different kind of relationship with their classteacher.

I always tried to be in school early enough to spend ten minutes with each classteacher, to get feedback on the child's week, and think with the teacher about the child. Most of the teachers I worked with found this time useful in enabling them to understand the child better and so formulate more effective strategies to help the child in class.

This kind of work in school is always a partnership, and as such is supported or sabotaged by one's colleagues in the classroom who function rather as a child's parents do in clinic-based psychotherapy. Time spent building a good relationship with a classteacher, a 'therapeutic alliance', is always well spent.

Working with parents

My contact with parents was generally limited, but important nonetheless. I always met with parents beforehand to explain what the work involved, and tried to meet for reviews once a term, and for a final review at the end of the work. Sometimes I became more involved, in one case writing to the Housing Department to support a family's request for a change of accommodation. However, the main work was in the individual sessions each week with the child, and supporting the child's teacher.

CASE HISTORIES

James was rather older than most of the children I saw. I worked with him for just over a term before he transferred to secondary school a term after stopping his sessions with me. I'd seen him for little more than a term. Despite the gloomy predictions of many staff at the primary school, he settled down well at secondary school, formed positive relationships with staff and peers, and succeeded academically. He had shown a very different picture to me from that generally perceived within the primary school, where he had been viewed as an arrogant bully. Through his drawings he showed an anxious perfectionist, highly critical of himself. Once he felt I could accept him as he was, and the mistakes in his drawings were not evidence of his lack of worth, he began to relax, draw more rapidly and fluently, take risks, try out new things and open up a bit in what he talked about.

James' nervous-looking 'Fierce Black Panther' (Figure 3.1) dramatically illustrates the gap between his conscious and unconscious understanding of himself. I made no comment about this drawing, but I believe the act of drawing it enabled James to begin a process of getting into more of a balance with himself.

Although he stopped his sessions earlier than I felt he should have done, and was quite ambivalent about his work with me, I felt important changes had begun. The headteacher was sure that without this intervention he would not have survived in secondary school.

Another boy, Simon, age 9, was prone to violent outbursts, smashing windows and hurling furniture, and found it difficult to concentrate in class for any length of time. Over the year I worked with him he calmed down considerably, he began to take some pride in his work and he was no longer the disruptive influence he had been. An understanding young male teacher helped considerably in this process. Simon had developed a good relationship with this teacher by the time the work had finished, which meant that when he went through a difficult patch, sparked off by suddenly seeing his father after many years' absence, he was able to talk to his teacher about it. Through being understood he was able to manage the strong feelings that had been aroused. Previously he would not have had the inner resources to take advantage of the help this teacher could give him.

In his weekly sessions Simon was extremely hesitant to draw or talk about anything at first. Gradually, with encouragement from me, he began to be able to make stories around some of his drawings, and talk of experiences of loss. Then over several months a story was created in pictures and through discussion of two boys on a space flight to different planets (Figures 3.2 and 3.3). When they finally returned to Earth, I felt Simon had revisited and safely worked through many painful experiences from his past. The imaginative vehicle for this work, the symbol

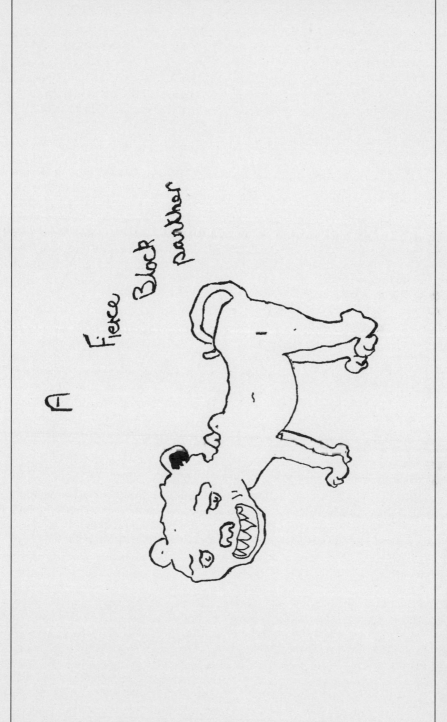

Figure 3.1 A fierce black panther

Figure 3.2 On the moon

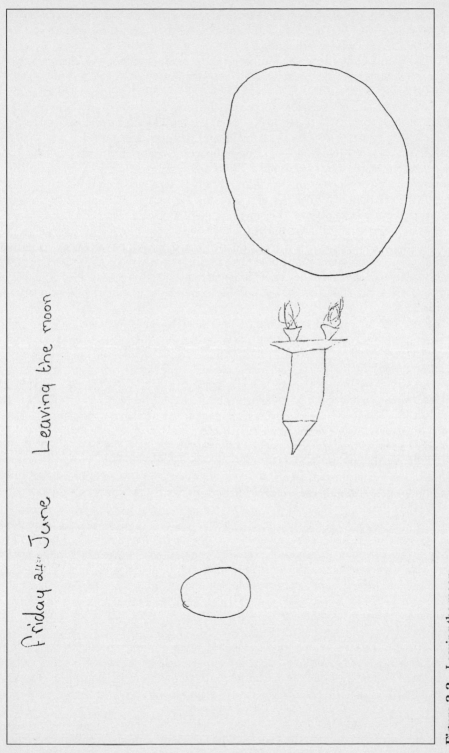

Figure 3.3 Leaving the moon

produced by the self of 'space travel', seemed to me strikingly apt for an exploration of one's inner worlds. The work with Simon came to an end soon afterwards. He knew he had done what was needed.

Simon's change in his view of himself can be seen clearly in the change in his 'person' drawing from the beginning to the end of his work with me, the tense figure floating omnipotently in the top left-hand corner (Figure 3.4) giving way to the more relaxed, larger figure securely placed in the middle of the page (Figure 3.5). Noticeably too this figure is clearly of African origins, like the boy himself, showing a fundamental change in his understanding and acceptance of himself.

Neelam was a rather overweight and unhappy 8-year-old girl who was highly disruptive in class. I was concerned about worrying overtones of abuse in the stories and pictures she made, although there was nothing other than this imaginative material to give me any grounds for further action. All my direct questions on the lines of, say, 'Has anything like this ever happened to you?' were met with a firm denial. Worries like this have to be largely held by the counsellor in this situation (with support from his or her own supervision) whilst at the same time I think any serious concerns should also be discussed with the headteacher and classteacher to ascertain if they have similar anxieties. In this case the head did have some worries about this child, but nothing concrete to justify a child protection referral.

By the end of our work together, which lasted a year, Neelam had stopped storming out of school and refusing to participate in class. She was making progress academically and also seemed to be getting on much better at home with her mother. If anything had happened to her, she had made her own decision about how to deal with it. Finding a space to give symbolic expression to whatever her difficulties were had enabled healing to take place. For Neelam, an additional support in school was a network of several teachers who had known her for some time. Regular reviews of her progress with this staff group, initially brought together to provide some support for her current classteacher who was having difficulty coping with her, gave her a sense of being thought about and cared for. Letters home from the school after each of these reviews, reporting how well she was doing, were a valued reward for her achievements. She is a different child today.

For these children a key factor for any change to take place is a sense of being understood. It is so easy to misunderstand children's defences, to see the aggression and the 'I don't care' attitude and not see the fear and hurt underneath. They are actually often desperate for adults to understand them, to see through their 'act', to help free them from the destructive patterns of relating which they are stuck in. Mary Sue Moore, a clinical psychologist and psychotherapist who began her professional career as a primary school teacher, has used children's drawings extensively in her work. She writes,

> Children's drawings can provide a means of communicating what cannot be expressed verbally, because it may not consciously be known. Thus, drawings become a pathway for adults to a better understanding of children and the world in which they live. (Moore 1990)

Children know when they are understood, or when adults are trying to understand them and accepting them as they are, without criticism. This enables them to begin

Figure 3.4 Person (beginning of contact)

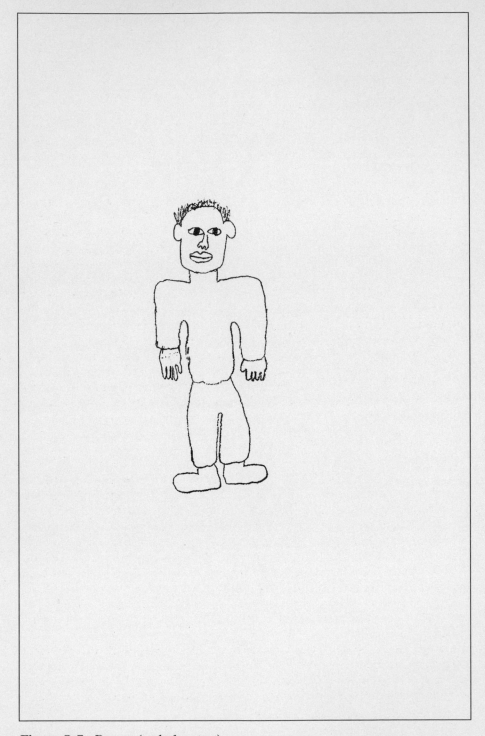

Figure 3.5 Person (end of contact)

trying to understand and accept themselves, and find more productive ways to engage with the world. It is a part of the containment that is necessary for the archetypal healing processes to begin, base camp for the journeys in imagination that can set them free.

GROUP STORYMAKING

While using an academic approach, storywriting, the children are learning new behaviours for working with others and are also being given an opportunity to release deeper emotional issues which are often underlying their behaviour. (Allan and Bertoia 1992)

Although Jung did not use his method with groups, I feel that it is nonetheless appropriate to think of the group work too as 'active imagination'. The individual members of a group can represent unconscious aspects of each other, enabling a creative dialogue between different parts of the personality. The imaginative task of the story provides a vehicle for the exploration of this 'group mind' which can contain and allow expression of forgotten, unwanted and buried parts of each person. The story becomes the dream in which they all consciously participate but which they do not have complete control over, carried along as they are by the narrative and kept safe, at moments when the archetypal forces might burst too much into consciousness, by the reassuring limit setting of the counsellor.

The basic idea for group storywriting is very simple, and I'm sure there are many teachers using variations on this technique already. After trying it out in one school alongside the individual method I've just described, I ran groups in several other schools. Attendance was excellent; the children seemed to relish the opportunity to create stories together.

The method

I saw four children for half an hour once a week. Every week the children made up a story round the table, each in turn dictating a sentence to carry the story on. I was group secretary, writing the stories down. If they didn't want to contribute that round they could 'pass'. I provided paper along with felt pens, pencils, rubbers and rulers (a set each to cut down on unnecessary friction). While waiting their turn to dictate they could draw whatever they chose. Talking was discouraged while each child was dictating a sentence. At the end of the session I read back the completed story and the children could share their drawings if they wished. Finally, I thanked each child for something they had contributed to the group that day: the helpful way they'd handed out paper, helping solve a conflict, finding a way of linking ideas in the story, etc. (Allan and Bertoia 1992).

I typed the stories up on my computer each week and stapled them together to make a booklet for every child, with each one's names and the title the child had picked in bold lettering on the front sheet. We read through the previous week's story at the beginning of each session; sometimes I read, sometimes the children read, as they preferred. The children had their own folders in which they kept their stories and drawings, which I looked after in between groups, but they could take home at the end of the group work. I let them know at the beginning that the sessions were confidential in that I would not be telling their teachers or their parents what they said or did in the groups, unless they told me something which indicated they were in danger, in which case I would need to make sure they were safe. I would, however, meet with their teachers and parents to think about how they were getting on. The groups ran for 10 sessions over a school term.

Setting up

I have found as an outsider going in to schools that careful preparation is essential. It is important to build the container (Jung 1935b, Bion 1970) for any kind of therapeutic work: the stronger the container, the more it can hold, the greater the possibility of allowing the powerful chemical/emotional reaction of change for those children participating. Put another way, the more secure the children feel, the more trust will be developed in the group, the more risks they will feel able to take, the deeper they will be able to go, the greater the potential for healing/change. Talking to the staff group beforehand, explaining what is proposed, enabling the classroom teachers to play a part in selecting children for the group, meeting regularly with the teachers whose children are in the group, all this helps build the therapeutic alliance with the school. Children, with their ultra-sensitive emotional antennae, will be aware of any conflict, resentment or rivalry between the teacher/counsellor running the group and school staff, and the resulting conflict of loyalties can destroy a group's potential. Having a 'safe' room where children will not be disturbed or overheard is also important. Establishing continuity is another part of this building of a sense of security, so the group must take place at the same time, in the same place, with the same children each week. If a child is away, teachers will sometimes ask if that absent child can be replaced by another child and this must be resisted. Losses need to be felt.

The type of children

The group work was aimed at children underachieving in school because of emotional and social factors. I like to work with a mixture of acting out and more passive, depressed children. This mix seems to help both kinds of children, and also avoids the groups having to be too carefully controlled. I prefer mixed sex groups, although the all-boys' group I ran as an experiment worked well. An all-girls' group seemed less successful. I'm not sure why, although one of the girls in that group did seem more disturbed than other children I had worked with. It must be stressed that this is not a method for working with very disturbed children who should be referred to local child and adolescent mental health services. The individual method described earlier could be used with such children as a last resort, if parental support for clinic-based work is not available, but a group like this is not appropriate for such a child.

How does it help?

At the beginning of the chapter I described processes through which a deep release of 'blocking' tension is made possible by giving expression to unconscious conflicts in imaginative work, making it possible for the self to find a new way forward. Robert

Bly, the American poet and social commentator who works with groups of men using myth and fairy tales, illuminates this idea further in a chapter of his book, *The Sibling Society* (Bly 1996). He talks of two parallel streams in our lives that he calls 'literal life' and 'mythological life'. Through 'ritual practice' we are able to enter into the mythological life, the world of archetypal imagery, of the unconscious, the world of the imagination. The particular ways in which a group is set up, the special rules that are different from ordinary school life, the confidentiality, even the use of particular objects to give a sense of ceremony to the proceedings, all give a sense of ritual, of difference, of other worldliness to the group.

In one group which needed more containment, I used a carved stone egg from east Africa as a 'talking object', passed from child to child as they added their section to the story. One child, who found coping with the loss of the group hard, became angry in the last session. She said she wouldn't miss coming to the group, but she would miss the egg. Some loss could be mourned.

Bly says,

> The idea of ritual is strange to our ears; it says that if something is healed in the other world, something is healed in this world also. Christ spoke of that precisely when he said, 'What is loosed in heaven is loosed on earth.' (Bly 1996)

Imaginative work has powerful effects in our literal worlds (I'm avoiding saying 'real' world here as this would deny the reality and importance of the 'imaginary' world). Solutions and resolutions 'there' open up new possibilities for us 'here'. Damage can be made good. Bly goes on to talk about another advantage of this kind of work, 'doing something in the mythological world means that we don't have to do it here'. If the container of the group is strong enough, terrible violence can be enacted in the mythological world, rage and fury can be vented, and nobody 'here' need get actually hurt. As violence runs its course in the other world, this world becomes a safer place. There are also more 'literal', conventionally understood ways in which this work helps children. As in all group activities, there are group dynamics operating that can be harnessed positively. The more withdrawn members of the group are able to experience lively behaviour in a safe context and can enjoy the energy and spontaneity of peers they might find threatening in a less contained environment. The impulsive children in turn get to appreciate the more thoughtful contributions of the quieter ones. In a group that's going well, some kind of mixing up together goes on at a deep level, like in a chemical reaction, and imbalances get adjusted. Further benefits come from skills that are developed through having to concentrate so as not to lose the thread of the story, and having to wait one's turn and not interrupt others. The children are having to build on each other's contributions, and thus learn to value others. It is a process of teamwork which the boys in particular may only have experienced previously on the football field. Making their own (often very gory) stories, an *academic* activity that they find exciting, gives them an incentive to persevere and work together, and in so doing they can pick up learning skills they may have missed earlier.

Additionally the children all get a massive boost to their self-esteem in seeing themselves in print as authors (as every teacher knows). The easy printing of smart looking 'books' that the widespread availability of computer technology makes possible is a tremendous asset for motivating children. A further boost comes from just being in a special group and knowing that their teachers and I meet to think about them. It all adds up to a feeling of being worth something.

At the end of each group I asked the children to pick the story they liked best to be made into a 'real' book for them, as a way of validating their achievement. A local print shop photocopied the masters onto thin card with a coloured card cover, then spiral bound each one with an acetate dust sheet. Their stories now looked even more impressive and the children took them away proudly. Some groups also chose to read their stories to their classes afterwards; I always made it clear that it had to be a group decision whether or not to share their stories. One group presented their stories to a junior school assembly, and preparing for this with their teacher provided a useful way of bringing the group's achievements and closeness back into the school context.

Contact with parents

I always left it with the school to explain to parents what kind of a group was being suggested for their children and to get their permission to go ahead. In retrospect it could have been useful to meet with parents beforehand, in visible partnership with the headteacher and/or Special Educational Needs Co-ordinator (SENCO), as there were times when parents seemed to get a rather different view of the kind of work I was doing. I set aside two meetings after school times during each group to see parents. The school SENCO wrote to the parents and arranged appointment times for them. To have some contact, however brief, always seemed important to me, and I managed this with all the children I worked with, thanks to a lot of work by the SENCO and classteachers in encouraging parents to come. It always made a lot of difference to the children, and provided further proof that the group really was 'private' when I didn't talk about what they did or said in the group, other than commenting that they used the time well.

One important aspect of my liaison with parents was around the kind of material the children tended to produce in the groups. Many of the stories – influenced to some extent by TV programmes like 'Power Rangers', and computer games such as 'Streetfighter' – were violent, gory tales, potentially rather shocking to some parents (although the stories produced by the girls' group seemed more influenced by TV soaps). Allowing as much freedom of expression as possible was essential to the method – to allow the unconscious material to come to the surface – although there were times I had to set limits, particularly around sexual material. In these cases I explained why such material could not be included in their stories, in the form in which they were first suggesting it, in terms of what their parents might think about work like this being done in school if they showed the stories to them. I made it clear that they could think what they wanted, but what I, as a teacher, could include in their books, and what we could acceptably talk about, was limited by the school setting we were working in. They were able to accept that reality and think about other ways to say what they wanted/needed to say.

For real change to become possible it is necessary for the children to be able to explore the darker, shadow areas of the psyche, in order to give the oppositional forces in the psyche full expression. Jung made it clear that 'the new symbol . . . cannot be a one sided product of the most highly differentiated mental functions but must derive equally from the lowest and most primitive levels of the psyche' (Jung

1923). The reality of working with a group in a school setting does require some compromise on this, but the principle remains that the children should experience the group as a place to freely express all aspects of their imagination. When it came near to the end of a group and the children would shortly be taking their stories home, I would send a letter home to the parents. I have included a version of this letter at the end of the chapter so anyone who thinks it might be useful can adapt it as they wish (see appendix). My experience with the parent of a child I was seeing individually at the child guidance unit had made me aware of how important it was to prepare parents for the strong nature of material produced in therapeutic work, and of the importance for the child of the parents' reaction to their stories. The value can be lost completely if a parent reacts to a story in a negative way, through failing to understand the purpose and meaning of a child's work. This is one of the reasons why in psychotherapy with children the rule is generally that any drawings or other creative work produced in the sessions stay in the clinic.

Only one parent so far has taken exception to the stories taken home. She came into the school to see the headteacher, furious at the 'suggestive' nature of what she had read. Despite the total support the headteacher gave me, she remained unconvinced of the work's value. Her daughter, a clever yet insecure girl with a very low opinion of herself, had thoroughly enjoyed the group. She had grown in confidence in expressing herself in the group time, and had begun to tackle more demanding tasks in class, with encouragement from her teacher. A stubborn streak in this girl – which didn't always help her in school – gave me hope that she could hang on to the changes she had begun to make for herself, despite her mother's denigration of the group work. For the most part though, I have found parents supportive of this work, and in several cases the involvement of their child in a storymaking group has resulted in a much more positive relationship with the school.

A story: 'The Baby Assassins'

The sky was light blue on Jupiter. The Jupitans were letters with bulging eyes. They wore fur pants and they had hairy arms. They also had special powers and strength. Their powers were hypnotism and whirlpools.

They pushed a button and a little tiny bomb fell out and hit the ground and went BOOM!

Before it hit the Earth it let out hypnotising powder. They flew down to Earth and started taking hostages from us, but a baby assassin beat them all up. They escaped with their magic powers, bruised and very hurt.

They got back to Jupiter and although the humans were dying, they put them in a special unit or prison. But the baby from earth had a baby gang, and suddenly they all started fighting and beat the Jupitans all up and punched them in their heads sixteen times.

They escaped with their lives, but their magic powers were almost gone.

The babies gave up their gang because they were always arguing, but before they split up they had a big fight. Legs were flying all over the place. Suddenly, one of the legs came off. He quickly dashed after his leg and glued it back on.

They all split up and then the aliens came to attack; tanks and bombers and everything. All the babies got back together, but they lost this time and the aliens took them as prisoners.

When they got into the jail they saw this big window and they climbed out and ran away. Just before they'd run away they'd found some diving breathing apparatus and they put them on and they beat up all the bombers, even the ones that weren't armed, and threw them into space where they just drifted away.

They returned to Earth, but some aliens were still alive and they attacked again and the babies lost this time, and they were taken hostage then thrown out to space to die where they couldn't breathe.

But they didn't die because some alien babies came to rescue them, and they were glad and after that they won. The Jupitans had holes in their hats and clothes and all over the place, so they said in the end, 'OK, you win. Mercy! Mercy!'

And the babies were children now and they said, 'Alright, but you must help us if more aliens come down and try to hurt us.' But the children, who were once babies, lost their touch in karate and the aliens said, 'Those stupid children . . .' and attacked them again.

And they did. But, in between, they'd been practising fencing, and got together all kinds of swords and weapons and attacked again and won.

This story was created by a lively mixed group about half way through a piece of group work. I've chosen this one because I think it provides good examples of the kinds of anxieties, left over from the very earliest developmental stages in infancy, that can continue to affect children's emotional development and thinking. In the story you can see how the letters of the alphabet are associated with frightening figures with sexual overtones (Klein 1932) – this, left in the unconscious, would make the business of meaningfully linking up letters in the mind to make words (a process essential in reading and writing) an activity fraught with danger.

Omnipotent infantile defences are described to protect against feelings of disintegration and of body parts not holding together (a 'baby assassin', 'magic powers'). Francis Tustin, a child psychotherapist, has described the same anxieties about body parts felt by autistic children: 'they feel that their limbs are stuck onto them and can easily become detached' (Tustin 1981). Autistic children may never be able to shed the defences they erect against these early childhood terrors.

Next in the story there is all-out war (infantile rage?). The babies lose to alien forces and are at their mercy. We see their terrible fears of being left to die in a place without air (birth fears?), of floating lost in space. Now we know more about how much infants are actually aware of (Stern 1985) it is easy to believe that they do experience such feelings of utter helplessness and vulnerability.

A passage written by the psychoanalyst Esther Bick provides an interesting parallel to the material in the story:

When the baby is born he is in the position of an astronaut who has been shot out into outer space without a space suit . . . The predominant terror of the baby is of falling to pieces or liquefying. One can see this in the infant trembling when the nipple is taken out of his mouth, but also when his clothes are taken off. (Bick 1986)

At the end of the story, the scary Jupitans, who seem to me to represent the adult world, have become allies. The magical defences of infancy have been replaced with a new *skill* of fencing that the children, 'who were once babies', have *learned*. The story is of a developmental progression, of triumphing over fear, of working to learn new skills, of growing up. It is a letter from the group to themselves, detailing their inner struggles and setting out the way forward. Much important work has been done.

Each group develops its own character and develops their own themes in the stories they make, according to the needs of the group. Sometimes the stories become fragmented, destructive elements become predominant, and it is fascinating to watch the struggle for growth, of hope fighting against despair, as embodied in different members of the group. Arguments can break out at these times and the containing, thinking role of the counsellor then becomes important, encouraging the group to find their solution through the story where the tensions can become resolved safely.

Drawing during storymaking

Having the freedom to draw while they work together on the story gives the children in a group a way of working simultaneously at two levels. With the demands of the story taking up much of their conscious attention, the drawings they do come from a deep area of the psyche. Concentrating on their drawings also enables rather less conscious attention to the stories so they can come more from the deeper self. I believe this part of the work to be equally as important as the actual storymaking. The two complementary activities correspond to the interlinked processes I described at the beginning of the chapter, each stimulating the other, conscious and unconscious interweaving in a creative dance.

Sometimes the shared material in the stories stimulates one child to produce a particular drawing, or series of drawings, relating to her individual concerns. At other times seeing what one child has drawn will strike a common chord, and others will produce drawings on the same theme. First pictures may well be a representation of the children's feelings about themselves; they may draw tiny figures showing their feelings of inadequacy, or a hard-looking man with tattoos and long scars, showing their hurts and the tough persona they have tried to construct as a defence. They may draw their current situation: a car stopped at the lights is a drawing I have seen many times, a powerful metaphor for blocked vital energies (Figure 3.6).

Later on in a group, drawings will show more clearly what an individual child is preoccupied with. Children seeking for a sense of identity may draw flags of different countries. I have observed black children seeking through the Stars and Stripes (Figure 3.7) and the Jamaican flag (Figure 3.8) a strong black identity to support them in a culture where they do not feel valued. Internal struggles can be expressed in violent battles (Figures 3.9 and 3.10) or struggles with monsters, including giant sharks (Figure 3.11); amongst other possibilities these drawings may express unresolved Oedipal conflicts, separation difficulties, or the working through of the shock of having witnessed violence in the home. Volcanoes, another frequent subject, are a vivid metaphor for the deep explosive anger some children feel, anger that they have sat on for too long (Figure 3.12). Trains and boats and planes provide movement, a sense of new possibilities. Regular geometric patterns meet a hunger for order and containment, and can express a new balance and order

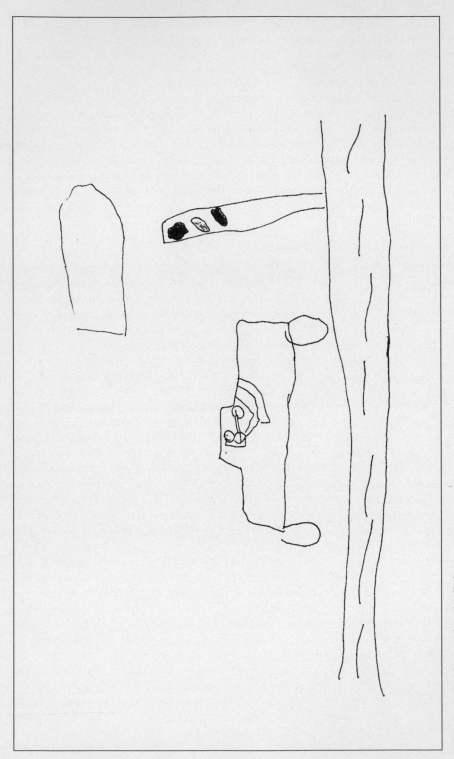

Figure 3.6 Stopped at the lights

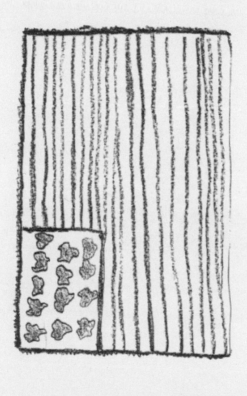

Figure 3.7 Stars and Stripes

Figure 3.8 Jamaican flag

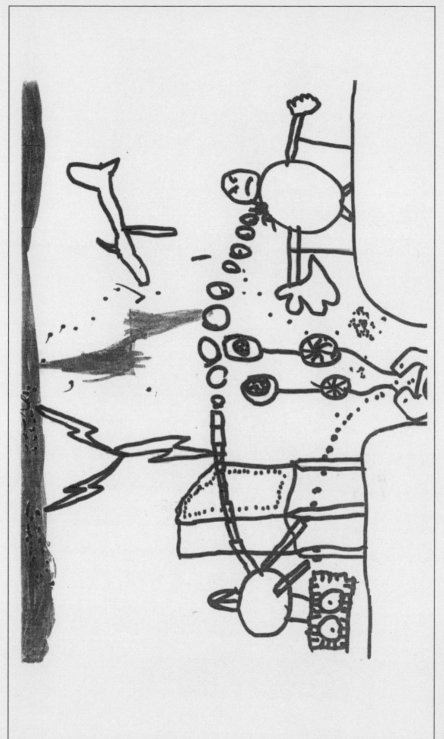

Figure 3.9 Battle

Figure 3.10 Sea war

Figure 3.11 Giant shark

Figure 3.12   Volcano

in the personality following a journey of inner exploration. Flowers and trees give a sense of growth and hope. (I don't interpret the drawings, but as I said earlier, I leave a few minutes at the end when the children can talk about what they have drawn, if they wish.) It is a real privilege to witness the creative powers of the self unfolding in the children's drawings, gradually changing the way they talk, the way they move, bringing a new-self confidence into their lives.

Changes

As interesting as the stories and drawings they produce are, the reason these children are in a group is to help them with their difficulties. It was important for me to know that they were actually benefiting from being in a group. My method for evaluating the work was to establish beforehand with their classteacher four 'hoped-for changes' and to return to these at each of three reviews during the group, with a final evaluation session at the end. Brief weekly progress reports kept me in touch with how each child was doing in class. I also tried to have termly follow-up meetings with the SENCO for a year afterwards. The same kinds of thinking and structures could be built into an Individual Education Plan.

As I found in using a group therapy technique in schools (see Chapter 8), in each group there seemed to be one child who did brilliantly and seemed transformed by the experience. Other members made significant changes. Yet always there was one who seemed somehow to benefit little at the time. The one who seemed to have gained nothing did often, on follow-up, turn out to have made some real improvements later. A brief, unmaintained improvement can provide a base memory for the classteacher and child to work with as a reference point, 'We know you can do it! Let's work together so you can do it again.' Sometimes it becomes clearer that an unresolved home situation lies at the root of a child's difficulties, and a referral to a child and family consultation service might become a possibility if some trust has been developed through the work.

Karl was referred to a group because, despite being a bright boy, tall and good-looking, he had very low self-esteem and spent most of the time huddled in his coat with the hood up. Work in class was often not completed: he'd say he couldn't do it or he would waste time in silly ways. In the group his imaginative talents became apparent almost immediately, and he became a powerful creative force in the storymaking. His skilful, sophisticated drawings took on an angrier, more primitive, violent appearance as the group developed and he absorbed some 'heat' from another, less inhibited child. He began to make much better progress in class, he was finishing work and becoming more outgoing, and to his surprise he was elected class representative for the school council. Unfortunately, he was taken back to his parents' home country unexpectedly shortly after the end of the group and he missed a lot of school. On his return he seemed to regress to his old unhappy state for a while, but at the last review I attended he seemed to be making some progress again. With plenty of positive reinforcement and reminders of what he had achieved before, Karl will hopefully be able to make the most of his considerable abilities. A few individual sessions with a school counsellor might have put him back on track faster, but this was not a resource the school had.

Sarah was the only girl in a group with three boys, and she was the smallest child in the group. She seemed much of the time to be not really there; often she 'passed' when it was her turn to add to the story and I really wondered how much she was getting out of the group. Her drawings, however, showed something important and powerful being expressed. A trilogy of bold, rather surreal, dreamlike drawings starts with a scene showing three figures, who look like little girls, in and around a swimming pool (Figure 3.13). The pool is at the end of a long flight of steps that descend from a house. One girl seems to be bouncing on a diving board, close to a red sun, her 'Oh no' expressing anxiety about going in the water. Another girl sits with her feet dangling in the water, the third floats peacefully in or under the water. Dark clouds and sharp black V-shaped birds complete the picture, giving a sense of worry and sadness. In the next picture (Figure 3.14) a female figure is now entering a pool of some kind, an animal at her side. She is saying, 'It real hot here.' The inky black pool fills the bottom of the page. Clouds, birds and sun form the upper half of the picture as before. The third drawing (Figure 3.15) has a larger figure in a yellow dress, a wistful look on her face as she stands in a garden setting with a tree and a row of flowers. Clouds, birds and sun remain constant, although the sun is now yellow.

Sarah went on to make a much more detailed picture of a little girl, floating in the middle of the paper in a red dress and red shoes (Figure 3.16). The girl seems to be also wearing red lipstick. The partly erased arms, from Sarah's first attempt at the picture, make her appear to have wings. There is a sad, longing, mournful feeling about the drawing to me, yet also a quiet assurance and a solidity about the figure. Her later drawings consisted mainly of regular patterns on a ruled out grid (Figure 3.17). None of Sarah's drawings seemed to relate directly to the group stories which were being made as Sarah was drawing, and they were very different from the bloodthirsty battle scenes the boys were producing.

Looking at her pictures now there seems to be an initial fear about entering some inner experience, symbolized by the pool. The staircase motif is a favourite in film noir to represent a descent into the underworld of the unconscious, inevitably preceding some encounter with dark forces which will either destroy or strengthen a character. The dark pool that the girl is in up to her waist suggests her getting in touch with the dark energy of the 'shadow' parts of herself, the parts she has disowned. The presence of an animal suggests that this may be about instinctual feelings, greedy, devouring or sexual, that could earlier have seemed overwhelming or lead to intense guilt. Here in the pictures, within the containment of the group, such fears could be faced and a new balance found between conscious and unconscious. In Jungian thinking this coming to terms with the 'shadow' which is taking place is an essential element in 'individuation', the process of becoming truly oneself. Split-off parts of the personality can be brought together and old wounds healed, but to do this you have to get in touch with deep, submerged parts of yourself, and that can feel very risky ('Oh no!').

Without my realizing it, Sarah seemed to have been doing just that. In the safety of the group she seems to have gone deep into her self and re-emerged with a new sense of herself. She found a garden to grow in, with a gentler, golden sun. Finding this nurturing space inside enabled her to grow in confidence and self-esteem. She became able to settle to her work and began to achieve academic success.

In another group I ran there was a similar situation with one girl and three boys. Again the girl seemed to be rather sidelined by the exuberant boys and not really getting much out of it, but Cecilia turned out in the end to benefit greatly from the

Figure 3.13 'Oh no!'

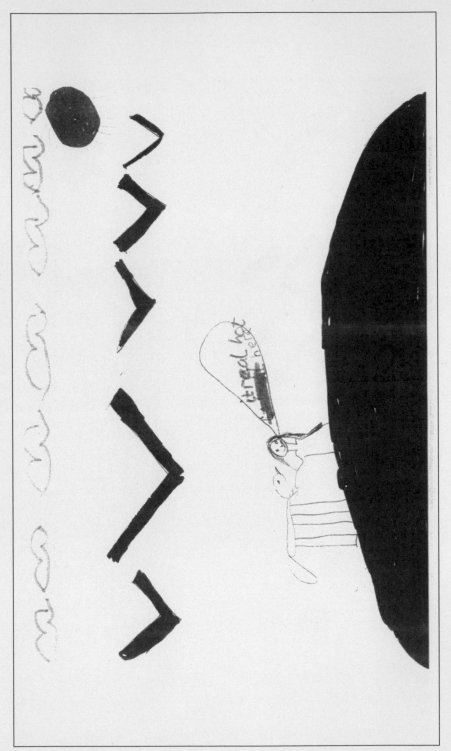

Figure 3.14 'It real hot here'

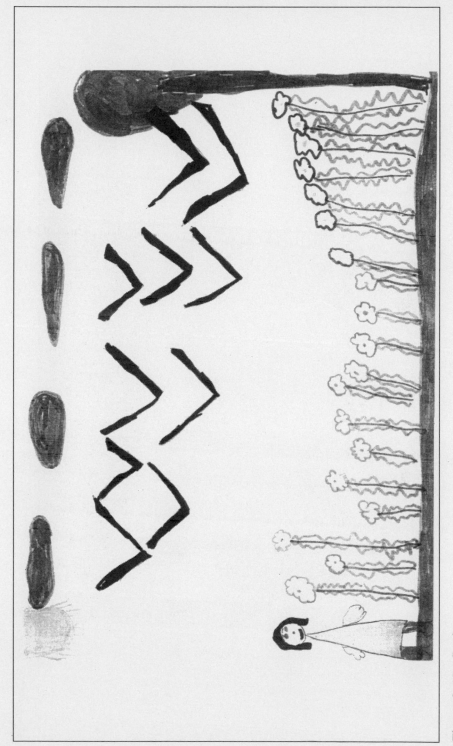

Figure 3.15 Garden

Figure 3.16 Red dress

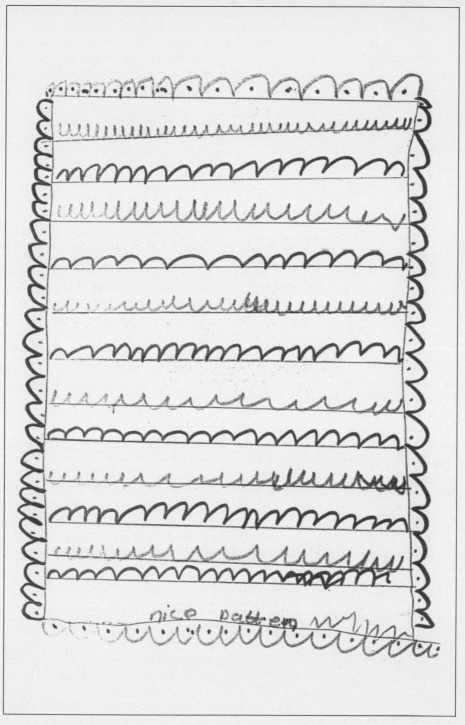

Figure 3.17 Nice pattern

group. From a girl who had been struggling with her reading she moved on to reading aloud to the class, and she developed a whole new bounciness in herself and pleasure in her work. In Cecilia's case in particular, the ability of her teacher to see change beginning and to nurture it was crucial. Although the group can create the conditions for change, each child must begin the process individually, and sensitive support is needed from the classteacher if the momentum is to be maintained outside of the group.

Sunil was referred to a group because he was almost mute in class. He was reluctant to seek help from his teacher with his work, and he said he disliked school. Although his basic skills were sound, he was underachieving considerably. In the group he quickly showed a rich imagination. He was able to maintain quite complex narrative structures and produced bright, lively drawings of warriors fighting. In class there was an instant transformation: he began talking to his classteacher, took a part in a class production for assembly, and by the end of the group was able to join in all class activities, including the deviant ones! He had really enjoyed the group where he had been able to find a way of expressing many aspects of himself. Of particular importance for Sunil was the opportunity to safely explore different approaches to disagreements with others. On one occasion he took a personal stand over an issue in the group and held his ground despite considerable pressure from the others (with my support for his right to do this). The next week he was able to modify his approach and find a compromise to enable that week's story to continue.

Sunil was very sad at the ending of the group. A few weeks later he wrote a long story for his teacher containing allegations about cruel treatment at home. In discussion with her he made further allegations and eventually a child protection enquiry was instigated. There was found to be little substance to his allegations, but the investigation uncovered the difficulties his parents had in setting limits for Sunil at home, and a tension between his parents and his grandmother who lived close by and who had virtually taken him over. Despite having his own room at home, Sunil slept at his grandmother's house. The family asked for help in resolving this situation and I met with them over several months with a social worker colleague from my team. The end result was Sunil returning home to live with his parents, freed from the heavy psychological burden of meeting his grandmother's emotional needs. At school he continued to make rapid progress in all areas. The experience of being in the group had given him the confidence to bring this problem to people's attention, through the medium of a story interestingly, so he and his family could be helped in finding a way through their enmeshed situation with its strong elements of fairy tale. The stolen child recovered from his enchantment and returned to his rejoicing family. His mother cried as she spoke of her joy at getting her son back.

Endings

The management of the ending is crucial for the lasting success of any piece of therapeutic work. The same principle also holds true for all aspects of endings in schools. The way the loss of a teacher is dealt with, the change of class at the end of a year, and even how a short holiday break is managed, will affect how easily children can adjust to another teacher, how much they can retain of what they have learned, and how quickly they can settle back after the holiday (Salzberger-Wittenberg, Henry and Osborne 1983).

Children rapidly become very attached to the group, enjoying the special relationships they build with the counsellor and the other children, and the very different freedom to express deep parts of themselves that the group provides. Although they know from the beginning how many sessions the group will run for, it's important to make the dates and timetable clear in the first session. They may well deny the coming ending to themselves, preferring not to think about it as they have learned to submerge other painful or uncomfortable feelings and thoughts. The half-term break provides a good opportunity to think with the children about how many sessions are left. Taking a register at the beginning of each group also provides a focus for counting up the sessions they have had and how many are to come. It is vital that the feelings about the coming ending are expressed by the children and acknowledged by the counsellor. I also make it clear that I'll miss the group too. Isca Salzberger-Wittenberg, organizing tutor on the Aspects of Counselling in Education course at the Tavistock Clinic, states,

> There is also real sadness at parting from a child or a class to whom we may have become attached. I believe there cannot be a good parting unless both partners in the relationship can acknowledge their loss and sadness. (Salzberger-Wittenberg 1989)

Children's difficulties in school are often bound up with unresolved feelings about loss. 'Any loss evokes feelings connected with earlier losses and the threat of future ones' (Ibid.). Children can be deeply affected by the 'loss' of their mother to a baby brother or sister, parental break-up, bereavement, and all the other things that can happen in families, particularly if there is no adult emotionally available to contain the child's feelings at the time. Having an anticipated, prepared-for ending can be a way of helping children with the other endings that couldn't be thought about.

Conflict can easily break out in a group in the last few sessions as children try to displace the pain they feel on to others. At such times it is important to relate what is happening to their sadness at the ending of the group and their anger at the counsellor for going away. 'I think some of these cross feelings in the group today are about the end of the group coming. You're letting me know that the group has been important to you, that you are going to miss working with me and the others on a Wednesday, and you're cross and sad about it coming to an end.' This makes it possible for thinking to continue and for the loss to be borne.

The sensitivity of the counsellor is vital at these times. Anyone planning to work like this, with groups or individual children, will be helped considerably by a personal experience of counselling or psychotherapy to develop their capacity to stay in touch with strong feelings. This is why personal psychotherapy is a basic requirement for anyone embarking on child psychotherapy or educational therapy training. The support of regular supervision is also important. If several local schools had counsellors working in them, a supervision group would be a cost-effective way of supporting the work.

Conclusion

In this chapter I have described two ways of working based on principles first described by Jung, but common to many healing traditions. With the support of classroom teachers, 'active imagination' can be highly successful in helping children whose learning is affected by emotional and social factors, transforming their thinking and their lives.

'if something is healed in the other world, something is healed in this world also.' (Bly 1996)

APPENDIX: LETTER TO PARENTS

Dear Parent

The group work that your child has been taking part in at —— School this term will shortly be coming to an end. I have enjoyed the work, and my contact both with the children's teachers and with you suggests that the children have both enjoyed the experience and found it beneficial.

When the group finishes, the children will be bringing home some of the stories they have made together in the group. How you react to these stories is important; if you appear to be disapproving of the sometimes powerful nature of the stories, your child may feel criticized and that their achievement is not being valued. This in turn may make it hard for them to value the experience of the group and what they learned from it. The stories children make up when free to unleash their imaginations often have the ruthless character of traditional fairy tales, and if you see these stories in this way it might make it easier to appreciate their worth, should you have any doubts about this.

In producing this work the children have had to work together and share ideas with the others in the group, to take their turn and concentrate hard so as not to lose the thread of the story they have been making. These are all skills that they need to succeed in class. Being able to work together in this way to produce these stories represents a very real achievement for the children who took part, all of whom contributed fully.

As well as building these academic and social skills, the group provides, through the storymaking, an outlet for the strong feelings children often have that they find hard to express directly. These strong feelings can remain bottled up inside, affecting their ability to think, or at other times can burst out in disruptive behaviour or over-reaction to situations they would otherwise find easy to deal with. Expressing such feelings in the group, in the events in the stories, can enable the children to come to terms with their feelings and move on to begin using their creativity and intelligence in class and developing better strategies to deal with situations that they may have been finding problematic. Self-confidence increases and the child can begin to achieve what they have always been capable of.

I will be meeting with the children's teachers for a final evaluation of the work when the group finishes, and will be monitoring their progress at termly intervals over the next year. A feature of this kind of group work is that further positive changes in children often occur after the group work has finished.

Should you wish to discuss anything in this letter further, or if you would like to meet with me again to discuss anything concerning your child, please contact me on the above phone number.

Yours sincerely

REFERENCES

Allan, J. (1988) *Inscapes of the Child's World: Jungian Counselling in Schools and Clinics.* Dallas: Spring.

Allan, J. and Bertoia, J. (1992) *Written Paths to Healing: Education and Jungian Child Counselling.* Dallas: Spring.

Astor, J. (1995) *Michael Fordham: Innovations in Analytical Psychology.* London: Routledge.

Bick, E. (1986) Further considerations of the function of the skin in early object relations. *British Journal of Psychotherapy,* 2, 292–9.

Bion, W. (1970) *Attention and Interpretation.* London: Tavistock.

Bly, R. (1996) *The Sibling Society.* London: Hamish Hamilton.

Fordham, M. (1994) *Children as Individuals.* London: Free Association.

Jung, C. G. (1923) *Psychological Types.* Republished (1971) as *Collected Works, Volume 6,* London: Routledge and Kegan Paul.

Jung, C. G. (1928) The relations between the ego and the unconscious. In *Collected Works, Volume 7, Two Essays on Analytical Psychology* (1953). London: Routledge and Kegan Paul.

Jung, C. G. (1935a) Series of lectures at the Tavistock Clinic. Published as *Analytical Psychology: Its Theory and Practice* (1968). London: Routledge and Kegan Paul.

Jung, C. G. (1935b) Marriage as a psychological relationship. In *Collected Works, Volume 17, The Development of Personality* (1954). London: Routledge and Kegan Paul.

Jung, C. G. (1963) *Memories, Dreams and Reflections.* London: Collins & Routledge and Kegan Paul.

Klein, M. (1932) *The Psychoanalysis of Children.* London: Hogarth.

Klein, M. (1935) A contribution to the psychogenesis of manic-depressive states. *International Journal of Psycho-Analysis,* 16, 145–74.

Koppitz, E. (1968) *Psychological Evaluation of Children's Drawings.* New York: Grune and Stratton.

Moore, M. S. (1990) Understanding children's drawings: developmental and emotional indicators in children's human figure drawings. *Journal of Education Therapy,* 3(2).

Salzberger-Wittenberg, I. (1989) The meaning and management of endings. *Journal of Education Therapy,* 2(3).

Salzberger-Wittenberg, I., Henry, G. and Osborne, E. (1983) *The Emotional Experience of Learning and Teaching.* London: Routledge and Kegan Paul.

Samuels, A., Shorter, B. and Plaut, F. (1986) *A Critical Dictionary of Jungian Analysis.* London: Routledge and Kegan Paul.

Segal, H. (1964) Phantasy and other mental processes. *International Journal of Psycho-Analysis,* 45, 191–4. In *The Work of Hanna Segal* (1981). New York: Jason Aronson.

Slade, A. (1994) Making meaning and making believe. In Slade, A. and Wolf, D. P. (eds) *Children at Play: Clinical and Developmental Approaches to Meaning and Representation.* Oxford: Oxford University Press.

Stern, D. N. (1985) *The Interpersonal World of the Infant.* New York: Basic Books.

Tustin, F. (1981) *Autistic States in Children.* London: Routledge and Kegan Paul.

Winnicott, D. W. (1971) *Playing and Reality.* London: Tavistock.

Wohl, A. and Kaufman, B. (1985) *Silent Screams and Hidden Cries: An Interpretation of Artwork by Children from Violent Homes.* New York: Brunner/Mazel.

CHAPTER 4

Stories and writing
Angela Greenwood

> We need to ride our images as one would ride a giant eagle, soaring up and down wherever they may take us . . . Who knows what lies behind and beyond our images until we trust them enough to ride them fully, even into the darkness and into the depths like a seed in the soil. Perhaps we will never know the gift that our images are until we ride them through to the other side, and only from that perspective will we see them for the first time. (Fox 1983)

I suppose what differentiates us from the animal kingdom is the gift and the potential (but also the problem!) of our imagination. We can dream dreams, realize hopes, understand and empathize with each other, but we can also block off that imagination when it becomes too terrifying, and we can get stuck through fear of failure. The trouble is that in doing so we may block off our learning and our opportunities at the same time.

In school, writing is one of the main opportunities for accessing this potential of the imagination. Through creating and writing stories we can begin to get in touch with that inner life which is our creative possibility, and which can be understood and loved in relationships. This chapter looks at the therapeutic value of children's storywriting, and at ways of understanding and working with the writing process. The stories included in the chapter come from various writing opportunities in school: individual educational therapy (a psychodynamic child therapy which works on children's learning difficulties at the same time as working on their underlying emotional difficulties), small writing groups and regular class writing sessions.

ENGAGING WITH STORIES
Story telling is an ancient, but sadly declining art. Stories bring pleasure and fun and rapt attention, as well as satisfaction and inspiration, as we are transported into another world, and as we identify with the characters and their struggles. All children love stories. With a little encouragement they love to tell them, and in a calm secure environment with a trusted adult and just a little familiarity and confidence with the writing process, they will love to write them too. Teachers are often very skilled at creating an atmosphere where children's imaginations can flow

onto the paper allowing them to 'write their hearts' a little into their stories, either freely or through given themes or poetry.

STORIES AS SELF-EXPRESSION

Children sharing their stories with adults is not just an opportunity for fun and drama. It can also be a safe and natural way for children to express some of their hopes, wishes, frustrations and fears in the once removed situation of their characters.

Richard's traumatic beginning, and his many serious operations, left him far behind with his learning, his size and his confidence. In school he struggled with everything, and he was often bullied and laughed at. After reading *Willy the Wimp* (Browne 1984) with his learning support teacher he dictated:

Willie wanted to be strong.
Willie wanted to be a star.
Willie wanted to be big.
Willie wanted to have a swimming pool.
Willie wanted to be nice to everyone.

Richard probably wished *he* could be big and strong, and everyone would be nice to him, and not make him feel so bad and useless.

Through stories we can express difficulties which we dare not acknowledge out loud. After drawing a picture of a dog Jimmy (age 8) wrote: 'This dog is happy every day. They feed very good stuff. Its not fair because people pick on him because they think he is fat.' Jimmy was fat.

Stories can also be hopeful. They can be places where we can try out in fantasy the possibility of struggle and transformation. Through stories we can accomplish in our imagination what we fear or are unable to do (yet?) in real life. After looking at a winter picture Jon (age 10), who had extreme difficulties with social relationships, told the story of 'Winter Boy' to his educational therapist:

It was winter. The boy used to play in the snow, and no one else used to play in the snow. No one liked him, so he built a frog out of snow to amaze them. But it didn't work, and he went to school and no one sat next to him. When the children went up in the second year, he had to stay in the first year because no one liked him, and the teacher in the other class didn't like him. But because he was a Winter Boy the snow stuck up the door and it couldn't open. Everyone was stuck inside with no food. One day Winter Boy said: 'I might be able to open the door.' The teacher said: 'I don't think you could open it but you could try.' When he opened it all the children ran to the door, and they said: 'Thank you Winter Boy,' and they all went home and told their mums about it, and Winter Boy was happy for the rest of his life.

This story was dictated and written in Jon's second educational therapy session, unconsciously communicating the possibility of hope and hidden potential under his outwardly rather depressed and tearful exterior.

Allan and Bertoia (1992) write: 'On one level the material presented by the child is just a story. On a symbolic level, however, it is significant because it [can be] a concrete representation of the images of the child's unconscious.'

SOME THEORETICAL CONSIDERATIONS

Containment, or emotional holding

Generally children have secure enough backgrounds and beginnings to enable them to develop the capacity to contain their own anxieties most of the time and feel free to learn; but for badly damaged or deprived children, something more is often needed to enable them to function and learn effectively in school. Paul Greenhalgh in Chapter 4 of his book *Emotional Growth and Learning* writes of the need of disturbed children for 'emotional holding' as well as for teaching:

> Emotional holding is the holding and containment of disturbed feelings which are inhibiting the capacity for relationship, emotional growth and learning. It involves demonstrating that distressing feelings can be tolerated, helping children to manage feelings, think about them, and understand something of their meaning. (Greenhalgh 1994)

This concept of 'containment' of distressing feelings was developed by W. R. Bion (1962) in relation to a mother being a container of her infant's feelings. After experiencing distress through the infant's cries which cannot be ignored, a mother thinks about the meaning of the cries and is able to respond helpfully. So infants learn that distressing feelings can be expressed and tolerated, because mother will understand and make them better, leaving them free to look around, take an interest in things and begin to learn.

As well as a secure accepting relationship and firm consistent boundaries providing the opportunity for 'emotional holding' in school, a story written, shared and remembered can also be like a container. When anxieties are deposited into the 'once removed' situation of a story and shared and thought about with a trusted adult, it is as if the child is being safely held. In the context of the story the difficult anxieties can become bearable, so they don't need to remain locked away or worried about so much, leaving the child freer to learn. In the regular weekly setting of individual educational therapy both the stories and the relationship are used in this way. In fact the two are interdependent. The presence of the understanding adult who remembers and holds the stories in mind, and keeps them in a safe place from week to week, facilitates the containing process. Without the reliable, trusted, remembering adult the stories could easily just slip away and lose their opportunity to become important, and act as stepping stones from which to grow.

Sharing stories and reflecting on stories together can enhance relationships and encourage the experience of being understood, because the feelings of the characters, which are probably also important to the child, are taken seriously. Janet, a very withdrawn teenager, was such a child. Her educational therapy sessions consisted of either long awkward silences or writing endless shared stories of arguments and conflicts. Although right up to the end (I saw her for about eight months) this pattern did not change much, in school and in class there were reports that she was 'coming out' of herself, speaking to teachers, and asking when she needed help. She began to acknowledge that she felt more confident and 'ready to finish'. It was noticeable that her stories were becoming more resolved and hopeful – and 'jokey' too!

Integrating the 'shadow'

In order to feel comfortable enough with ourselves, and in order to conform to the image others expect of us, we all hide away and suppress those uncomfortable, destructive and wild parts of our natures, hoping that they will not erupt at unguarded moments and depress us, or get us into trouble. We are mostly unaware of these *shadow* parts (Jung 1958) and would often earnestly deny that we should have such qualities – tending rather to notice and criticize or ridicule them in others (or admire them wistfully – for we can lock up our strengths and our gifts too). However, not only does this hiding away deplete our energy and our ability to learn and create and think, but also particularly for the more 'disturbed' children (whose ability to contain their uncomfortable or unacknowledged bits may be damaged or undeveloped) it does not work, and they can find themselves more and more 'leaking out' the qualities they wish to avoid and deny. For healthy growth and development we need to feel and become comfortable enough with the whole of our natures, so that our lives can flow freely.

Fairy tales

Engaging with stories, and with fairy tales in particular, can resonate with the voice of our shadow parts, enabling us to grow a little more open and tolerant, as we identify with the different characters, their plights and behaviours. For example, we can sympathize with Goldilocks, who only ate the bears' porridge because she was hungry, and who fell asleep in baby bear's bed because she was tired – although the bears may have seen her rather differently!

The fairy tale message of hope and help through struggles faced with courage, can inspire us to want to try to make a difference and be brave and patient when things get difficult – like Hansel, perhaps, who bravely sneaked into the garden at night in order to gather pebbles in the dark, knowing he and his sister might be left stranded in the forest on the following day. Familiarizing children with fairy tales can give them a language and a structure, as well as a host of harmful and helpful characters

> to enable them to think about seemingly unjust or dangerous situations. The solutions the characters in fairy tales use to overcome their difficulties can give children clues to the kinds of resources they need to develop, to deal with their own difficulties in life . . . In writing their own fairy story children can take an active part in this 'healing' process. (Green 1996)

I suppose I know a little about this process 'from the inside'. As well as using fairy tales with children, a few years ago I was also encouraged to write a fairy story, as part of my own journey of self-awareness and development. I sat down with pad and pencil, and without any preparation apart from a short period of conscious stillness and relaxation, I began to write, and the story began, and it seemed to take on its own form and struggle until it was ended. Later I was amazed to see just how much understanding and insight I could gain from the story – my story, which continues to be a source of inspiration, and an opportunity for integration and hope to this day. It seemed as if the process of just allowing the story to grow and be written down without too much conscious intention was important. My familiarity with fairy stories from childhood was no doubt important too. Michael Green talks of the need to 'prime the pump' (Green 1996). We need to provide the atmosphere, the familiarity with the genre, and the secure relationship for the story to flow. Openness to the voice of the imagination also makes a difference. David Holbrook writes:

> The primary and urgent need of the less able child . . . is for the exploration of inward fantasy, and the expression of it in many forms . . . This should be the basis of all their work, not only in English, but in English it is [also] the root of literacy. Without a great deal of such work they can neither begin to bring their personalities into order, nor become effectively articulate for normal social life, and literate. (Holbrook 1964)

Importance of a safe space and a trusted adult

Of course vivid and symbolic expressions of conflicts, anxieties and dreams do not just occur in a vacuum. Children need to feel safe, valued and cared about as individuals for them to consciously or unconsciously allow their imaginations to ride and flow out in stories such as these. To release this special potential children need opportunities both to write creatively in the presence of a trusted adult and to have their writing content taken seriously and thought about. Gill Morton talks of creating a special writing *frame* which also includes a regular time and place each week and a special book or folder to keep the stories in (Morton 1996). Such opportunities could be in a supportive small group situation, in a class where caring, trusting relationships had been fostered through processes such as circle time (see Chapter 10), or in the context of a closer one-to-one relationship of individual special needs support or educational therapy.

Importance of regularity and consistency

Although many children may be able to *express and communicate* difficulties and anxieties through initial stories (or drawings) with a sympathetic adult, the transformative potential of creative arts like storymaking grows slowly. As trust and engagement with the therapist or teacher and with the regular session time develops, and through cumulative experiences of writing or creating stories and having them held in mind and thought about, children really become able to make use of stories for symbolic representation, and their transformative and integrative potential is realized and observed. When children begin to feel understood and taken seriously, changes can often be observed in their writing from week to week. Michael was a child with very low self-esteem – expressed in his minute, rather messy handwriting, his very poor work output, and the fact that he hardly ever finished anything. Understandably teachers found it hard to be patient with him. For many years he had received special needs support, but these tendencies remained. In his final primary year it was suggested that he should have just 20 minutes' educational therapy per week, when we mostly wrote stories together. In these two stories, written just a few weeks apart, his growing stronger and braver can be observed:

> I have got a story about a beanstlak. It was growing right up through the clouds a boy called Jack and one day Jack looked at the beanstlak. He felt he was going up there but he was a bit nervous to go. He did not know that a giant was up there and the giant was very horrible. Jack went up the beanstalk although he was nervous and he did not know that the Ball [bell] was noisy. He looked up at the top of the carstle. He felt nervous. He thought he might go back home. He dsided [decided] thet he did want to go back home so he did. The end. (Shared writing after reading the story and drawing the beanstalk picture.)

> A monkey came to a maze. It looked very hard to Find the treasure and he miad it to the treasure. He walked all the way.

In class his handwriting was growing larger!

Ways of responding to children's stories

The way that children's stories are received by both teacher (or therapist) and peers is crucial. Taking their stories seriously is important. Giving a little time to thinking with children about the feelings and dilemmas of their characters, as well as seeing their stories in the context of their previous stories and characters, would all indicate our serious attention and acceptance. Sometimes it feels affirming and helpful to respond in the context of the story itself, by adding a few words or a sentence to the writing. This can both move the story on a little (for reluctant writers) and serve as a device for acknowledging and reflecting back seemingly important bits, although we must always be careful to keep to the child's agenda and only make bland or reflective contributions to the story. Although educational therapy training can equip teachers to understand some of the symbolic content of children's stories, interpreting personal meanings to the content of their stories would obviously not be appropriate in class, and is usually better just borne in mind, as it could cause a child to feel vulnerable and exposed.

Sensitivity is important. Too much attention or direct questions could feel intrusive or persecutory, particularly in the case of an abused child, whilst not noticing little hints or uncomfortable allusions could indicate that we could not bear to think about such themes, or that we were not really tuned into them. Gill Morton writes of the importance of 'hearing small signals'. When a child repeats a word or an image or an idea, it may

> be thought of as a small signal about a child's inner world, and may help the observant teacher or therapist to work towards a joint 'language' with the child about difficulties and preoccupations. Using the word or image yourself and feeding it back to the child (or including it in your part of the story) shows that it has been heard. If it is not important your use of it won't matter. If it has been a very tentative indication of how a child sees a difficult idea, then the child may feel permission to say more. (Morton 1996)

Counselling skills like empathy and unconditonal acceptance are very helpful when responding to children's stories. Sometimes, depending on our priorities for the child and for the task, it is more important to accept the story as it is than to make suggestions for improvements (although this is not easy for us as teachers!). Sometimes, as with counselling, it is necessary to be able to bear the discomfort of the characters without needing to reassure or encourage premature happy endings for the child to really feel understood as in 'Pinocchio and His Friend' (see below). Sometimes a little understanding silence is the most appropriate response. For particularly in educational therapy, it is the quality of our thinking and remembering that leads eventually to understanding, and to the important experience of 'containment' of anxieties, which are buried or difficult to talk about, for the child.

Ways to facilitate children's stories

Probably the most important way to develop and facilitate children's storywriting is to read stories to them. With the tightening and filling up of the National Curriculum, and with the advent of television and computers at home, children are much more deprived of this 'food of the imagination' than they used to be. Educational therapists and teachers will often have a special collection of fairy stories, and stories of struggles, worries and hope for example, from which to select.

Children's pictures, sand worlds and plasticine models will also have stories to tell. The famous child psychiatrist D. W. Winnicott developed the squiggle technique whereby the adult does a quick squiggle on the paper, and then the child turns it into something (Winnicott 1971). Surprisingly satisfying pictures can result from this technique, and often the picture becomes important and sparks off a revealing story which can be helpful to think about with the child. After drawing a squiggle creature in her educational therapy session, Natalie (age 10), who lived a very restricted life, expressed her hesitations and her frustrations as her wishes tumbled out, when she wrote:

> This creature is Wondring what to think. May be he would go and play with his firends then he will go down the Park and Play but then Want will he do I kown he will go to the siwnming pool but he wouldn be a louid in oh Well. The end.

Evocative colour supplement pictures stimulated some quite primitive needs and fears in the small therapeutic writing group. Heather (age 8) found a picture of a rather straggly looking boy she called Ben:

> Once upon a time there was a boy called Ben. He cept hiding so his mum cod [could] find him and he hide agen behand the cate hang [behind the coat hangers] and his mum find him and gave him a big cubol [cuddle].

Cindy chose a picture of a lady squashed up in a crowded shop.

> help me help me I nede help I am shwasd [squashed] with all the pepller I want to get out of this shop ahhhhhhhhhh . . . help me pleas help me i'm criying I hate this shop get me out of this shop good biye evrebody I wont bey seying you agen then they started a fite.

In individual learning support or educational therapy sharing the writing is a very motivating possibility. This can be either writing alternate lines or paragraphs, or writing a shared conversation or play. Polly Burridge writes that 'sharing a story together is something very special: something organic perhaps like a living metaphor to be played around with in the shared space, something with possibilities' (Burridge 1992).

'Pinocchio and His Friend' was written by Billy and his educational therapist together using sequential speech bubbles, after reading the story and drawing the characters.

Friend:	How are things Pinocchio?
Pinocchio:	They are all right.
Friend:	What is it like being made out of wood?
Pinocchio:	It is very, very, horrible.
Friend:	That sounds very difficult for you.
Pinocchio:	Yes. It is so horrible, I feel like setting myself on fire sometimes.
Friend:	Oh Pinocchio you would get hurt.
Pinocchio:	Yes. That is the whole point of doing it.
Friend:	The point. What is the point, Pinocchio?
Pinocchio:	Because everybody is so horrible to me.
Friend:	That sounds very difficult for you Pinocchio.
Pinocchio:	Yes, that is right, but you are my friend.
Friend:	Yes, I am your friend, Pinocchio. But why do you think everybody hates you Pinocchio?
Pinocchio:	I do not know.
Friend:	That must make you feel . . . well, how does it make you feel, Pinocchio?
Pinocchio:	Very, very horrible.
Friend:	Like you are no good?
Pinocchio:	Yes, that is perfectly right.

This story was written by a boy who could not talk directly about his feelings at all, although he could obviously use writing very effectively to communicate.

Storywriting in class

I have been fortunate to work in a school where creative and developmental writing has been fostered on a weekly basis in every class for many years.

At the start of a session the teacher and children settle down to write quietly without disturbance for 10 minutes. This peaceful settling-in time with the teacher also writing is crucial to enable everyone to get 'stuck into' their writing. The children are mostly free to choose what to write about, although in the beginning and on occasions they may need help with (or be given) ideas. In this first draft it is important that the children's thoughts can flow fluently onto the paper without interruptions. Children are encouraged to underline any words they want to check later, and to write on alternate lines, and even alternate pages, so space is available for editing. Editing is, as far as possible, a self-help process with the children being expected to check and reflect on their own work, and to support each other before having a 'conference' with the teacher. A wide variety of dictionaries and word banks are available, and some children may have 'spelling partners' to whom they can turn for help when editing their work. After the 10 minutes' quiet writing time teachers – and sometimes special needs teachers and teacher assistants – sit in a quiet place to conference children individually on their writing, focusing on receiving the content with interest and empathy, perhaps reflecting on similar themes in literature or in life, before moving on to working on one or two (often self-chosen) technical points. During conferences other children must manage any difficulties or questions independently and not interrupt another child's conference. Various options are available for children to work on if they are 'waiting' or stuck. Obviously with this level of individual support it is not possible (or necessary) for every piece of work to be conferenced, but children do value the fact that teachers read and take an interest in their work each week, as they read the comments written in response to it. For example:

'I can't wait to find out what is going to happen next, Samantha.'
'I'm glad the monkey got back down safely, Joe.'
'I hope I never meet a monster like that, Elizabeth.'

Teachers create various systems to manage the time and the conferencing. For example, children sign up on the blackboard for a conference when they feel they need one, or when they have completed their self-help editing; children must have a conference on at least 1 in 4 'stories'; certain children must have a conference after every page or session. Genuine accepting, empathic listening is important during conferencing, as it is in the whole class sharing times at the ends of the sessions. As well as being encouraged to share and think about their writing with friends, the sharing time at the ends of the sessions is a crucial part of the 'Graves Writing' process (after Donald Graves, who inspired us with his book *Writing: Teachers and Children at Work,* 1983). Children or teachers may request a particular piece of work to be read out – either their own or someone else's which they particularly enjoyed. Ideally this should be done in a circle, but however the children are arranged everyone listens intently and reflectively as the writer reads. At the end the writer may take questions or comments. For a moment the roles are reversed, and the writer is the authority with the knowledge and the ideas and the power to accept or reject the suggestions. If during this sharing time the teacher takes a back seat the children will tend to develop the ability to play the supportive, thoughtful, encouraging roles for each other; although there will obviously need to be some negotiated 'ground rules', e.g. in some classes only two questions are allowed for each writer in order to make room for more sharing turns. Children can learn a lot from reflecting on each other's writing, particularly the occasional vivid or moving piece which inspires or amuses – not necessarily from the most able pupil! For example:

One day Mrs Ourbote was washing-up her husebande said don't just stande there listen to me. I whon't listen to you Ourbote all white don't. I'm leving enyway to scotloande. Pleaces don't I will liston to you. Its to laite for that I said I was laeving ennyway its not you she said i'm having a baby goriller.

This was written in response to a colour supplement picture by 9-year-old Tina, a very slow-thinking but imaginative child who had been receiving special needs support throughout her primary schooling. Like other children who write regularly, Tina had obviously 'found her voice'. She could write with confidence and power, despite her spelling difficulties – for which she was having extra help.

Pieces of writing children are particularly proud of can be 'published' in various ways. Having their stories published by hand or computer – perhaps being made into a book for younger children, or into a magazine article – can provide the children with the feeling of being valued and empowered. Not only is it empowering for the writers to see their work in print, but the interest and obvious enjoyment their stories evoke in other children reinforces this. David Holbrook writes of using the duplicated writing of 3C as readers for 4B: 'It always worked – there was always the naturally engaged concentrated silence, and acute critical interest. Other teachers confirmed this impression – and the procedure led to a remarkable advance in reading capacity' (Holbrook 1964).

Of course it must also be acknowledged that children and classes can sometimes 'get in a rut' with their stories and writing. Teachers may need, for example, to limit the number of football or television stories! They may sometimes suggest or offer a stimulus to the class or to an individual; and such regular story and free writing opportunities are also supported by many stories, excerpts, poems, etc. being read to the class. So 'Graves Writing' is a time when children can feel completely free to write, without needing to worry about their secretarial skills. Initially they just allow their thoughts and ideas to flow out onto the paper as fast and as fluently as possible. Thinking about such matters as spelling can come later.

Scribing

For children who are unable (or unwilling) to write we can act as their scribe or their secretary. As they talk and we write, they (and we!) discover there are powerful stories inside them which can be written down, and in a sense they can become writers too. It is as if we are making a bridge into their world, accompanying them on their first difficult steps into literacy. Polly Burridge writes: 'What registers for them is that we show that we value their words by our seriousness in writing them down. By acting as their secretaries we demonstrate how well we listen and attend to them' (Burridge 1992). Probably many special needs teachers and teaching assistants have used this technique as a way in to teaching a child to read. Remembering your own story can be so much more motivating than reading someone else's – as well as, perhaps, being a helpful way to contain some of one's anxieties within a story and a trusting relationship.

Sam had moderate learning difficulties as well as having been very damaged by sexual abuse. Through her choice of *monster* stories to dictate and to read, and later to write, she was able to progress a long way towards becoming a coping healthy reader and person. 'Big Hairy' was dictated when she was 9, after drawing a picture of a big hairy monster (Figure 4.1).

One day Batman had gone and Maggie went on and on and on with mummy with a story about a big hairy monster. The monster was fat and hairy. He climbed into a high cave, the big hairy monster. He frightened her, he found out where Maggie

Figure 4.1 Big Hairy

lived. She lived at 72 and he had two guns to blow up the house and he done something. He roared, and he got spikes on his head and he is saying: 'I am coming to get yoouu.'

In Sam's case to dictate the story and to have it written down was enough. To know that someone else could hold it in their mind and bear to write it down was a relief, but to read it through again in the early days was just too much. Although it was only a story, the associations were obviously too powerful to be re-experienced and this was understood. Whereas normally teachers would try to encourage children to write a variety of stories, understanding the symbolic content of Sam's monster stories as a bearable way of letting out repressed and unbearable memories was important, and meant that we were happy for her to continue to dictate and write monster stories for as long as she needed to. Later she came to want to read her stories again and again, and amazingly she began to learn to read and to write. Predictably the *Monster Books* (for example, Blance and Cook 1973) were special favourites!

For many children the writing and reading go together. As Burridge continues:

As I write their words they start to show wonder that their story looks so long, and when it is finished I suggest that after all their hard work, they can sit back comfortably while I read their story to them. As they listen a grin spreads over their faces – they react as if I had given them a rare present – it is their creation but they did not know such a thing was possible. (Burridge 1992)

As we concentrate on and appreciate their stories, for a few moments they can feel that the knowledge and the good things are inside them (for once!). If for a short time they are able to experience what it is like to have something good to share perhaps they may begin to feel that other changes are possible. Burridge writes: 'As their story grows so the child also seems to grow.'

Writing for real purposes

John Holt wrote:

It cannot be said too often [that] we get better at using words, whether hearing, speaking or writing [them] under one condition only – when we use these words to say something we want to say, to people we want to say them to; and for purposes of our own. (Holt 1964)

Too often these days in our 'top-down' approach to education it is hard for children to write for their own purposes and to their own audiences although skilful and wise teachers will find ways to facilitate opportunities. Sometimes they can arise unexpectedly. In the 1960s David Holbrook was developing the use of 'creative and imaginative writing', both as a way to enable children to explore their fantasies, fears and dreams, and as a way to enable them to become literate and to find their 'voice'. One day he was criticized by a writer to the *Guardian* who said that he was being 'over indulgent' and 'over protective' (Holbrook 1964). He goes on to describe the fury and indignation of his (Year 10) C and D stream pupils who requested to reply to the letter:

'Can we tell 'im 'e's a clot sir?'
'No,' I said, 'you must write carefully written, proper and polite letters saying what
you think.'

He continues:

We had as yet done no practice in letter writing . . . But now they wanted to write
letters. So I produced some single sheets of paper for them, and they began. All
the letters were neat and set out in the proper way, and nearly all were postable.
Every letter had its own characteristic way of putting the arguments. What
surprised me most of all was that they not only wrote with efficiency, but they
showed that they knew why we worked in the way we did. Far from being
deceived about the world, they were very realistic, in the way a child can only
become by attention to the needs and realities of his psyche.

'We write a lot of stories but we nearly all enjoy writing them.' (Judith)

'We have to work hard, and it tacks hard work to write thoses story and it very
hard when people say he soft on us.' (Joan)

'I should never get anything done if all my spelling were perfect. I would be
looking in the Dictonary all Lesson insted of getting on with my work and I can
right a letter and right a postcard . . . and Mr Holbrook can be srict.' (John)

At other times such real purposes may be planned for, or arise through the
curriculum. Children who have found their 'writing voice' and who feel secure
within the setting can often use these opportunities creatively – and sometimes
unexpectedly. At the end of the school year Susan was asked, along with the rest of
the class, to write a letter introducing herself to her next teacher. It rather surprised
and disturbed her present teacher to find her letter full of anguished experiences of
bullying both from a child at school and from her brothers. Susan had obviously
internalized her teacher and the school as a caring place where children were
listened to and taken seriously, and the opportunity of the letter enabled her to
express her hurts. She had always been a child who found talking difficult, but after
the letter she greatly appreciated being able to talk things through with her
teachers, her parents and the offending 'bullies'.

Other teachers have used 'private journals' (10 minutes a day), writing reviews
and reports, requests for help and messages to children as valuable real purposes
for writing. In educational therapy, writing messages to children can sometimes be
more bearable than saying anything. Polly Burridge writes of how a child came in to
see her in a state of such anger and despair one day that it was hard to know how to
start communicating helpfully with him. So she wrote: 'Hello Abi, I know you are
unhappy today [and] it is hard for you to think. When you feel better I will read you
a story' (Burridge 1992). As a result she released the tension and stimulated his
curiosity. He was soon able to relax a little and they were able to begin the story.

Teachers also write messages to children and vice versa. Instead of the usual 'well
done' and 'good work' comments Katie's teacher would write such comments as
'good idea', 'I didn't know that' and 'this is fascinating' both at the end of her work

and anywhere she felt the need to respond to the child's writing. Katie's parents were also invited to make comments on her work. On one occasion her father wrote:

> It was good to see you working quietly at your table Katie, bit by bit doing more of the work until it was complete. That is the way to do it, asking questions when you need an answer. Dad.

Mrs L found Michael's constant complaints about the other children very trying and disruptive, so she put a special book and pencil near her table where he could write down any complaints or behaviour problems, with the agreement that they would read them before he went out to play. The number of complaints declined considerably!

SOME THOUGHTS ABOUT THE WRITING PROCESS

Children with writing inhibitions

There will unfortunately be some children for whom writing does not feel exciting, creative and productive. Children who have been the recipients of too much destructive criticism may be reluctant to commit words and spellings to paper. They may have got into the habit of avoiding work for fear of getting it wrong and being criticized again. For some just getting started is fraught with difficulties. They may fear to start in case they mess it up, when they so much want it to be perfect. Getting things not quite right, an experience we all have to go through when we learn or try something new, can threaten such children with unbearable feelings of humiliation.

For others it may be humiliating and even agonizing as they are caught in the conflict between needing to think about what to write, and trying to keep their thinking lid down, in case what comes up might be too disturbing.

Traumatic experiences, if not dealt with adequately at the time, can cause blockages in writing as in other learning. Sometimes talking things through with the child and family, together with making a special effort to give time and understanding to the child, can be enough to begin to release the blockage, but sometimes more specialized help is needed.

Therapeutic writing group

As an educational therapist I was able to offer a small group of children with various writing anxieties and inhibitions a weekly therapeutic storywriting group for a term, where a space to talk was combined with a space to write stories without pressure. No one was forced to do anything and eventually everyone found their writing voice. But sometimes they just could not manage it and we needed to understand how hard it could be to write, when we had so much on our minds. I would write too – sometimes about the feelings and anxieties which had surfaced in the group. For example:

> Sometimes it is hard to get started. We don't know what to write about. We don't know if our writing will be all right. We worry in case the others might think it is silly. But in the writing group it is OK to write about whatever we like.

or:

> Today we have found out that we can help each other. Darren needed to know about cocoons and Elizabeth could tell him a lot. Christopher was delighted to find a book he could read easily and enjoy. Darren was worried about his pencil case.

Raymond used his time in the writing group to work through some of the very intense feelings aroused in his whole family by the death of his much loved grandfather, whom they had all only recently got to know. He wrote: 'My grandad is a nic [nice] man and I love him so dus everdody ews [else] in my fanmle [family] and I am upset but I am getting betu [better] as the days go biy.'

Children with extreme difficulties

Children with extreme learning difficulties can have anxieties relating to their difficulties which most of us can't imagine. It is especially important for their self-esteem that the content of their writing be accepted and valued as it is, before any mistakes are noticed and worked on. Asking 'What would you like to work on today?' can give them a feeling of control over the help they receive; this may compensate for the humiliation they can experience when mistakes are noticed. Some children are stuck in the double bind of having real problems with spellings and writing and hearing blends (for example), and feeling that they need to be perfect – perhaps because their parents need them to be so when other things are not so perfect and cause such anxiety. They can become frozen avoiders or manipulative pretenders with beautiful handwriting, hoping that no one will notice their difficulties, and the way they need to sneak help from those around them. Children with serious learning difficulties obviously need skilled and targeted support with writing and spelling. However, for some children this help may be hard to make use of, when other troubling and even damaging circumstances compound their problems and anxieties, making it hard for them to face their difficulties, or to take in and hold on to what they are taught. They are like babies who have been badly treated, neglected or fed the wrong sort of food, for whom memories of feeding cause inhibiting anxieties, even though they are desperately hungry. Such children (amongst others) may benefit from educational therapy, a psychodynamic child therapy which works on the child's learning difficulties at the same time as working on the underlying emotional difficulties.

Roger was a child with severe dyslexic difficulties who had also been stuck in the middle of his parents' very antagonistic relationship and divorce. In many ways he may have acted as the focus for their anxieties. His problems had perhaps held them together for a while, but in the end a messy separation ensued, and he could have felt to blame for that too. He certainly found it very hard to use and hold on to the special needs support he received, particularly as his home circumstances fell apart. In his educational therapy sessions he was able little by little to communicate his desperate helplessness. After drawing a picture of a drowning boy attached to my squiggly line which he turned into a rope (Figure 4.2) I encouraged him to write down what the boy might be saying:

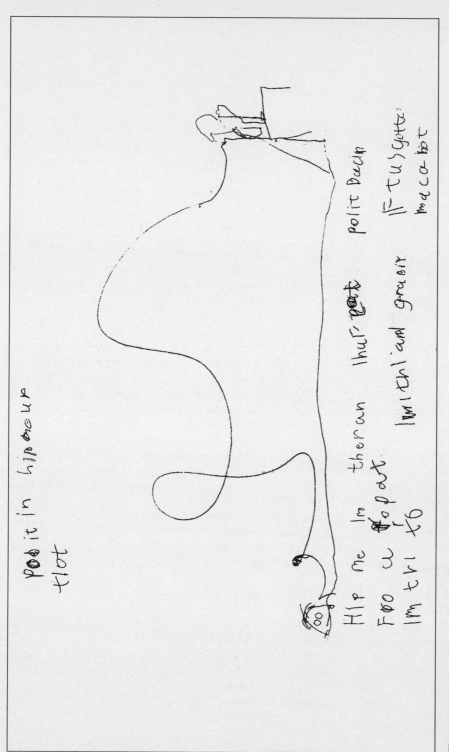

Figure 4.2 Roger's 'squiggle' picture and desperate story

Roger: hlp me Im theran [drowning].
Me: How shall I help you?
Roger: Fro a rop at.
Me: Catch the rope. Here it comes.
Roger: Im tri to.
Me: It is behind you.
Roger: I haf got . . .
Me: It sounds hard to grab it.
Roger: Im train to grab it.
Me: You have got it?
Roger: If jus got to mac a not.
Me: OK.
Roger: Pol it bac in.
Me: I'm pulling hard.
Roger: Pol it in.
Me: OK.
Roger: Hlp me up.
Me: OK. Here you are. How are you feeling?
Roger: Tiot [tired].
Me: Then lie down and have a sleep.

Writing and reading were really hard for Roger. Even when he was trying his very best things were difficult. Remembering the letter patterns was hard. Remembering which way round to write the letters was hard. Thinking and remembering was doubly hard when the thoughts which might pop up about home and about his own uselessness were so uncomfortable. He began to write and tell stories about 'Hard Harry' which expressed some of these useless feelings:

> There was once a boy called Harry. Everything was hard for Harry. They called him Hard Harry. One day Harry went for a walk and 'he met [went] in the rcds [arcades] and met [went] on a mhen [machine] and it was to hab [hard] f [for] him so he wet back ho [home] he had din [dinner] and the suc [steak] was to hrt [hard] fr Hare to cut so he rs [asked] his mum to cut it.'

One day I drew a 'circle creature' opposite his duck. Our characters began to have a 'paper conversation' (share writing a cartoon-type conversation):

Circle creature: Hallo Duck.
Duck: Hallo Sal.
Circle creature: What are you doing?
Duck: Swimin.
Circle creature: Tell me about swimming.
Duck: Yo waf yo rs and ck yo lgs [You wave your arms and kick your legs].
Circle creature: I have not got arms and legs.
Duck: Then yo crt swim.
Circle creature: But you can swim.
Duck: I'f got rs and legs.

Circle creature:	It's hard for me. I can't do much.
Duck:	Yo can toc. Yo can et.
Circle creature:	Yes. I had forgotten. You think I can do some things?
Duck:	Yor jus as clcf [clever] as I am.
Circle creature:	I think you are trying to cheer me up.

In the context of our 'conversation' we could play about with changing roles. He could see me as the circle creature feeling useless and depressed and envious of his skills perhaps, and experience vicariously that I might understand a little how he sometimes felt. Amongst his many problems were his poor visual perception and his poor visual memory. Many letters were problems for him. 'M's were muddled with 'w's, 'p's with 'g's, 'b's with 'd's, etc. In addition to more direct teaching on the letters, creating letter land stories with muddled and angry characters was a helpful way to acknowledge and work through this difficulty. At the same time this was a way of safely letting out his aggressive fantasies which were very much around, both in his very ambivalent learning relationship and in his situation at home. Examples are:

The messy mole with his two holes was mesin up the to hos in the mountains. They was so messy he couldn't get in so he timd them up and he was not messy any more. (Figure 4.3)

and:

The wicked witch went to the weird and wonderful park. She made everything loose so that when the children went on them they fell off and after it was all tightened up she put grease on the seats so they slipped off and she put water in the bottom of the sandput so they sunk under. (Figure 4.4)

So his educational therapy sessions and the stories we wrote together became an opportunity for us to hear and contain his huge anxieties, and to think about them in the safer 'once removed' situation of the story characters and their dilemmas, as well as an opportunity for practising his reading and writing skills. A large amount of anxiety was experienced and tolerated by both of us in the sessions as well as in the stories at this time, and it was interesting to hear from his teacher how in class his reading and writing were really beginning to relax and 'take off' just as we were experiencing more of the difficulties.

In addition to the importance of understanding responses and facilitating opportunities there are various practical ways teachers have developed to make things easier for children with writing difficulties. This is not the place to go into the wide range of learning support techniques and approaches which are possible, but perhaps one or two deserve mention as they relate more directly to developing children's self-esteem and making their frustrations bearable. The application of scribing mentioned above also serves as a way of separating the process of creating a story from that of writing down the words. For some children, coping with the two challenges together is just too much. The use of tapes, 'language master cards' (single sentence tape recording cards) and concept keyboards are other ways to separate out the two processes. Danny was given a set of four numbered language master cards on which to record his story. He then listened to each card in turn on

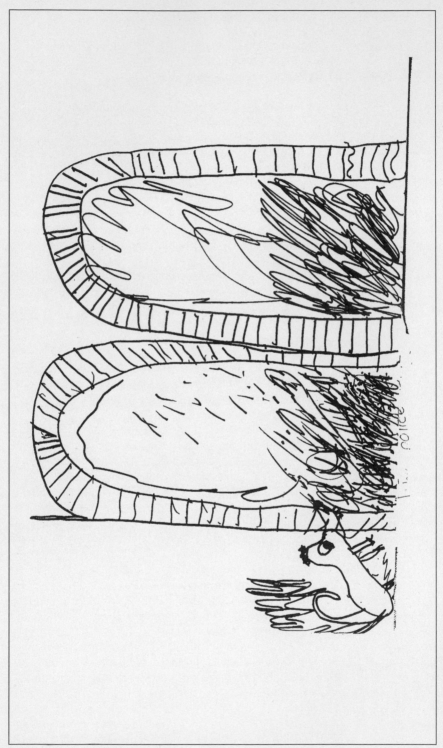

Figure 4.3 The messy mole messing up the mountains

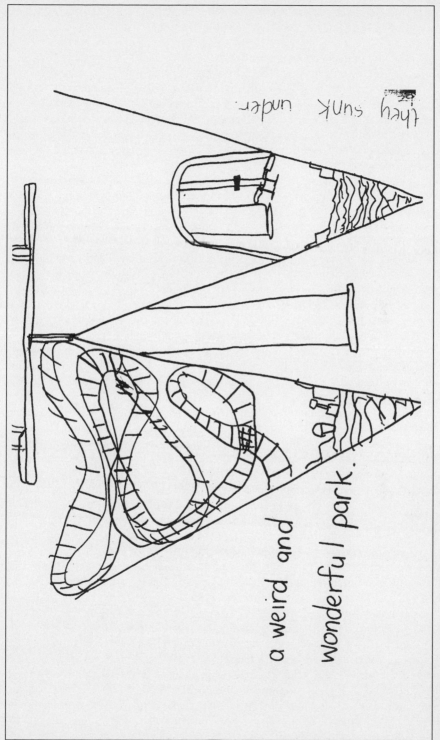

a weird and
wonderful park.

they sunk under.

Figure 4.4 A weird and wonderful park

his earphones and wrote down the words as he heard his own voice saying them, enabling him to concentrate more fully on the writing process without disturbance as he wrote.

The value and importance of accepting inventive spellings in first drafts has also been mentioned. Encouraging children to identify words to check is the first step towards correcting spellings. For children with fragile self-esteem it may be important not even to draw attention to other misspellings, unless the work is to be published. Of course expectations are important and should be consistent and realistic, and spelling skills need to be taught, but in order to encourage confidence the power needs to remain with the child as far as possible. They may need to grow into independence one step at a time.

Whilst in general being an advocate of independent or inventive spellings in first drafts, if nervous and vulnerable children appear very uncomfortable attempting their own spellings I would say 'Do you want to have a go first?' when asked for a spelling. For a while they may say no and I would just give the spelling, but there usually comes a time when they decide to have a go.

Affirmation of children's good efforts by ticking the correct letters (on a nearly correct word) can be helpful and can even amaze them. With such children teacher assistants have tried 'Have a go books' as a step along the road to independence – whereby children who lack confidence gain a 'well done' stamp on a facing page for every word they 'have a go' at, although they can choose to ask for spellings if they prefer. No comments are made about their attempts unless they request it.

Of course computers and word processors are very useful both for drafting and for editing. They can be particularly helpful for children with extreme spelling and handwriting difficulties and for those with fragile self-esteem since their work can look beautiful in the end.

Some writers are reluctant to edit their work for fear of drawing attention to their mistakes and feeling just awful again. If such children can earn a point for every word underlined and checked in a dictionary they may be able to bear to approach and correct some of their mistakes. We all feel slightly uncomfortable when our faults and failings are pointed out, although we know that it is through acknowledging our mistakes and trying again that we learn. For children who have had a difficult start this discomfort is more acute, but that does not mean that it should be avoided. Such children are likely to find it easier to learn and to hold on to what they have learned if they are encouraged to take small manageable steps in the direction of independence. If by just working on one or two things during a conference, and if help is offered in the context of their being taken seriously and treated with understanding, they are more likely to be able to move into becoming people who can use writing for their own purposes, and people who can share their stories when they find a good listener.

So we return to the gift of imagination in our fears and in our dreams. We can create monsters – or we can create free soaring birds (Burridge 1992). Just as it is important to allow our stories of struggle to come alive and perhaps become transformed or resolved, so it is important for us all to acknowledge our dreams. (Otherwise how could any of them be realized!) Magical stories, bird stories, rainbow stories, etc. will come out anyway when the time is right in educational therapy. But in class we may wish to provide children with opportunities to focus on their 'dreams' – to get in touch with their other, less well-known, more spiritual sides

– through suggestions to read and write fairy stories, bird stories, magical journeys, etc., through taking them into 'special places' in guided fantasies, or through music or poetry.

In response to a suggestion to write a magical story in class Robert wrote 'The Magical Tree':

> He was a magical tree. He lived in the woods. He made magic with his leaves. He grew flowers with his leaaves. He dusted the floor with his branches and leaves. He flopped down in the night. He woke up in the morning on Saturday night. He fell asleep in the daytime. A boy climbed up in his branches and the boy fell down on the floor. The boy had to go to hospital to have an X-ray. The tree made some magic and sent it to the boy. It made him well and now the boy can play in the tree whenever he likes.

It has been said that all children have stories inside them. Facilitating their safe expression can be therapeutic, in the sense that they can express and perhaps 'work through' some of their anxieties in the struggles of their characters, either in the more focused opportunity of educational therapy or in regular storywriting groups or class sessions. They can be a motivating way into literacy, enabling children to want to refine their writing skills, as well as enabling them to find their writing 'voice'. In addition their stories, and even their writing difficulties, can enable us to understand and respond to them more helpfully, as we enter into their world and their struggles – discovering perhaps 'that in fact they are very much like ourselves, trying to make sense of life in exactly the same bewildered way as we are' (Holbrook 1964), suffering perhaps from the fear of exposing their weaknesses as we all do, and hoping that their struggles will be bearable and help will be available when they need it – and that happy endings will be possible finally.

Perhaps also, in our present troubled world, it is not just we as individuals who need happy endings, but the whole world too. If through finding our healthy, authentic writing voices we can develop our abilities to think and act and solve problems creatively, it will be no small thing. There is a danger that in our present rat race towards qualifications and 'progress', and in our tendency to let the likes of political leaders and TV do our thinking for us, we might forget to educate for reflectiveness, authenticity and courage – qualities we are going to need rather a lot in future.

REFERENCES

Allan, J. and Bertoia, J. (1992) *Written Paths to Healing: Education and Jungian Child Counselling.* Dallas: Spring.

Bion, W. R. (1962) *Learning from Experience.* London: Heinemann.

Blance, E. and Cook, A. (1973) *Monster Cleans His House.* London: Longman.

Browne, A. (1984) *Willy the Wimp.* London: Little Mammoth.

Burridge, P. (1992) The story behind the words. In *Making Links: How Children Learn*, Oslo: Yrkeslitteratur.

Fox, M. (1983) *Original Blessing.* Santa Fe: Bear.

Graves, D. (1983) *Writing: Teachers and Children at Work.* London: Heinemann Educational.

Green, M. (1996) 'Where the Wild Things Are': the use of fairy tales with children. *Educational Therapy and Therapeutic Teaching*, April.

Greenhalgh, P. (1994) *Emotional Growth and Learning.* London: Routledge.

Holbrook, D. (1964) *English for the Rejected.* London: Cambridge University Press.

Holt, J. (1964) *How Children Fail.* London: Pitman.

Jung, C. (1958) *Collected Works 11, Psychology and Religion: West and East.* London: Routledge and Kegan Paul.

Morton, G. (1996) The therapeutic potential of storymaking with children. *Educational Therapy and Therapeutic Teaching*, April.

Winnicott, D. W. (1971) *Playing and Reality.* London: Tavistock.

CHAPTER 5

A place to be, an ear to hear: working therapeutically with children in a primary school

Jean Lloyd

I was angry with my friend;
I told my wrath, my wrath did end.
I was angry with my foe:
I told it not, my wrath did grow.
William Blake, *Songs of Experience*

Daniel Goleman, journalist, author and former Harvard lecturer, has been so concerned as a parent that his children were growing up in times of unprecedented violence and anxiety amongst American youth that he is now engaged in a serious attempt to change the way the USA brings up its children. His thinking has caused controversy, but the evidence to support his theory is obvious enough: gang warfare, children turning up at school with knives and guns, petty disputes which should have been easily diffused blowing up into fatal conflicts. Goleman (1996) has theorized 'that this was because children had somehow lost the ability to control their emotions and did not know how to interpret others'.

He set out to prove his radical theory by drawing together the threads of a decade of research. The result is his best-selling book entitled *Emotional Intelligence*, which has caused media sensation in the USA, and is now published here in Britain. It proposes a new way of educating children to recognize feelings such as anger or fear and to deal with them appropriately. It asserts also that emotional intelligence is just as important an indicator of personal ability as is IQ, and that it is only in taking emotional intelligence seriously that we will be educating the whole person. It is tempting to be dismissive, to maintain that social conditions in America hardly equate with our own, but Goleman goes on to describe much more familiar areas of concern as he expounds his theory:

There is an African saying that it takes a village to raise a child . . . We have lost the village. In many families both parents work, so they have less time with their children; neighbourhoods are no longer cosy places to grow up in; more children spend more time glued to television or to a computer screen, not playing with others. There has been a precipitous drop in the opportunity to learn basic social skills.

The central thrust of Goleman's argument for developing the whole person is based on recent discoveries about the brain – crucially the way in which the area governing emotions complements, and sometimes overwhelms, rational thinking. This would account for the kind of behaviour Goleman relates and the type of its manifestations in the classroom. Such behaviour sits uneasily, and such discoveries about the brain's function are not necessarily enlightening, but rather formidable without offering solution. Goleman describes a series of experimental teaching courses in the USA which seem to have brought encouraging results, such as a reduction in the number of fights in one school, and an improvement in classroom discipline.

My own personal optimism was also encouraged by research findings which suggest that emotional response mechanisms in humans are not fully developed until late adolescence, indicating that children who have not learned to control and use emotion within their family can experience doing so in a more formal setting. These findings bear out what I have felt intuitively and witnessed in actuality when working with children and their emotional needs. They also pose the question of rights and obligations if we are to assume that our education system is to enable our young people to realize their full potential. This chapter leads on from Goleman's analysis, and offers further practical proof of the importance of educating the 'whole person'. Although my case studies have their origins in very different social contexts from those described by Goleman, and the children's emotional needs may be very differently expressed, strong similarities lie in the emphasis placed on understanding gained by individuals of themselves and their relationships with others through the expression of associated emotions.

When I look back over my career as a primary teacher, before ever the thought or the value of counselling young children had occurred to me, I realize that the needs of the children themselves had been setting the scene for me and I had been responding automatically, as the majority of teachers do, to my pupils' requests for understanding as a matter of course, whether by way of open recognition or by more subtly following their hidden trail. Alongside the more structured and more directed aspects of school life pertaining to academic achievement, children have been inviting me into their worlds, sometimes seemingly chaotic and frightening, making it evident that emotional and psychological wellbeing is as crucial to development as is intellectual capacity. I have worked with children whose barrier to learning has not been so much the result of disability or incapacity, but as a result of emotional preoccupation which is either long-term or resulting from temporary trauma or personal difficulty at a particular time.

Such experiences happen on a continuous basis in every classroom, but recognition of the value of therapeutic intervention is slow to be acknowledged. Yet I feel sure that an investment into the emotional wellbeing of our children in schools would not only be instrumental in helping to 'raise standards', a top priority in the current political climate, but would also release the children themselves to take more control of and responsibility for their actions. In this chapter I wish to demonstrate the value of taking time to listen to and really hear what children are telling those of us who work closely with them about their needs.

It is time to meet the children who trusted me with their innermost fears and anxieties, and whose worlds I was privileged to enter.

By way of an example, a small boy of 6 years old once attempted to explain to me, his busy preoccupied teacher, how his preference for the long, flowing, female items of clothing hanging up in the role-play area of our infant classroom was helping him to experience the gentle, soft and feminine side of his nature. The clothes were always there in the home corner for all the children to choose in their free play time after the completion of more formal classroom activities. It began to be noticed how David invariably dressed up in girls' clothes, making deliberate choices about the colour, length and type of fabric he preferred for his role-play. This was despite the fact that there was an equal array of smart men's suits and casual men's clothing. He would go the whole way to identifying himself with the female including balancing precariously on high heels, adorning himself with a chiffon scarf and never leaving the area without his handbag. When suitably attired, he would then parade, often making deliberate sweeping actions with his long, flowing robes. Other children had made comments, although their understanding of the purpose of this kind of role-play which enabled you to become at any one time the baby, the nurturing mother, the authoritarian older sister, the working father, gave permission to David to feel comfortable experimenting in this way. The people who were not so sure about it were, of course, the adults who observed from a distance and were uncomfortable with what they saw. It was not long before David's mother came to see me, concerned about his female tendencies at home and aware that he seemed to be telling her that he enjoyed dressing up in the girls' clothes at school. Was I actively encouraging him towards abnormal tendencies and why wasn't I discouraging him from this latest preoccupation? I had to admit to her that whilst I was also aware of what he was choosing to do in his free choice time, I did not impose direction or restriction on any of the children in that setting, unless it was in the interests of safety or destruction. I could, however, see her concern and agreed to try to find the opportunity to talk to David, although I would not be making an issue out if it but rather waiting for an occasion to arise naturally. Such an opportunity arose quite spontaneously a short time later when some new clothes had been introduced into the role-play area, which happened from time to time.

David had chosen to try on a colourful evening dress which reached to the floor and which invited swirling movements to show it off to its full advantage. He was obviously delighted with it and as he came towards me in the classroom, it felt natural to make a passing comment. I reflected to him that he seemed to be enjoying the experience of the dress and I wondered if it were the colours which so attracted him to it. He replied straight away and without embarrassment that he liked the softness of the material next to his skin. This was my first indication of a deeper significance for David in his use of the role-play materials. In subsequent conversations that we had, he was able to explain to me that he enjoyed the role-play area because it felt safe to be gentle and kind there. In fact the clothes he chose to wear when playing there actually encouraged and allowed him to behave in that way. He was, I'm sure, identifying gentle, soft, caring ways of being with the feminine persona. This contrasted sharply with what he was experiencing as a boy in the playground and our conversations turned to bullying. David's preference to play with the girls had been picked upon, and his attempts at relating with the boys met with taunts and ridicule. In actual fact he enjoyed the rough and tumble of the boys' play as much as any other, was a skilful footballer as I recall, but was somehow not being accepted by his peers and felt bullied by them. It began to be obvious why he relished the opportunity to experience the female side of his personality within the secure environment of the play area, and why it was so difficult for him to reconcile his maleness with the other boys. With the benefit of hindsight, I can now see that his school work had been erratic and untidy for some time with lots of crossings out in his written attempts to communicate, as if reflecting the confusion he felt inside about his identity. It took some time for him to work through his own feelings as well as those of significant people around him, but the fact that he had been taken seriously by the adults he encountered allowed him to be more open. This was especially true in terms of his family when, with their realization that he was more likely to be trying to deal with a specific problem in the here and now rather than displaying general homosexual tendencies, they became much more able to talk openly and supportively with him.

In contrast Sarah's difficulties during one term of her infant schooling when she was 7 were much more acute, resulting as they did from a traumatic occurrence in her family life. She had witnessed the death of a close family member in a particularly distressing way, and had been involved in police investigations, receiving support and counselling from them at the time. But somehow life had to go on and very quickly afterwards Sarah was back at school to resume 'normal life'. She had been in my class on entry to school, but was now with another teacher. In my role as a deputy head with responsibility for personal and social education within the school, and as a member of staff whom Sarah would know and hopefully trust, it was agreed that the particular events in her life warranted some special provision at this time. With her parents' permission and with the headteacher's support I was released from classroom teaching at regular times in order to offer Sarah one-to-one counselling on a daily basis over a period of six weeks leading up to the end of the summer term. We didn't actually call it counselling, but what I offered her was a place to be – an old, spare, demountable classroom, with toys, paper, paints and crayons and books. At first the books were the only things that interested her, and one in particular seemed to hold a singular fascination. It was a picture book by Janet and Allan Ahlberg entitled *Funnybones,* a popular choice with all the children who liked it for its humour and cartoon-like style. But Sarah was drawn to it for a different reason. It possibly held the secret of her fears and her natural curiosity about what had happened. She began to ask questions about the skeleton figures she saw on every page of the book, wanting to know specific details about human anatomy. She asked many questions about the different bones in the body, especially the ribs – 'bones with holes' as she called them. I explained the bones' functions – the skull, the backbone, the connection of bones to each other, the ribs as protection. She asked what the ribs were protecting, and was keen to feel her own ribs. We had discussions about the protective nature of the skeleton and the vulnerability of the internal organs as she led me down her path of discovery. She worked out for herself the effect of a knife penetrating one of the internal organs and didn't have to ask me that question. But it was important that I was there at that time, able to stay with her curiosity and not frightened off by the horror of her discovery. Through her play and our conversations she was able to add to her knowledge and satisfy her need for exploration and enquiry, as when she chose to tell me about her school trip to Mountfitchet Castle in Essex. I felt it was more than coincidental that she concentrated on a particular aspect of her visit:

Sarah: I want to show you some of the things we saw at Mountfitchet. (She wrote a word which she said was 'surgeon' and drew a picture of the hut.)

Me: Do you know what a surgeon is?

Sarah: A doctor who cuts you with a knife when you are ill. The surgeon at Mountfitchet had a knife and you could see that he had cut open a person.

I went on to explain the specialist nature of a surgeon's work as distinct from that of a general practitioner, and of the advances in surgical practice since the Mountfitchet tableau. She changed the subject quickly at that point, telling me about a chart that had been devised at home to encourage Sarah and her younger brother to behave well, and letting me know that she had explored enough for the time being. In her later play during our sessions, she made several references to the knife which was an item of the tea set I had provided, asking what it could be used for. She set the table for tea on many occasions, using soft toys as invited guests and making sure that they were well looked after. On one occasion she used the toy telephone to reprimand an imaginary parent for not coming to meet her child from the party when all the others had long since gone home. Her request to bring her own soft toys to our sessions became an important way in which she could work through her grief, as well as reconcile conflicting feelings about her own social integration:

Sarah: Daddy says I can bring some of my own toys and games to school. I'd like to have my own toys to play with.

Me: What kind of toys?

Sarah: I've got some cuddly toys.

Me: Oh . . . like Squeaky? (This was a toy referred to by Sarah from the start of our sessions.) How is Squeaky?

Sarah: He gets up in the night and wakes me up . . . He is starting to make friends because I've got a lot of other cuddly toys. He is making friends with Algie and Charlotte [two mice]. They are twins – a boy and a girl – that's unusual.

The above conversation was synonymous with Sarah's own tentative social strategies within the school and classroom environment where she, too, had been experiencing difficulties making and sustaining friendships over a prolonged period. She was therefore using these sessions, which became very important to her, to work through a number of important issues which allowed her to express intense anger, violent temper, destructive impulses as well as to restore, if only in imaginary scenarios, some semblance of normality to her life. My crucial role during this time was to engage fully with her, receiving her instructions and commands, supporting her in her discoveries and feeling the intensity of her frustrations and helplessness. She desperately needed a constant environment with a trusting adult who could be accepting of her and her world as it was in reality for her at that time.

Children can be very aware of the difficulty of expressing such feelings to or making such enquiries of those closest to them at home. When parents or carers are also experiencing similar emotional crises, the risk of upsetting them further becomes very real. It is not surprising, therefore, that children bring their anxieties in to school, which serves as a secure environment where they can confide in a trusted adult.

But Sarah also needed far more than a classroom teacher, with responsibility for upwards of 30 children, could provide. The two examples described above contrast in this respect, and reflect the varying nature of emotional difficulties which can present themselves in any classroom over the period of any one academic year. The problems which were surfacing for David were of a kind which could be worked through as part of normal classroom practice. Provision in the classroom meant that David himself could draw attention to his needs. Classteacher awareness, together with parental liaison, support and co-operation, meant that his needs could then be taken seriously and put into perspective. Increasing awareness on the part of classteachers of the emotional needs of their pupils will mean that children like David can feel supported within the classroom without the need for outside intervention. There is a need for us as professionals to recognize, perhaps urgently, the needs of pupils like Sarah who face emotional trauma, or the increasing number of children who experience prolonged emotional turmoil which interferes with their learning and which invariably manifests itself in behavioural abnormalities and socially related problems. Special needs provision as it exists at present serves largely as a learning support to enhance academic learning. Despite the fact that research by Lawrence (1988) consisting of a series of experiments with primary age children who were retarded in reading demonstrated overwhelmingly that the inclusion of counselling sessions and some drama techniques significantly enhanced self-esteem as well as reading attainment, little recognition of comparable benefits to emotionally disturbed children appears to exist as a result. My personal feelings are that an investment in counselling in the primary phase as part of special needs provision could indeed benefit such children in a similar way. Consequently I was very interested in a telephone message I received recently from a local headteacher enquiring whether I would consider working with some children in school in a counselling capacity. Having left full-time teaching to take up a part-time post in teacher education and to pursue my counselling training, I had the flexibility to consider such a proposal. The work that I was to undertake would bring me into contact on a one-to-one basis with individual children, as well as with a group of 10 to 11-year-old pupils. So I put together a proposal, an outline plan of possible ways to use the three hours on a Wednesday morning that I would be able to commit to the project, and presented it to the headteacher. My term's work with these children, which I now describe, was both rewarding in itself, and also served as an opportunity to develop my own thinking about the value of counselling in primary education.

FORMULATING MY OWN PHILOSOPHY

Before embarking on such a commitment, my first consideration was to formulate my own personal philosophy of counselling. Central to this philosophy is a person-centred approach which recognizes the capacity of the individual to know best how to take responsibility and thereby reach her own potential. I have experienced its benefits myself and know that personal development can take place within a climate of acceptance, genuineness and empathy. My approach to working with children in a counselling capacity would, therefore, be based on those same principles, respecting the child, and understanding alongside the child the difficulties she may be experiencing. Little children are unlikely to be able to express in words what their worries and problems are about, so close observation of their ways of behaving and relating, their artistic impressions, and their choices and uses of play materials are important, and might each, in a veiled way, indicate inner conflicts. Prior knowledge of particular circumstances can also assist the counsellor towards greater understanding. The ability to speak the child's language is also helpful, although this does not mean being patronising which has the effect of widening the gap between child and adult, but rather the ability to proceed on equal terms. Children can be helped to think for themselves and express ideas and feelings if they are allowed to control the pace and direction of the conversation, just as in adult therapy. The counsellor's role is to listen to both words and feelings and to reflect back to the child that such feelings do exist and can be expressed. It may be that the child is unable to express, or fears divulging, exact details of personal circumstances, so that an ability on the part of the counsellor to make connections, to pick up hints or to appreciate the links that are alluded to is helpful in leading the child gradually towards greater awareness. And the child needs to see the counsellor as someone who is reliable, whom she can trust as the relationship develops, and who is secure in maintaining boundaries for the benefit of their relationship.

Lastly, a belief in the intrinsically positive nature of the counselling process is essential, both for the counsellor and for the school, since its effects spill over into many other areas of life. However, equally important is the recognition that it is a gradual process which cannot be hurried, and I have found that this applies equally to children and adults.

My next consideration in wanting to provide this opportunity was to ask myself what I would be aiming to offer the children within this extra provision. I was aware that those who were being referred to me were causing concern as a result of their low attainment in class, low self-esteem and difficult behaviour, all common areas of concern in the classroom. I decided, therefore, that my principal objective would be to provide them with a good experience based on consistency and reliability and an acknowledgement of their feelings. Evidence of wide research in this area (e.g. Axline 1947 and 1989, McMahon 1992) suggests that it is positive experiences of a pleasurable and rewarding nature which help children to develop a sense of their own worth together with the confidence to cope with life's challenges. These can then lead to an ability to control what happens to them subsequently. Confidentiality is an important issue and one that can be discussed honestly with the child as part of the agreed contract. In order to feel secure about exploring difficult feelings and uncertain relationships, the child must be able to trust the counsellor who makes an undertaking not to divulge any of the content of the session without her permission. But the child might also need to understand that there may arise an occasion when, in the interests of her safety, another person may need to be informed of a particular issue. However, this would be discussed and agreed with the child. Permission is something not always agreed with children, and some may view it as a novel prospect, or may be suspicious as a result. And so the development of trust becomes a central feature of the relationship in which the child receives respect, consideration and concern. I would hope then to be able to build on children's own strengths and to give them some experience, however briefly, of an adult in whom they can trust and confide.

In planning any project, even a short-term one, an awareness of possible outcomes is advantageous. Because the children I was to work alongside in this particular situation were being referred for a range of personal difficulties related to self-concept, I hoped more than anything that increased self-esteem would be a recognizable outcome together with a more acceptable (to the child) way of relating. Denis Lawrence has written extensively on the subject of self-esteem, saying that the process of development can be equated with 'the process of becoming more and more aware of one's own characteristics and consequent feelings about them' (Lawrence 1988). He goes on to define *self-image* as what people actually are or perceive themselves to be, as opposed to the *ideal self* which is what a person would like to be. Self-esteem then is the result of what the person feels about the discrepancy between what she actually is and what she would really like to be. Self-concept is the umbrella term used to encompass this.

I had a poignant reminder of this system at work when the final session of my group therapy was drawing to an end. The children in the group were preparing in different ways for their ending – some wrapping up presents of small items which had been part of our time together, some drawing pictures, both of which were coming my way. But one child was busy composing a letter which she then requested should be read aloud to the group while she remained out of sight. It was addressed to 'My really nice friend' and talked about how she would miss her when they parted at the end of term. She concluded with the words 'I know I am not the best girl in the school' which reflects very openly her self-image at that time. In a personal letter to me on another occasion, she talks about a boy in the group whom she perceives as having feelings for other people, and expresses a desire to be like that, thus revealing her ideal self. It was of great importance to her to articulate those feelings at that particular time and demonstrates her courage and insight, which are among her own strengths to be built on in further counselling sessions.

THE PLANNING STAGE

Having received confirmation from the headteacher that the school would be 'delighted' to take up my offer of working with some children in a counselling capacity, I set about planning in my own mind how such provision would take shape, and subsequently made an appointment to visit the school to confirm my intentions.

First of all there were the practical arrangements, including agreed times and venue for the sessions to take place. Then came the important opportunity for me to meet the parents of the two boys with whom I was to start the individual work, to provide us with a forum for discussion. I had been assured that both families had agreed to the offer and welcomed it as a means of additional help and support for their sons. The meeting I subsequently had with one set of parents in the presence also of the Learning Support teachers who had selected the two boys was, I feel, extremely useful for all parties. It offered me the opportunity to outline the nature of the work I was intending to do and to assure the parents that their involvement in terms of monitoring their son's progress and giving feedback would be welcomed. It was also stressed that if they had any concerns during that time there was an open door policy at the school, and I would also be able to make myself available to them for a short time at the end of each session should they wish to talk to me. They also provided much additional information during the meeting about their son's difficulties as they perceived them, as well as about his likes and dislikes, which gave me the kind of insight into his world referred to earlier. More specific issues were also able to be voiced and agreed upon such as that of confidentiality of the content of our sessions, and specific questions raised by the other parties could be addressed.

One such question raised by the father was: 'What happens if his behaviour deteriorates significantly while he is having counselling?' I felt this to be a crucial question and explained that such a thing could indeed happen because a child might be tapping into feelings and emotions that have hitherto remained repressed. There could, as a result, be repercussions in both home and school life which it would be helpful for us to share. In addition to the above, this initial meeting provided the opportunity for agreement about procedure from this point on:

- their son would be aware that his parents had come to this meeting.
- it was agreed that it was in the best interests of the child to leave the parents to decide whether to tell their son what was being arranged for him in school. This decision was reached mainly because of the timing of our meeting before the school Easter holidays. As I was not starting the counselling sessions until the beginning of the next term, we felt jointly that knowledge of it may cause him unnecessary anxiety during the interim period. It was for this reason also that I decided not to meet the child on that occasion.
- we were able to agree on the date and timing of the first session although I made the point that I would not be offering choice to the boys about whether they attended or not, but I would discuss with them any reluctance they might have, should it arise.

The discussion of such important preliminary issues strengthened my belief in the necessity of ongoing liaison with parents and with all involved parties. I did not have this advantage with the other parents although verbal permission for the counselling to go ahead was given, and it was hoped at the beginning that the social worker involved with the family would be able to elicit their written permission. I did meet the other mother informally during the course of her son's counselling, which she seemed at ease with, and I did wonder whether, on occasions, we may need to consider alternative ways of communicating with parents in this situation.

Negotiating the practical issue of the venue proved problematic, since ideally the counselling place should remain as constant as possible and the safety of the children is paramount. There is also the consideration of confidentiality. A classroom corner, a staff room, the school library and a resource room were all offered as possibilities but, while each may offer some degree of privacy, I felt that we were likely to be disturbed, and it would be difficult to maintain a constant environment. I had noted with interest that there was a demountable classroom on the site, and was pleased to learn that, although the room was used regularly for other purposes, I could have the use of it for my counselling sessions. It raised the question of safety and security, moving to and from the main school but, with assurances from me that I would always escort the children back and forth from their sessions, it was agreed that I could use the demountable, and I would make any issues surrounding the journey part of my contract with them. And so I had a base from which to work, with the freedom to create my own counselling space. I had agreed to restore the arrangement of the room at the end of my sessions but, during the Wednesday mornings that I was there, I could have a free rein! It was an ideal way of working within the school environment and one for which I was very grateful.

My next step, therefore, was to plan the arrangement of the room which I intended to keep the same as far as possible, displaying some basic resources supplied by the school and some of my own play materials. These included paper of various sizes and colours, thick and thin card, pens, pencils, crayons, paints, scissors and glue. I had a box of books which I used to create a book corner. There were puppets, soft toys, modelling mediums, junk materials and offcuts of wood, Lego bricks, figures and knights in armour and a selection of board games.

MY APPROACH TO COUNSELLING WITH THE CHILDREN

The two children I was to work with, Tony and Matt, were of primary school age at the time of starting, 10 and 8 years respectively. They had each experienced learning support in school, but were seen to have in addition emotional difficulties, problems of isolation and difficulty with friendships. I got the feeling that insecurity and lack of trust could also be presenting problems. Having read extensively on play therapy, and as a result of my own training in counselling, I decided to adopt a non-directive approach and modelled my sessions on Virginia Axline's non-directive play therapy (1947 and 1989), using the counselling technique of reflective listening. My years as an infant teacher have served to establish for me the therapeutic value of play and to recognize the need we all have, children and adults alike, 'to let our minds wander around a problem' in the words of Linnet McMahon (1993), who goes on to describe play as 'a spontaneous and active process in which thinking, feeling and doing can flourish since they are separated from the fear of failure or disastrous consequences'.

The above recognition, together with Axline's eight basic principles of non-directive play therapy, were to formulate my philosophy and approach in this experimental undertaking. Some of the principles have already been mentioned, such as a relationship of warmth and empathy, acceptance and respect of the child, permission to express feelings, and recognition of the gradual process of therapy as well as its limitations. But specific to the non-directive approach is that the counsellor does not seek to direct the play or conversation in any way, but allows the child to lead. The counsellor remains alert to the feelings being expressed through play and seeks to reflect them back to the child in such a way that enables insight to be gained gradually.

My own personal approach also incorporated other principles in addition to those stated above, and ones which may not meet with the agreement of other therapists working in this way. I found myself, for instance, feeling quite strongly that respect for the child could be extended to include suggestions by the child as to how we might proceed in certain circumstances, and so being adaptive became one of my fundamental philosophies. It could be argued that setting firm boundaries which are non-negotiable are at the centre of all counselling work, and indeed in my time with these children such boundaries were established. These included the time and place of our sessions, limitations such as the non-destruction of, or damage to, the play materials and equipment in the room, and injury to self or to me. But over and above these constraints, the occasional negotiation of particular features of our work together I regard as of potential benefit to the progress of the individual, to the extent that it might actually be influential in reinforcing self-esteem, as well as to assist in the development of relationships. Both of these aspects of development were central to my work with the two boys selected. An example of a way in which we negotiated for change was when I was asked by Tony if I would provide some additional tools for use with the offcuts of wood supplied by the school. Both boys were using the junk materials creatively at this point and as the activity seemed to facilitate conversation, and the tools requested could probably be obtained without difficulty, I agreed to try to do as he had asked. He wrote down his requirements on a piece of paper taken from his own ring binder that he was bringing to the sessions. I was careful not to make any promises, but could see how such a request might open up opportunities to explore specific issues. It did in fact allow certain realizations for him in that, because I was unable to obtain one of the tools he requested, he was able justifiably to express his annoyance and frustration. He was able to say to me in this connection 'I might have to get cross with you if you can't bring it next time', serving as a timely reminder of his own powerlessness in his family situation. It gave him the opportunity to give commands and state preferences, to have his wishes and needs taken seriously, all of which are rare occurrences for him. The situation also allowed him to use the therapeutic relationship to experiment with different ways of relating and to observe the consequences.

A more striking example of negotiating change came about when a request was made by both boys, who are friends outside school, to have their sessions together. It was first requested by Tony around the time his stepfather had died. My initial feeling that it might be helpful for him to have the support of his friend at such a critical time was tempered by the practical impossibility of changing the arrangements immediately, as well as my reflection that it would be better to determine whether that was really what he wanted in the longer term. We discussed the reasons why he was wanting to have his counselling together with his friend as well as possible reasons why it might not be such a good idea. In support of his request he put forward the fact that 'it's boring playing with Lego on your own' and 'there isn't anything that I wouldn't want Matt to know'. By way of a caution against it he said, 'because it could get out of hand'. The reasoning I expressed to him was that while I could see how he might feel reassured and perhaps more at ease with his friend there, I wanted to make sure that he had every opportunity to express his feelings in private first. I could see that there was a natural break coming in our counselling in the form of the school's half-term holiday week when I would not be seeing the boys and, having confirmed with their respective classteachers that a change in arrangements would not cause problems, I put it to the boys that we would continue until half term individually, but they could have their sessions together after the break if that was still what they both wanted. I had in mind 'Excerpts from Group Therapy Records' from Axline (1989) in which she talks about the increased opportunities for interaction where there is more than one child present, and the facilitating effect of increased security in the taking of risks. With that in mind, the arrangement was changed so that the boys could have their five remaining sessions together, except that unfortunately Tony was absent for the final two sessions. But that in itself offered opportunities, as when Matt, who was obviously missing his friend, suggested that we wrote him a letter which he would then deliver. The letter was to express our regret that Tony had not been able to attend our final session and to wish him a good summer holiday. The content of the letter was decided by Matt but written by me and given to Matt to deliver. It seemed a fitting end to our time together, and enabled Matt to demonstrate the caring side of his nature through an actual act of concern which was implemented. I think that adaptability, as well as the willingness to be receptive to the changing needs of the child, is an important factor in enabling children to take control of their lives within a safe and trusting environment. In fact, I feel that the rewards of pursuing an adaptive approach far outweigh the possible disadvantages, certainly within the context of this work.

THE DEVELOPMENT OF THE COUNSELLING

Having established the boundaries with each child separately in our first sessions, giving permission for the full range of feelings and emotions to be expressed, it became immediately evident to me that children have the same complex mixture of emotions that we have as adults. They can in turn be feeling happy, fearful, angry, guilty, sad, confused to varying degrees, and they are capable also of being preoccupied or depressed. They may have difficulty expressing their feelings openly, but they have a similar need for them to be acknowledged. During the course of our 11 short weeks together I witnessed many occasions when both boys made use of the play materials to express their feelings, and when tentatively they made use of me to put into words their innermost thoughts. I observed the subtle ways in which, through their drawings and paintings, they incorporated aspects of their external and internal worlds into their pictures. There was the picture painted by Matt with bright yellows and greens depicting the sun and the natural setting, which was then dominated by proportionally much larger black birds which seemed to catch the eye. It felt like a window into his inner struggle at that time.

It is a measure of the trust that builds up within the counselling relationship that such difficult and extremely risky feelings can come out into the open. For Tony who lives in the precarious world of his warring parents, both of whom want to keep him, threats of damage, destruction and even death are very real. He has experienced the actual death of his stepfather whose loss was painfully explored, as when he shared with me the ways in which he would say his goodbyes. He arrived at one of our sessions in a red, fleecy-lined jacket zipped up to the neck, which he kept that way for the whole hour. He told me it had belonged to his stepdad, and it was immediately obvious that he had found a way of keeping this special person close to him. It is not surprising that Tony played frequently, sometimes violently, with the Lego figures, especially the knights in armour. He would prepare them for battle, often lining them up opposite each other, then systematically destroy their defences, leaving them vulnerable to certain attack and inevitable death. His deaths were often prolonged, with repeated injury. Through his play he was able to act out the destructive elements of his life as he saw it, and give vent to his anger about death and its aftermath. Later, he was able to talk more calmly about important personal issues such as justice and the rights and wrongs of life. He remained fearful of his anger, although it lurked very near the surface and was at times very intense, as when he was 'grounded' for one month, a punishment he felt was excessive and unreasonable. But his anger about it could only be displayed in covert ways. In Tony's world you acted in a certain way, that is you kept occupied 'to take your mind off things', and so he had to be helped first to recognize his feelings, then to give them expression in a safe enough way.

For Matt who was his friend, the timing of his counselling, coinciding as it did with Tony's difficult circumstances, gave him the opportunity to identify and empathize with the plight of his friend. He often chose to talk about Tony in his sessions, and left him things to look at when it was his turn. When the two boys started coming together, Matt would sometimes strike up a conversation with Tony about his circumstances showing that he was not afraid to enter Tony's world. For both boys there were significant signs of growth, trust and ability to sustain a relationship during the counselling period. Some difficulties did arise in other areas of their lives, which reinforces the importance of liaison in order to facilitate understanding. But the school reported a particularly marked improvement in Matt's attitude towards the end of his counselling, in terms of both his own self-esteem and his interaction with others.

CONCLUSION

In presenting my argument for the inclusion of counselling and/or play therapy as part of special needs provision, I have concentrated on four case studies as examples of opportunities which have arisen for me over a number of years of involvement in the primary sector of education. Each case study focuses on an individual child's needs at a particular time, differing in terms of the specific nature and the duration of the emotional disturbance created. Each case is highly individual and unique, and yet my own conclusions, which have been reached through the practical experiences I have described, indicate that these diverse needs can be met through a common approach that gives time and respect to the child's inner voice. Sometimes a listening ear combined with being taken seriously will be sufficient to effect a change of attitude. In certain circumstances, however, a child may need the support of a trusted adult in order to take tentative steps into an unknown inner world. This may suggest a lengthy commitment, and undeniably some long-term emotional disturbance may require correspondingly long-term work, but equally the results of my involvement with these children, though not conclusive, would suggest that short-term intervention can also claim therapeutic value and effect visible change. I heard recently of Sarah who, five years after our term's work together, is well integrated into secondary school and more able to make mutually satisfying friendships. Whilst obviously not claiming to have worked through all her difficulties, I felt that the intervention at that crucial point was highly significant, both in what it offered her at the time and in enabling her to seek help for herself at a later stage in school. Matt's teacher also remarked on his improved self-esteem and his ability to acknowledge other pupils' needs. When he first came to our sessions he rarely finished anything and took little pride in achievement. The combination of being able to express care and concern for his friend both verbally and through art work, as well as his letter, gave purpose to his creativity and subsequently value to his success. Both these examples would have been hard to achieve in the classroom, yet the progress in our therapy sessions happened naturally, the important factors being an unconditional acceptance of each individual, and an understanding of the need to proceed at the child's pace and to take seriously their ways of communicating. Being able to stay with them in their most difficult or distressing moments was also vital and is perhaps what reduces a classteacher's ability to empathize fully in certain situations given that teacher's responsibility for the other children in the class. However, teachers are increasingly aware of the demands such emotionally troubled children can create, and may need support themselves if they are to be able to give access to a broad and balanced curriculum for all children.

Sadly, in these days of severe financial constraints, especially in respect of primary school budgets, it is not surprising that schools are reluctant, and in all probability unable, to commit funds to a service which cannot guarantee either tangible results or a definite timescale. My point about considering short-term intervention at a significant time for a given pupil may be a starting point towards the recognition of the value of counselling as one of a range of support services. It is clear from a recent survey (Moore et al. 1994) that schools would welcome greater access to a wider range of support, with some evidence that therapeutic approaches would feature among schools' preferences. Since the results of this survey suggest that learning difficulties and certain emotional needs are often interrelated, an investment in counselling services could benefit both the individuals and the school.

It is increasingly common now for schools to belong to a 'cluster group' or consortium where corporate decisions can be made on behalf of all parties. Perhaps a combined contribution to buy in counselling services will become the way in which they can operate and be shared by all. What would be even more facilitating would be government recognition of the value of such provision in the form of grants or funds for which schools could apply. The services which schools sought could then be provided through an agency, which would have the responsibility of confirming the qualifications, skills and experience of the counsellors or therapists. As this is a relatively new area of provision, and one which is potentially open to abuse by way of the ease with which it is possible to acquire a counselling qualification, a rigorous selection process for those offering the service to schools would be essential. Recognition and value of any service by a higher authority will contribute to the confidence of the consumer, and if governments are serious about entitlement for all, giving access to support for emotional disturbance would be providing for this particular area of need as well as meeting equal opportunities criteria. In addition, the investment needed to provide support for emotionally troubled children would be offset by an almost certain reduction in truancy rates, vandalism, delinquency, state dependency and all the attendant services and costs.

Enriching young people's lives must be an investment for the future, an important basis of which is the ability to make sound relationships. When I consider the relationships I was able to develop with these troubled children, the trust which became implicit in our work together and the potential for growth that recognition of their needs allowed, the investment of time and money seems only relative. If you combine that with the willingness of children of this age to communicate their needs and to enquire about their world, there seems to be an overwhelming case for recognition of the value of therapeutic intervention for children in both the short and the long term.

REFERENCES

Ahlberg, J. and A. (1982) *Funnybones*. London: Collins.

Axline, V. (1947) *Play Therapy*. Boston: Houghton Mifflin.

Axline, V. (1989) *Play Therapy*. Edinburgh: Churchill Livingstone.

Goleman, D. (1996) *Emotional Intelligence*. London: Bloomsbury.

Lawrence, D. (1988) *Enhancing Self-Esteem in the Classroom*. London: Paul Chapman.

McMahon, L. (1992) *The Handbook of Play Therapy*. London: Routledge.

McMahon, L. (1993) Autonomy through play. *Special Children*, November/December.

Moore, D. et al. (1994) Helping the emotionally troubled child. *Topic*, 12.

CHAPTER 6

Support for young people through counselling: the experience of working in a secondary school

Sandy Kirby

Having worked as a teacher for many years, particularly in the pastoral area of school life, I have been acutely aware of the need for a facility for young people to be able to have someone to talk to, not casually, but in an environment that is safe and empathic. Several years ago a number of schools employed their own counsellors. However, the present stringent economic climate seems to have caused the demise of the school counsellor, and any facilities that do exist seem to be the result of individual enterprise. Present government policy focuses upon specific initiatives related to a particular problem, such as drug abuse and under-age pregnancy. These initiatives tend to take the form of monetary funds for training and supplying the young people with information and drop-in centres, but not so much upon providing a general counselling facility. Following research with a group of colleagues (Moore et al. 1993, 1996) which confirmed our belief that there was a need for counselling provision for young people, we set up a counselling service for students of secondary school age in one comprehensive school. It is from the experience of working with these young people that I take my client case studies. From these I will illustrate the benefit and frustrations of working with young people in this way and reflect upon the value of using different therapeutic models, whilst also highlighting the constraints that exist when working as an external agency for an institution.

THEORETICAL PERSPECTIVES

My working frame is dictated mainly by a person-centred approach, with psychodynamic insights. I have a strong belief in the quality of the relationship being the major vehicle enabling clients to effect their own change. To establish such a relationship it is important to develop and communicate the core conditions of acceptance, empathy and genuineness (Rogers 1951). I do not plan a session, but trust that my client will initiate a direction for the therapy to progress. If I listen, reflect, empathize and respond to her thoughts, she will be able to clarify her difficulties. As the sessions progress, my main task is to create a non-judgemental climate of openness, trust and caring so that she can feel safe to use the therapeutic relationship to develop and move forward. Alongside this frame I also consider the possibility that difficulties with specific relationships, in my client's younger years, may affect how she relates to others in the present time. Therefore, I would be observant of her relationship with me and look for the possible transference in our relationship. I may also be interested in any dreams she may choose to present, as clues to her unconscious thinking.

In appropriate situations I sometimes work in a brief focused way. This way of working begins not by exploring the problem (however big), but by seeking solutions (however distant those may seem to be) and then figuring out how to get there. Each client is seen as individual and having the ability to adjust if given the opportunity. Steve de Shazer suggests: 'The client often knows what the problem is but doesn't know that he knows' (de Shazer 1996).

Within this frame one works with the client establishing the possible solutions to the presenting problem. This is a fairly directed way of working, in as much as one asks similar questions of each client. Initial questions, such as 'What brought you here today?' and 'How would you like us to help?', direct the session to the presenting issue and these are followed by the 'Miracle question': 'Imagine that a miracle happens tonight while you are asleep. Because you are asleep you are not aware that it has happened. When you wake up in the morning, the difficulty that you came here with no longer exists What will be the first thing that you will notice that tells you the problem has gone?' Answers to this and subsequent questions, such as 'What will happen next?' and 'What will other people notice?', focus the client on a direction towards concrete goals. Scaling questions are introduced to gauge the client's present perception of the problem. The client is asked, 'On a scale of 0–10, where 0 is the worst, and 10 is the best that you can expect, where are you today?' The scaling question is used in subsequent sessions to monitor progress and to reinforce a positive philosophy. Even if the client returns a scaling number of 1 or lower, the question 'How come you are not at 0, what keeps you above 0?' can be posed. The emphasis is always to reinforce the positive and the focus is upon the anticipated change and the motivation that the client has to make the desired change. The therapist will then reflect upon the information presented by the client. Initially genuine compliments are reflected back to illustrate what the client is already achieving and this is followed by a task or goal, which the client may wish to focus upon. The nature of the task has usually been determined by the client in some way within the session and may be very specific or more general. Clients are usually invited to return to a further session. (For further discussion of this approach see O'Hanlon and Weiner-Davis 1989.)

The clients

The school makes referrals. We offer an assessment session to evaluate whether counselling will be helpful to the young person. This includes allowing the client to fully understand what is on offer, explaining the client's part in the process and right to confidentiality. We also take into consideration whether the client would be more comfortable working with a male or a female therapist. Parents are asked to the assessment session and are invited to discuss the process with the young person also present. I would normally spend 40 minutes with the client and a further 20 minutes with the parent/s and the client together. The inclusion of the parent has developed in negotiation with the school and follows the practice of other supportive agencies that work with young people in schools, e.g. the educational psychologist.

However, initial barriers can be created if it detracts from the autonomy of the young client and it may raise questions for them, as to whether they have confidentiality. On the other hand, parents find it comforting to know whom their child is seeing and it can help them to establish an understanding of the process and the boundaries that will be put in place. For example, they will get to hear only what their daughter/son wants to tell them. Some parents can feel resentful that someone else is being told private thoughts and feelings, which perhaps they believe should be their prerogative to know. Below I now present two case studies to illustrate the different models outlined above and then reflect upon their value within the institutional setting of a school.

PHOEBE, 13 YEARS OLD

Referral and the first meeting with the client

Her school referred Phoebe to me. They were concerned that she had not been attending school regularly. My initial information was fairly brief. The school said that she was of average intelligence (whatever that means), lived with her mother and saw her father at weekends. The parents had divorced when Phoebe was 7 years old. She frequently did not attend school on a Monday and if she did come into school she refused to attend certain lessons. This pattern had continued for several months. She and her mum had agreed to an assessment session, which they both attended. I met Phoebe with her mother in the reception area of the school. We briefly shook hands and then I led Phoebe away to my room. She was about the same height as I am (5 feet 4 inches), but thin; her long dark hair was swept back in a hair band at the back of her head. As we sat down, she closed up, curling her legs around each other and folding her arms; she looked down and gave me very little eye contact. The following half hour was spent asking prompting questions and getting monosyllabic replies. She clearly felt that she did not want to be here. Mum, however, was a little more open and told me it was difficult to force Phoebe to come to school, particularly when she came home late from her father's place at the end of the weekend and further alluded to the friction between herself and Phoebe's father. She also had a small cry saying that she probably needed the counselling too. Phoebe seemed to be a bit embarrassed that her mum had started crying. I had spent more than the 20 minutes with both of them because the first half hour had been very uneventful. Mum and Phoebe seemed as if they needed each other to be reassured and it was also difficult for the mother to come into conflict with Phoebe.

Following sessions

The first few sessions were hard going. Phoebe continued to start the sessions with little eye contact and answering anything I said as a prompt with monosyllables. In one session, I used some photographs she had with her as a vehicle for discussion. She let down her defences for a little while and seemed to enjoy talking, in particular as she spoke about her two sisters and pets, but this was short-lived. In other sessions I used Winnicott's squiggle game (Winnicott 1971) to see if that would help her to feel more relaxed. She liked drawing and this seemed to help free her to start talking. The drawings did have some interesting aspects and I gently suggested these to her, but I met with very little response. And so we continued, little words, a few smiles and lots of pictures.

I began to feel all at sea. I did not appear to be making any progress in allowing her to feel safe enough to work with the difficult issues and feelings; she still seemed very defensive.

Before I had started training to be a counsellor I really did not understand what supervision was all about: what was the point of going and telling someone or a group of people what is going on in the therapeutic relationship? As time has passed and I have acquired more experience, I have come to realize that this process is essential. It has many functions, the most important being the protection of the client from any of the counsellor's own negative transferences and providing support for the counsellor when the client transfers intense feelings within the session.

The following week I did not want to go to the session with Phoebe, as I had little belief that I could help make any difference. The session began in the same way, with little input from Phoebe. I asked if I could pose a question. I chose a more solution-focused question and asked her what she wanted from the sessions and in the future. The session became a lot more vocal and we seemed clearer about the goals that she wanted to achieve – in particular, getting to school without feeling sick, and attending all her lessons. We also touched on some feelings, which enabled Phoebe to cry for a short while. I had noticed that she kept mentioning her homes as her father's or her mother's, and I commented that it felt like she didn't belong in either home. She made no reply, but she looked sad and small. She continued with:

'I got up on Monday and felt sick, I told my mum I was worried about school, she said that she knew.'

'Then what did she say?'

'Nothing.'

'How did that feel?'

'At first I thought that she didn't care about me.'

'Do you think that she doesn't care about you now?'

She began to cry, gently and then more intensely, saying: 'Don't want to talk about this any more.'

It was very painful to stay with these feelings and she wanted to leave. I asked her to remain for a while, so that she was a little more calm before she left. I feel that this is a necessary consideration when working within an institution with young people, particularly as Phoebe walked home on her own. I also reflected on how painful these feelings had been for her and made it clear that when she felt able to, I would be there to help her with those feelings.

This had been a powerful session for Phoebe; she had come into school the following day and gone to her support teacher and asked if I was OK. The support teacher phoned me, and I decided to call Phoebe to tell her that I was well and that I was looking forward to seeing her on the following Monday. She clearly had a fantasy that these powerful feelings were capable of harming me. Sometimes feelings that have been stored up inside, from an earlier experience which appeared to be too difficult to be dealt with, create a sense of dread in the client and the belief that these collective feelings have the ability to actually harm others.

Phoebe was much more talkative in the following two sessions, but she still found it difficult to connect with the feelings. I wondered whether a visualization exercise at this point might help her. She understood what we were going to do and was quite happy to take part. However, once she had completed the exercise she resisted any conversation about it and didn't want to draw or write about her visual images. On the way home my feelings were a mixture of anger and frustration. Was this in fact projective identification? (A non-verbal communication from the client's feelings, which the client unconsciously perceives as unmanageable and therefore has suppressed, but in a session projects on to the therapist in order for them to be heard and survived. This understanding has usually been created by these feelings not being heard or understood by significant persons in their earlier life.) Would Phoebe be able to continue to give me the difficult feelings?

The session before the Christmas holidays was good. She had attended school all week and had missed only two lessons. She was very pleased with herself and drew pictures of Christmas trees and a picture of snakes and ladders. We talked about the break and noted that we had one more session before the holiday. She said that she might be late because she had a hospital appointment.

Unfortunately Phoebe did not make the last session and this made the break four weeks. I sent a card to try to support the gap. I wrote on the card that I had been there for the session and had been sorry to miss her.

The returning session seemed fine; she thanked me for her card and she continued to be quite chatty. The first week at school had also been good, so when in the following session she had decided to ask if she could have a gap of two sessions to see if she could deal with it herself, I was surprised. Do I interpret this as a denial or a defence against her feelings, or do I support a healthy move towards independence? I decided to be more solution focused and to build upon her positive approach. With hindsight I might have dealt with it differently and tried to be more in touch with the needy side of her that was well hidden.

Here I felt the pressure from the institution, to come up with a result. They needed something tangible, such as full-time attendance, or a change in her behaviour. However, this was for meeting their needs but not necessarily those of Phoebe.

Again, another difficulty in working within an institution occurs where there is unhappiness if the client misses a session. In therapeutic terms this could be useful and the feelings resulting from a missed session could be talked through. However, on occasion some clients who chose not to attend would actually be reprimanded by a teacher, which would be quite counter-productive.

I tried to re-establish our working frame when I next met Phoebe, but somehow, as the time passed, it felt as though we were caught in a transference situation, where despite the renewed frame she kept repeating the breaks through minor illnesses, colds and upset stomachs. The transference can be seen in the abandonment that she had experienced when her parents divorced. Maybe her minor illnesses were her way of gaining her father's attention. He had been sufficiently moved by her continued absence to visit the school to try to sort the situation out.

This is a good example of the client's resistance to progress and to the therapist. We seemed to be trapped in a cyclical pattern by her fear that these feelings were dangerous. She found ways to maintain the contact with me, but to control the sessions so they felt safe. Besides the absenteeism, she further asked to reduce the length and frequency of the sessions and she went along with the visualization exercises but then would not continue by drawing or talking about them. Maybe she offered me a cue in a picture that she drew of snakes and ladders in the tenth session, before Christmas. I wonder whether she was saying the time she was getting (one session a week) wasn't enough, because she felt that like the game, you take steps forward, only to slip backwards. Maybe two sessions a week would have felt safer with the gaps in-between being shorter, to hold on to the difficult feelings.

Phoebe's resistance might be understood in different ways, depending upon the framework used. In psychoanalytical terms resistance refers to everything the client may do or say that prevents them gaining insight into their unconscious thinking. This concept was introduced by Freud (1961). He discovered that confrontation and persuasion would not overcome the resistance in a client. He further suggested that to understand the resistance was to get closer to the repressed feelings of the unconscious.

In contrast the brief focused approach assumes that the client really does want to change, and that there is no such thing as resistance. Clients may not always follow what the therapist suggests, but this is not viewed as resistance. This is seen as the client educating the therapist to the most productive way of helping them change. My understanding of Phoebe's behaviour was more sympathetic to the psycho-analytic frame.

Phoebe's sessions numbered 18, but they had stretched over a period of 10 months, which meant that at times the work became very fragmented. She had made some progress; however, this was negligible as far as the school was concerned. She had regained some attendance at school, but this pattern had deteriorated while she was not attending the sessions. The school decided that they were not prepared to spend any more money on her therapy and told her so the day before the summer break. I was unaware that this was about to happen and heard it first from Phoebe. She was very distressed and angry with the school for just stopping the sessions and I echoed her, feeling equally frustrated that I had not been allowed to work through this with my client. Following discussion the school allowed me to meet with Phoebe after the school break so that an appropriate ending to the therapy could be achieved. Phoebe's mother was also keen for Phoebe to receive further sessions and asked for them to continue if she made the payment.

My feelings of anger surfaced when I discussed this in supervision. I felt that I had been ignored by the institution and that they did not have an idea of what I had been trying to achieve with Phoebe. More importantly, I did not wish to leave her without a satisfactory ending. If we failed to meet again I felt it might leave her with similar feelings of rejection to those she experienced after her parents separated. Finally it was decided that I would work with Phoebe for six more sessions. During these sessions we reflected and celebrated the things she had accomplished during the time we had been meeting. It was important to work together upon this ending so that she felt she had more autonomy over the process and was not left with any feelings of abandonment.

SUSAN, 15 YEARS OLD

Referral and the first meeting with the client

Susan was 15 years old and in her last term at school. There was no time to progress through the usual procedures of assessment sessions and early reviews of progress, as her time in school was coming rapidly to an end and exams were looming on the horizon. The phone call I received from the school suggested that she had poor communication with adults, being mostly done in monosyllables; she seemingly had low self-esteem and no sense of actually motivating herself towards a job or study beyond school. The school's assessment had also been based upon the fact that she had had a disastrous time on her work experience placement in a pet shop. The owner had become dissatisfied with her when she refused to get involved with serving many of the customers, despite the fact that this placement was her first choice. Would I see her for a few sessions and see what I could do? It seemed like a fairly impossible task, but my curiosity got the better of me. Could I make a difference in six sessions? What an admission – I was already exerting power over her and I hadn't even met her. That was the Thursday and she walked into the room on the following Monday afternoon.

My counselling room is a small teacher's office tucked away in a corridor out of the main thoroughfare. The school is mostly deserted when I meet my clients as it is usually at the end of the school day. I quickly rearranged the furniture, so that there was no physical barrier between the client and me. Susan caught me still struggling with the over-cumbersome chairs as she stuck her head around the door. 'Susan?' I enquired. She nodded. As she entered the room I felt dwarfed by her presence: she was very tall for her 15 years. Her legs seemed to go on forever; she certainly fitted the phrase 'gawky adolescent'. I invited her to tell me why she felt she needed to come. Without much hesitation she said: 'Because I find it difficult to talk to teachers in school and I didn't have a very good work experience.' There was an immediate resonance of words from the phone call I had heard the previous Thursday. Were these her thoughts or some that had been given to her? My second thought was that I had asked for some information and I had got an answer in sentences not in monosyllables. I asked her to complete a Lawseq questionnaire (Lawrence 1981), which would give me a rough guide as to her self-esteem. I did not calculate it then, but took it away with me to work out at home. The maximum score for high self-esteem is 24; Susan had scored 22. It would seem that the school was wrong in its assessment of her self-esteem too. As the session progressed she told me about her family, mum, dad, brother and favourite pets. She even laughed here and there. Her body language became more relaxed, and we began to talk about the way she had felt when she was in a situation where a teacher had shouted and been 'powerful' over her. She said that she had felt quite cross when he had shouted.

'How did that make you feel?'

'Cross. I would think it isn't fair, you don't need to shout.'

'Right, you think it to yourself, but it is difficult to say?'

She nodded.

'What if you imagined I was the teacher and I had just shouted at you, could you say what you were thinking to me?'

She nodded, and we engaged in some role-play. She very gently told me that she didn't think it was fair that I had shouted at her. I felt she had been very brave as her face screwed up a bit in anticipation of the reply. All in all I found her very friendly and quite easy to talk to. We even exchanged stories about our cats and how we frequently rescued them from situations. Suddenly I realized that we were two thirds of the way through the time and I had not negotiated the structure for the remaining five sessions. As this work was being done in such a confined space of time, I had previously felt that it was probably best to work in a solution-focused way.

Now I had a more genuine, accurate sense of Susan as opposed to the brief outline I had received from the school. I asked her what she wanted to be different in the future. She replied that she wanted to be able to talk more easily to adults, particularly those with some authority over her, and maybe look at how she could go about getting a job. I reflected these ideas back to her so that she was clear that I had heard what she had said. Then I recalled my first thoughts of power over this client and reflected that actually I had found other clients far less easy to talk to at the first session. The time was up and since we had spent a large part of the session talking, I said that I had enjoyed our time together and pointed out that she had very little difficulty talking to me, a complete stranger.

Following sessions

In the following sessions the main tasks were to support her in looking for possible jobs and strengthening her ability to speak up for herself.

I acquired research material on working with animals and sport, as these were the areas that she wanted to work in. At the beginning of each session I would focus on a positive aspect in the previous session, and ask her to reflect on the previous week. We spent much time talking about the teachers who shout in school and the man in the pet shop. I also looked at her more equal relationships where she felt she could say what she wanted to. We role-played her time in the pet shop; I put on a deeper male voice, which gave us plenty to laugh at. She was very good at using this method and responded very purposefully. She was really fun to be with and I had to be careful not to just enjoy myself and forget the time-frame. At the end of each session I would negotiate a task for her to work on in the intervening week. This usually took the form of buying a paper and looking in the job section for possible positions, reading material or saying out loud things that she had not said but wanted to. On a practical level I talked her through the process of applying for a job. We looked at adverts and considered how to lay out a curriculum vitae and phone for application forms, which, of course, led us to more role-play. This all gave me an easy task of watching Susan respond and feeding her the positive comments she justly deserved.

There were other issues in her life that came to light as we worked together, but they had to be put to one side as the main direction of the work was brief focused and there was not the time to digress.

Following the fifth session there was a break of one week since I was unwell. This gave me concern as I thought I might have missed the chance of our last session altogether. I phoned the school and rearranged the time to the following week. I felt that it was important that we practise the interview situation and have a proper ending to this brief encounter.

The last session

Susan arrived smiling and pleased to see me. She sat down and I began by apologizing for failing to attend the previous week. I continued to talk.

'Shall we have a go at a role-play of an interview situation?'

I had not paid attention to her face and was really on my own agenda.

She replied: 'I've already had one.'

It was then that I focused on her face; it was beaming.

'Great, tell me more.'

She proceeded to tell me how she had seen a job for a dental receptionist. She had planned her phone call before she made it, had laid out a CV, and had been called for an interview in the following week, when I had cancelled the session. I encouraged her to tell me about the interview, how she had practised beforehand and planned some questions.

'When he asked me at the end if I had any questions, I said yes as I had planned a few, like we had planned before.'

The dentist had offered her the job and given her a starting date in July. Time was fast running out so I felt it important to tie all her achievements together so that they presented a positive celebration and a strong foundation upon which she could build in the future. The end was upon us and I was overtaken by sadness. I was so pleased that she had been successful with finding a job and that she seemed more relaxed in herself. I struggled with saying 'keep in touch, let me know how you get on' as that was for my benefit. Maybe it might suggest to her that she needed to keep the link because I wasn't confident that she could cope on her own. My need to know was stronger, and I invited her to make contact once she had settled into the job, perhaps via a postcard to the school.

CONCLUSION

Whilst it is interesting to work with the children in this way, working within the constraints laid down by an institution (e.g. the school) can be very restricting. Having discussed the development of the consultancy with the school, it is clear that its goals are determined by time and money. Its response to Susan was that it had been very successful, it could see a tangible outcome, whereas Phoebe's progress was slow, expensive, not easy to measure, and not so positive in the school's terms, i.e. whilst her attendance had improved, she was not attending school regularly. My brief focused approach to the work with Susan was more straightforward, with only six sessions and clear set goals. However, other issues surfaced that we could have discussed and worked with, but, because these were not part of the frame within which we were working, they were not addressed. In the case of Phoebe, working in a more analytical way meant that the aims were not defined at the beginning and the work was more open-ended, allowing for the more hidden agendas to surface. In this case the school had its goal, which was for Phoebe to return regularly to school. However, my goals for Phoebe changed as it became more apparent that the root of her problem lay more with the feelings she had when she was 7, being related to the break-up of her parents' marriage. I could have worked in a more behaviourist way with Phoebe, which may have got her back into school initially, but the root problem would still have been there and in the longer term the symptoms may well have returned, in this case not attending school.

There seems little doubt that the brief focused style lends itself to working for such an institution. 'Treatment that meets the client's needs in a cost-effective manner is of importance to the health purchasers and insurance companies alike' (Wilgosh et al. 1994) – and increasingly the needs of educational institutions. Whilst it can be successful, I feel there are certain clients that would not be helped by working in this way.

On reflection, Susan had no formal assessment session at the beginning of her work, which would normally have included her parents. I wonder whether she had felt more autonomous, which therefore created greater confidentiality and a safer therapeutic space. Phoebe's mother, however, had been to two sessions. I also wonder if Phoebe was relaying a message in her picture of snakes and ladders, which she had drawn at the end of the tenth session. We had talked about how in the game you progress forward only to slip backwards down a snake. Maybe she was referring to the fact that the time wasn't sufficient and the gap between sessions was too great, thus making it feel impossible to hang on to the difficult feelings. If one is coping with very powerful feelings, working with the difficulty on a more regular basis can make the client feel more secure. In Phoebe's case it may have been more helpful for her to have been able to have two sessions a week, which would have felt safer. This, however, was not practical within the institutional framework.

Writing about my clients has made me dissect and reassess the issues several times over, which is always a worthwhile task. It has made me more aware of the effect of breaks on the client, the feeling of loss. I have experienced struggling with resistance, the feelings that this creates within myself and feelings transferred to me from within the client. I now have a fuller understanding of endings, and how important it is to work towards them and not to allow them to happen suddenly. Even after only working with Susan for six sessions the feelings were very powerful. In the last session, I felt a need to want to keep in contact, which I had to work through for myself.

The work I have been engaged in to date continues to confirm my belief that it is the quality of the relationship between client and therapist which is a very important element in enabling a client to change and grow. Irvin Yalom describes such indefinable elements as the 'throw-ins':

> Texts, journal articles and lectures portray therapy as precise and systematic, with carefully delineated stages, strategic technical interventions, the methodical development and resolution of the transference, analysis of object relations and a careful program of insight, offering interpretations. Yet I believe deeply that when no one is looking, the therapist throws in the 'real thing'. (Yalom 1980)

He suggests that what makes the difference are these crucial ingredients which are very difficult to define: 'Indeed is it possible to define and teach such qualities as compassion, "presence", caring, extending oneself, touching the patient at a deep level, or – that most elusive one of all – wisdom?' I'm not sure I believe that it is only the therapist who throws things in. I believe more that it is the sum of the two interacting people within the therapeutic relationship that creates the positive atmosphere for change.

In this present economic and political climate one has to continually consider what is cost-effective. Everything, including education and young people's wellbeing, is managed in terms of money and timescales. The government's focus is upon results, examinations both for the students and for their teachers, setting goals and targets to be achieved and improved upon within predetermined deadlines. The emphasis has been drawn away from a focus upon the person as an individual. There can be nothing wrong with supporting young people therapeutically in the shortest recovery time possible. However, it is essential that we are clear about whom the outcome is for when setting timescales for therapeutic work. A short-term result does not necessarily mean that in the long term the young person will have fully recovered from the difficulties that were the cause of dysfunction. Perhaps it is time for there to be a rebalance in the way we educate and support our young people and within therapeutic areas allow greater flexibility, so that different therapeutic methods can be used alongside each other. Those that may take the young person a longer period of time should be accepted as valuing the individual and not addressed in terms of finance. Both methods I have illustrated within this chapter have equal value used with the right person at the right time.

REFERENCES

de Shazer, S. (1996) Solution-focussed Therapy. Lecture given at the Brief Therapy Practice Conference, Regent's College, London, April.

Freud, S. (1961) *Beyond the Pleasure Principle.* London: Hogarth.

Lawrence, D. (1981) The development of a self-esteem questionnaire. *British Journal of Educational Psychology,* 51, 245–51.

Moore, D., Decker, S., Greenwood, A. and Kirby, S. (1993) Research into demand for counselling/therapeutic provision in a group of primary schools. *Educational Research,* 35(3), 276–81.

Moore, D., Decker, S., Greenwood, A. and Kirby, S. (1996) Research into demand for counselling/therapeutic provision in a group of secondary schools. *Pastoral Care in Education,* 14(1), 3–6.

O'Hanlon, W. H. and Weiner-Davis, M. (1989) *In Search of Solutions.* London: Norton.

Rogers, C. (1951) *Client-Centred Therapy.* London: Constable.

Wilgosh, R., Hawkes, D. and Marsh, I. (1994) Solution-focused therapy in promoting mental health. *Mental Health Nursing,* 14(6), 18–21.

Winnicott, D.W. (1971) *Playing and Reality.* London: Tavistock.

Yalom, I. D. (1980) *Existential Psychotherapy.* New York: Basic Books.

CHAPTER 7

Promoting Alternative Thinking Strategies (PATHS): mental health promotion with deaf children in school

Peter Hindley and Helen Reed

The vast majority of deaf children are born into hearing families, with little or no previous experience of deafness. The majority of deaf children will grow up to use sign language (Gregory, Bishop and Sheldon 1995), although most of their parents will have no prior knowledge of it. These differences in communication can lead to significant language delays and many deaf children will be exposed to a more limited vocabulary than that which hearing children experience. Parents and professionals working with deaf children often simplify their language, using words that their child is more likely to understand, e.g. using 'sad' rather than 'disappointed' or 'angry' instead of 'jealous'. In addition, as they grow up, deaf children are likely to experience language primarily as a means of communicating with other people, in contrast to hearing children who will quickly realize that adults often use language to talk to themselves (self-talk), e.g. when completing difficult tasks or to talk themselves through periods of emotional arousal. Deaf children often discover self-talk by accident, but many hearing people misconstrue deaf children signing to themselves in mirrors as a sign of psychological disturbance rather than self-talk. Finally, deaf children have limited access to the kinds of incidental learning (overhearing discussions between their parents or siblings, hearing pieces of information on the radio or TV) that support the development of social understanding.

This combination of language delay and communication differences has significant effects on deaf children's social and emotional development. Deaf children are more likely to be impulsive, have limited social-problem-solving skills and have greater difficulty in identifying and naming their own and other people's emotional states (Greenberg and Kusché 1988). As a result, deaf children are at greater risk of developing mental health problems than their hearing peers (Hindley et al. 1994). An effective mental health promotion package that addresses the social and emotional developmental delays outlined above would make a significant impact on deaf children's long-term mental health needs.

PROMOTING ALTERNATIVE THINKING STRATEGIES (PATHS)

PATHS (Greenberg and Kusché 1993) is a school-based curriculum, which has been developed in the USA and is aimed at promoting the development of a range of social and emotional cognitive skills that underpin social problem-solving. The curriculum promotes children's development in five broad areas: self-control; self-esteem; understanding and recognition of emotions; and social-problem-solving skills.

Establishing self-control and the ability to regulate emotional arousal during difficult social situations are essential problem-solving skills. Greater levels of impulsivity amongst deaf children are often manifested in self-control difficulties such as throwing temper tantrums (Gregory 1995). The first component of PATHS (the Readiness and Self-Control Unit) uses a behavioural technique (Doing Turtle) to establish self-control skills. Children are presented with a story about a young turtle who has great difficulty in school but consults a wise old turtle who teaches him to 'do turtle' by going into his shell to calm down and then begin to solve his problem. The child is taught to calm down by using a three-step technique: stop; take a deep breath; say what the problem is and say how I am feeling. Although this technique is initially reinforced by a contingency programme (Turtle stamps, etc.) and by visual materials such as the Control Signals Poster (using traffic lights as a metaphor for establishing control), these are rapidly faded and the technique becomes self-reinforcing.

The Readiness and Self Control unit introduces two further techniques that run through the curriculum. The first is the use of role-play. Initially this is introduced in an undemanding way, but it is used later in the curriculum to explore difficult emotional experiences. The children develop an understanding of the use of role-play – signalling when they are in role, distinguishing role-play from real life, de-roling, etc. The second technique, the Compliments List, is intended to build children's self-esteem and self-confidence, complimenting their growing self-control. Each day a child in the class is selected as the PATHS Child for the Day (the PATHS Kid for the Day in the original American version) to help the teacher during PATHS time. The PATHS Child for the Day is a daily activity at the end of a PATHS lesson, in which every child and adult in the class is asked to give compliments to the PATHS child for the day. Although initially children need considerable support, they rapidly take part in this activity of their own accord. Encouraging children to compliment each other builds mutual trust and is an important part of developing a supportive atmosphere in which to explore emotional experiences.

As children establish the capacity to self-control, they move on to the next part of the curriculum, the Feelings and Relationships Unit. The Feelings and Relationships Unit contains lessons about specific feelings which are taught in pairs of opposing feelings: happy/sad; scared/safe; etc. A variety of teaching techniques is used, including stories, role-plays and art activities. Each child has a box of cards with faces for each emotion, Feelings Faces. As each emotion is taught, children are encouraged to tell people about how they are feeling by displaying the Feelings Face on a stand on their desk, as are teachers and classroom assistants who have their own packs. The Feelings Faces now become part of the self-control technique and the basis of social problem-solving. When children run into difficult situations they are taught to stop, think about how they are feeling and then say what the problem is. The process of identifying feeling states has two functions. Firstly, it assists in calming down – leafing through their Feelings Faces means children have to stop and think. Secondly, identifying your emotional state helps in understanding the nature of a problem: understanding that you are angry because you are jealous of another person is much more helpful in identifying the right way to solve a problem than just knowing that you are angry. As the children develop a better understanding of their own and other people's feelings, they can then use this understanding to develop more effective skills in understanding and managing relationships.

As the Feelings and Relationships Unit comes to an end, teachers begin to teach informal problem-solving. They initially use the Turtle technique of: Stop and calm down; Say how you are feeling; Say the Problem. This can be done individually, in pairs and in groups. This then moves on to more formal problem-solving in the Problem Solving Unit. Children are taught an 11-step problem-solving technique using both real and imagined problems. Real problems can be drawn from the child's immediate environment or from the wider world.

Although PATHS is taught in the classroom, it works best when it generalizes throughout the school. Control Signals Posters in dining halls, corridors and playgrounds (sometimes painted onto the playground itself) reinforce the self-control and problem-solving techniques. Senior staff are encouraged to use their own Feelings Faces pack to identify how they are feeling and all members of the school are encouraged to join in. The curriculum is supported by a variety of home-based activities that inform parents of their children's activities in class and encourage families to participate. However, the authors emphasize that PATHS is a social education experience and not psychotherapy or counselling. If discussion during PATHS lessons leads to a child disclosing serious personal distress, teachers are advised to ask the child to talk to them later in a quiet and private time and then take appropriate action. In some circumstances, after full discussion with parents and the child, this has led to personal experiences at home becoming a focus for discussion in PATHS time, e.g. a boy discussing his feelings about his parents' divorce led to a classroom discussion.

PATHS IN THE UK

As already stated, PATHS has been developed in the USA. Hence, although it has been used in a variety of different countries (the Netherlands, Israel and France), the original version contains many American cultural references such as baseball and gum. With the support of the Department of Health and the National Deaf Children's Society we have adapted part of the curriculum (the Readiness and Self-Control Unit and half of the Feelings and Relationships Unit). This adapted curriculum has been piloted in primary classes (Years 5 and 6) in 4 schools for deaf children and 3 Hearing Impaired Units (HIUs). A total of 64 children were involved. PATHS is now being used in a total of 18 schools for deaf children, HIUs and other schools in Essex and the north-east of England, in addition to the original pilot group. PATHS has recently been introduced in hearing primary schools in north Wales as part of a prevention programme.

The pilot study

The first group of schools have used PATHS in various sections of the National Curriculum (personal health and social education (PHSE), religious education (RE), English) and have shown that it is possible to incorporate it into the primary school day. Each school has modified the curriculum to suit its particular needs. Overall we have found that the wholehearted commitment of the entire school and the senior management team in particular is vital for the curriculum to be successful. However, one school, a 'resourced' school in which the teachers had to balance the timetable of the children's school for deaf children and their 'host' school, found that it could not introduce the curriculum and dropped out of the pilot project. In addition to the curriculum, we provided whole family weekends for families in each of the two groups during the year that the curriculum was first introduced (see below). We have evaluated the curriculum in three main ways. Firstly, there were regular discussions with teachers on an individual basis and, less frequently, on a group basis. Secondly, the children were assessed by using a number of formal measures (see appendix). These assessments by the project co-ordinator also allowed her to develop a more intuitive sense of how the children were developing. This cannot be measured, but has informed our understanding of how the curriculum works. Finally, we have maintained contact with parents, partly by face to face contact at PATHS weekends and partly by asking them to complete formal measures.

The schools' experiences: creating time in the curriculum

The schools in the pilot study used the curriculum in different ways. Some had half-hour PATHS lessons four times a week, whilst others used one-hour lessons twice a week. On the whole the schools for deaf children had greater flexibility than the Hearing Impaired Units in creating time within the National Curriculum. As teachers in all schools became familiar with PATHS, they were able to justify it as part of various aspects of the National Curriculum: English, RE and PHSE. Five inspections of schools by the Office for Standards in Education (OFSTED) occurred during the pilot project. All of the inspection reports made positive comments about the use of PATHS in the schools.

Preparing the school and generalizing the curriculum

PATHS is most effective when it generalizes throughout the school, both in and out of classrooms. All schools who were involved in the project were offered an initial presentation to the senior management team, explaining the principles of PATHS. Teachers were then offered a three-day training programme, prior to introducing PATHS to their school. This training was most effective when more than one teacher attended. In some schools the teacher most closely involved in PATHS arranged meetings with *all* members of staff. This included dinner ladies and playground supervisors. All the members of staff could not be fully trained, but it was important that they were aware of aspects of the curriculum, e.g. praising a child for doing Turtle or encouraging children to problem-solve a dispute. The enthusiasm of the senior management team was vital and some headteachers displayed their own Feelings Faces on their desks and encouraged children to ask them how they were feeling. Throughout the project, the project co-ordinator made regular visits to the schools, observing and participating in class and offering consultation to teachers.

Schools did different things to generalize PATHS in the school environment. One school painted two sets of red traffic lights, two sets of amber traffic lights and one green traffic light in the playground. If two children were in dispute, they could go to the red lights to stop and think, move on to the amber light when they could speak how they felt and say the problem, and then advance to the green light to think together how to solve the problem. In another school, children on a family weekend painted a mural of the Turtle Story to remind the children during playtime.

The views and experiences of teachers and children

PATHS calls for a different relationship between teachers and children. Teachers become more self-disclosing, while letting children know that they have feelings can come as quite a shock to some children. Teachers need to be judicious about their use of self-disclosure. Following a late night, a teacher came into her class at school in something of a bad mood the next morning. Her children recognized this immediately and the teacher identified that she was feeling grumpy, using her Feelings Faces. When asked why, she explained that she had been working late the night before. Similarly, teachers need to feel comfortable with the use of role-play and need to be prepared to play an active part in role-plays, particularly in the beginning when the children may feel less certain. Establishing trust and confidence in each other within the classroom is vital. The curriculum encourages teachers to develop PATHS time rules with the children (Figure 7.1). This spirit of a collaborative relationship between the teacher and the children is central to the curriculum. Later in the curriculum the children begin to use problem-solving techniques and some children may feel unfamiliar with 'dialoguing' about a problem. Some teachers found it useful to fill in the two roles in the discussion so that the children understood the purpose of the activity and could then play an active part. At other times teachers asked classroom assistants to take the other role. Teachers described a variety of changes in the children that they taught. These changes were most obvious in children who were more impulsive and had less self-control. The children began to do Turtle to establish self-control, adapting it for themselves. Older children said that they found that folding their hands across their chest (the technique suggested in the curriculum) singled them out. They were encouraged to find alternative signals such as putting their hands in their pockets or crossing them behind their backs. Some children found that they could use Turtle to avoid unpleasant tasks; one boy consistently said that he didn't feel calm enough to go into science and would do Turtle when he wanted his teacher's attention. The curriculum suggests that neither of these would be appropriate uses of Turtle and should not be rewarded. One of the aims of the curriculum at this stage is to help children to distinguish between behaviours and feelings, emphasizing that all feelings are OK but that some behaviours are OK and some are not. Teachers used a variety of techniques to reinforce this important concept (Figures 7.2 and 7.3).

Most children found the idea of giving compliments unfamiliar. At the beginning many gave compliments that centred on physical attributes ('I like your hair') or possessions ('I like your Nike trainers'). However, as they used the curriculum, their compliments moved towards comments on psychological and emotional attributes

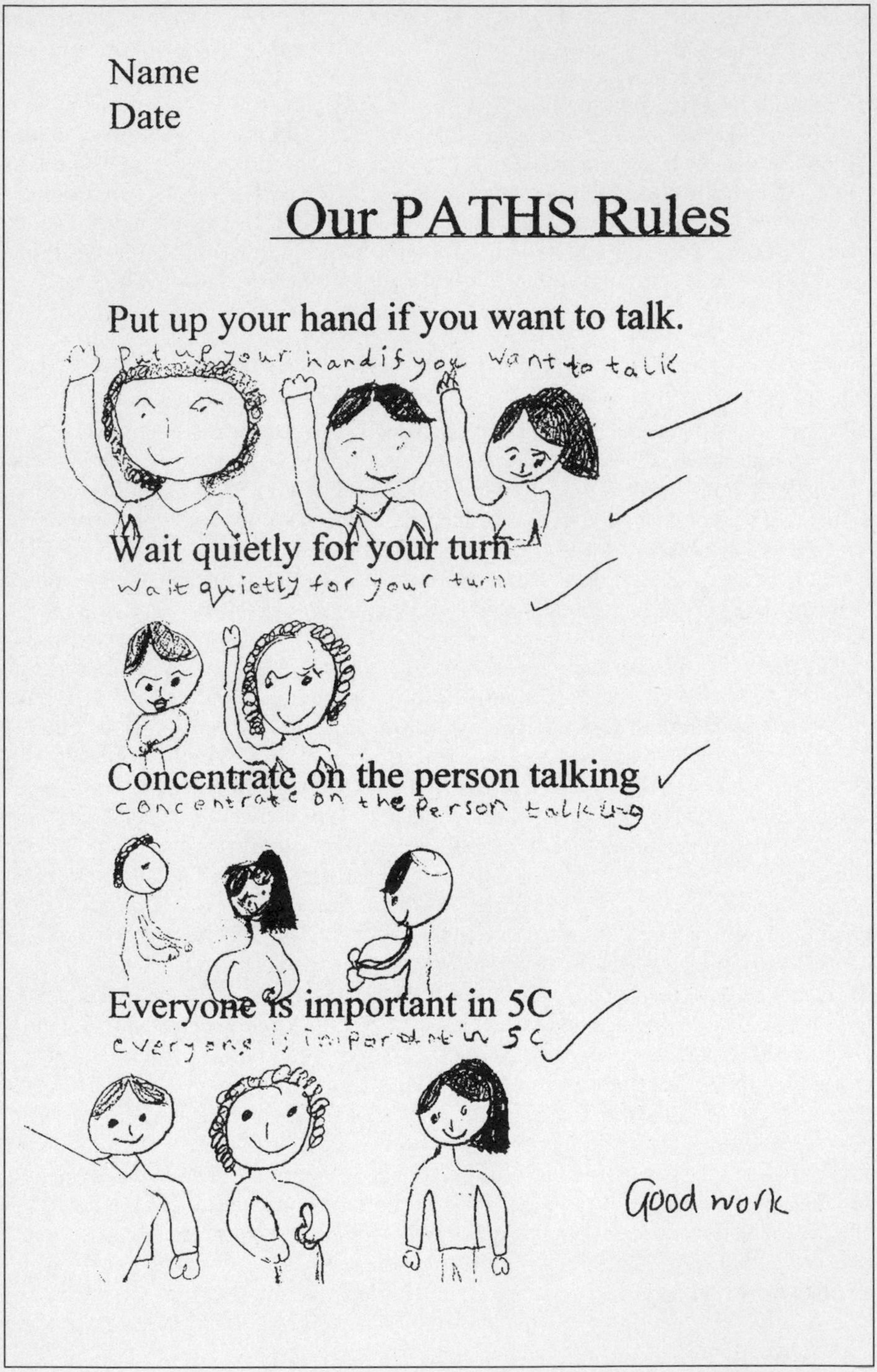

Name
Date

Our PATHS Rules

Put up your hand if you want to talk.

Wait quietly for your turn

Concentrate on the person talking ✓

Everyone is important in 5C

Good work

Figure 7.1 Our PATHS rules

Name   _3/2/97_

Feelings and Behaviour

I feel these things on the inside

✓ I am very quiet

✓ I want to hit someone

✓ my stomach feels funny

my heart is beating strongly.

✓ my face feels hot

✓ my breathing is fast

✓ my body feels tight

✓ I want to break something

✓ my teeth are stuck together

I behave like this. I show this on the outside.

✓ I look angry in my eyes

✓ I am shouting at someone.

✓ I am stamping my feet

✓ I am making a fist

✓ I break something

✓ I am crying

✓ I hurt someone

✓ I have shaky signs.

✓ I find it difficult to talk

Good boy ☺ *.

Figure 7.2   Feelings and behaviour

Date _6th november_

How are you feeling?

How are you feeling today?

I am feeling Happy

How do you look?

I have big eyes
I am smiling

Is your feeling comfortable or uncomfotable?

I am feeling Comfortable

Why are you feeling like this?

Figure 7.3 How are you feeling?

such as 'I like you because you helped me in class' or 'I like you because you were kind to me in playground'. We gained the impression that this apparently simple technique had far-reaching effects. In particular, asking children to pay each other compliments played a significant part in promoting the children's empathic development. The PATHS Child for the Day and the Compliments List also had a powerful effect on less self-confident and assertive children. We have referred to positive effects for impulsive children, and it was reassuring to see that the curriculum was effective with a wide range of children.

The children found the Feelings Faces a useful and fun activity. The children's skills in role-play combined with the Feelings and Relationships Unit began to have a powerful effect in the schools. In one school a group of shy, quiet deaf children began to explore emotions. Their skills developed rapidly and, in combination with the earlier components of the curriculum, their sense of self-confidence grew. Their teacher arranged a whole school assembly about emotions and recognizing other people's emotions. The children demonstrated that their skills in these areas were significantly advanced when compared with the hearing children, much to their delight. The Feelings and Relationships Unit also proved useful in helping the children cope with more extreme experiences. The schools in the early intervention group had started using Feelings Faces when the Dunblane shootings occurred. Several teachers reported that their children had used their PATHS lessons to talk about the wide range of emotions that the tragedy had evoked in them. As the children became more skilled at recognizing and talking about feelings, they began to use their vocabulary and concepts in various parts of their lives. Understanding more complex emotions such as jealousy and frustration helped them to make sense of relationships at home and at school. The examples from children's work show how they began to use their new understanding and vocabulary (see also Figure 7.4). It is important to emphasize that the aim of PATHS is to encourage emotional expression and understanding – the children's work may not be grammatically correct but it clearly shows their thoughts and feelings:

My cousin had a big ball. I wanted the same as my cousin. My ball was small and soft because my brother stuck a pin in it. I felt jealous. My brother had new clothes I want the same as my brother I had old clothes. I felt jealous my friend had a new bicycle. I had a old bicycle. I felt jealous my sister. I new had a sonic game. I want same old sonic game. My baby had a new clothes. My mummy please, clean. I felt jealous.

Yesterday in school Mrs C. give me my homework, maths. In the bus I was talk with my friend. I happy in bus. Yesterday I went home. I said hello to mummy, said bye to Mary. Then it was food, then homework time. My brother took my bag, I can't find my homework. I look in the bedroom, I can't find in bedroom. I was frustrated. I hit the table. I went in my bedroom. I hid in my bed. I waited. I calmed down.

However, these developments presented a challenge to parents. Their children were now returning from school with a range of emotional vocabulary with which the parents were unfamiliar. In response to this, the National Deaf Children's Society, the London Deaf Access Project and Hamilton Lodge School created a video dictionary of emotional signs and distributed it to all the parents in the project.

Jealous

14th OCTOBER

my Friend is go in to
America. I am not happy
About This. I Feel Very
Jealous Mickey Mouse is
lovely and I Wanted
to go.

Well done ✱ ✱

Figure 7.4   Using feeling vocabulary

Not all of the schools were able to make the final transition from the Feelings and Relationships Unit to the Problem Solving Unit. Two of the schools had children with complex additional needs and took much more time to work their way through the Turtle Unit and the Feelings and Relationships Unit. Teachers who made the transition to the Problem Solving Unit were impressed by their children's ability to engage in complex problem-solving. In one school the children moved rapidly from using problem-solving techniques for everyday problems in the school and class to world problems. The teacher and children would bring in stories from current affairs for discussion in problem-solving groups.

At a more personal level it has been striking to see the children develop. During their individual interviews the children have become more reflective and thoughtful, clearly developing a greater awareness of their emotions and other people's. This has been most obvious in their descriptions and explanations of emotional states. One picture that the children have been shown has a young girl looking at a mother holding a baby, with the girl looking resentful. At the beginning many of the children experienced the primary emotions that constitute jealousy, but did not have the sign vocabulary to label it nor an understanding of the meaning of jealousy. Initially many children described the girl as angry. As the children progressed through the curriculum, they began to describe her as jealous and then explain how she felt about having a baby brother or sister and what that meant to her.

Finally, teachers have described positive effects on children's academic functioning as a result of the curriculum. Academic tasks that depend heavily on English language skills are frustrating and demoralizing for many deaf children. Several teachers described children using techniques from PATHS to cope when faced by difficult tasks in class. One teacher proudly recalled one of her children's response to her assessment in the Standard Assessment Tasks (SATS). This girl found that staying on task was very difficult and that reading was particularly challenging. When faced with her SATS text she had looked at the clock, appeared increasingly frustrated and aroused, and then seemed to remember PATHS. She did Turtle to calm herself down, signed to herself 'CALM DOWN' and was then able to complete her SATS successfully.

The parents' experience

An open evening for parents was conducted by one of the authors (HR) at each of the schools during the first term of the first year in which PATHS was introduced. Parents were kept informed about developments in the classroom by regular letters, examples of work and constant liaison with teachers. The residential family weekend provided parents with more information about PATHS, a variety of workshops on subjects ranging from behaviour management and emotional sign language to non-verbal communication. Deaf children took part in a variety of confidence-building exercises, with and without their hearing siblings. Hearing siblings took part in a workshop on the experiences of having deaf brothers and sisters. The weekends were staffed by a combination of deaf and hearing people, and the parents and children appeared to appreciate the opportunity of meeting a wide range of deaf people.

We have less detailed information from parents. However, our overall impression is that the majority of parents welcomed the curriculum and reported positive outcomes for their children. Our face-to-face contact with parents at family weekends gave us more of a feel for parental views. Many described powerful feelings when their children first began to talk about feelings at home. Most asked for more work to help develop the effects of the curriculum at home.

CONCLUSION

This pilot study of the use of PATHS in British schools and HIUs for deaf children shows that the curriculum can be used effectively. Teachers have shown enthusiasm for the curriculum and have found it a useful and effective means of promoting deaf children's social and emotional competence. In turn, teachers have described positive impacts on children's academic functioning. The children involved have greatly enjoyed the experience of taking part in PATHS and have taken this enthusiasm home. Parents have welcomed the changes that they have seen in their children and have needed additional support to respond to their children's developing skills. Informal observations of the children, both in their class groups as individuals and in their schools as a whole, have confirmed these views. Formal assessments, using standardized measures, have partially confirmed these observations. Sadly, as a result of weaknesses in the design, the formal evaluation cannot confirm the teachers' impressions that the children's academic functioning improved.

Many deaf children grow up with a sense of disempowerment, difficulties in maintaining self-esteem and with low expectations of themselves. These feelings are in part a consequence of the experience of hearing people taking responsibility for their actions. PATHS offers a means of correcting that experience and compensating for many of the restrictions of experience that arise from being a deaf child in a hearing world. In this respect PATHS may reduce deaf children's need to access mental health services.

The experience of teachers, children, parents and the authors in the use of PATHS has confirmed the importance of the role of schools in promoting children's social and emotional competence. PATHS offers an effective and clearly structured means of achieving this aim. Enabling children to manage difficult situations is a central aim of mental health prevention: according to Clulow, 'Prevention . . . is not about stopping something from happening, but about establishing a framework within which potentially difficult experiences can be managed creatively.' In this respect, the pilot study highlights the importance of similar initiatives for all children. Schools play a vital role in promoting children's social and emotional competence and this role needs wider recognition. Wider recognition could lead to better understanding of the need to enhance social and emotional development within the framework of the National Curriculum.

APPENDIX

Study design

The pilot project used a waiting list control design with 2 schools and 1 unit receiving the curriculum in the first year (the early intervention group, Group 1). The children in the 2 other schools and units acted as controls for the first year and then received the curriculum the following year (the late intervention group, Group 2).

Subjects

There was a total of 64 children in the original study group. However, one of the HIUs in group 1 dropped out at the beginning of the study, leaving 55 children. There were 24 children in group 1, 14 boys and 10 girls aged 7.33–11.00 years, mean age 9.06. There were 31 children in group 2, 20 boys and 11 girls aged 7.00–11.00 years, mean age 8.76 years. All of the children were severely to profoundly deaf and used either Sign Supported English or British Sign Language as their main means of communication. All of the children's parents were hearing. Ten families from group 1 took part in a residential family weekend designed to reinforce aspects of the PATHS curriculum.

Measures at baseline

(a) Emotional vocabulary, understanding and recognition: teachers and parents were asked to complete a checklist of emotional signs used by the children; children were asked by HR to name emotions expressed by children and adults in photographs and explain what the children and adults were experiencing; the Kusché Emotional Inventories (KEI), assessing emotional recognition (I) and emotional labelling (II), were administered to all children in sign language by HR.

(b) Social and emotional adjustment and behaviour: the Meadow and Kendall Social Emotional Adjustment Inventory or SEAI (Meadow-Orlans 1983), a 59-item teacher's checklist, specifically developed to assess deaf children's social and emotional adjustment and the Strengths and Difficulties Questionnaire (Goodman 1997), a 25-item checklist completed by parents were completed on all children.

(c) Measures of cognitive ability and educational attainment: the Raven's Progressive Matrices (Standard and Coloured) were administered to classroom groups by HR's colleague, MM. Classroom teachers administered the Edinburgh Reading Test (University of Edinburgh 1981) to classroom groups.

(d) A measure of impulsivity: the Maze sub-test of the WISC III was administered individually by HR.

(e) Self-concept: HR administered pilot measures of the children's self-concept, using visual representations and 5-point Likert scales. Children were also asked to draw themselves, themselves in their family and themselves at school.

(f) Teachers and parents were asked to rate the communication competence of the children using a 5-point Likert scale.

Measures at follow-up

(a) Emotional vocabulary, understanding and recognition: all measures were repeated at times 1, 2 and 3.

(b) Social and emotional adjustment and behaviour: both the SEAI and the

Strengths and Difficulties Questionnaire were repeated at times 1, 2 and 3.

(c) Measures of educational attainment: the Edinburgh Reading Test was repeated at times 1, 2 and 3.

(d) A measure of impulsivity: the Maze sub-test was repeated at times 1, 2 and 3.

(e) Self-concept: Pilot measures of self-concept and children's drawings were repeated at times 1, 2 and 3.

(f) Teachers and parents were asked to re-rate the communication competence of the children using a 5-point Likert scale at T2.

Results

Mean scores on selected variables are summarized in Table 7.1. At T0, there was no significant difference between the children's total scores on recognizing photographs of emotional states. Using Analysis of Repeated Measures (ARM), there was a significant difference between the two groups over the 18/12 period and T3 between T0 ($F(1,55) = 26$; $p = 0.000$), with the early intervention group showing a more rapid rate of development. Similarly, there were no significant differences between the two groups at T0 on scores using the Kusché Emotional Inventory I and II. However, significant differences emerged between the two groups over time with the early intervention group showing more rapid development of both recognition and labelling of emotions ($F(1,56) = 4.71$, $p = 0.035$ and $F(1,56) = 6.83$, $p<0.0025$, respectively). There were no significant differences between the two groups in scores on the three subscales of the SEAI at T0. Using ARM, significant differences emerged between the early and late intervention groups on the Self-Image subscale ($F(1,56) = 4.53$, $p = 0.038$) and the Emotional Adjustment Subscale ($F(1,56) = 4.12$, $p = 0.47$). The early intervention group had significantly higher raw scores on the Edinburgh Reading Test at T0 ($p = 0.018$), but there was no significant difference over time ($F(1,53) = 2.49$, $p = 0.121$). This is probably because the children's scores were scattered over a wide range with a CI including zero. There was no significant difference between the two groups on scores on the Maze sub-test at T0. No significant difference emerged between the groups over time ($F(1,56) = 2.80$, $p = 0.100$).

Changes in means on these tests are illustrated in Figures 7.5 to 7.12.

Discussion

All of the children in the study group will have developed during the evaluation period. Our interest lies in whether or not PATHS can have an influence on the rate of children's development. Informal observation suggest that PATHS does have an influence and our formal evaluation lends support to those observations.

The influence of PATHS is most clearly seen in the development of the children's emotional skills. Four assessments of the children's ability to recognize, label and understand emotions and the teacher's assessment of the children's use of emotional vocabulary all show significantly more rapid development in the children in the early intervention group. The finding that the rate of development of the children in the late intervention group accelerated once the PATHS curriculum was introduced suggests that this effect was a direct result of the curriculum.

The findings relating to the children's overall social and emotional adjustment

Table 7.1 Summaries of selected variables, showing the mean (standard deviations) scores of the summary variables by gender and by time

	Gender	Time 0	Time 1	Time 2	Time 3
Photos					
Intervention	F	22.1 (7.2)	29.4 (3.3)	32.1 (2.2)	31.3 (1.8)
	M	24.7 (4.2)	29.8 (3.2)	31.9 (2.5)	30.8 (2.5)
Late	F	24.1 (4.9)	27.1 (5.2)	34.3 (5.8)	29.4 (2.1)
Intervention	M	19.7 (4.4)	24.3 (3.6)	24.3 (4.6)	28.7 (3.7)
Maze Test					
Intervention	F	17.9 (7.0)	19.1 (4.8)	17.8 (3.9)	20.0 (2.8)
	M	18.4 (3.1)	21.7 (3.5)	20.8 (3.0)	23.7 (4.0)
Late	F	15.6 (7.6)	19.8 (7.3)	17.8 (5.9)	18.5 (7.1)
Intervention	M	15.5 (6.3)	19.6 (4.2)	16.7 (6.2)	19.3 (6.2)
Kusché Emotional Inventory (Emotional Recognition)					
Intervention	F	59.9 (12.9)	73.3 (5.2)	74.4 (4.1)	77.8 (2.8)
	M	59.0 (10.3)	69.4 (6.5)	72.9 (4.7)	76.4 (3.8)
Late	F	63.6 (9.8)	65.8 (8.1)	64.0 (11.4)	76.0 (2.4)
Intervention	M	60.1 (8.9)	64.7 (8.5)	60.2 (13.8)	74.4 (3.9)
Kusché Emotional Inventory (Emotional Labelling)					
Intervention	F	59.0 (11.3)	73.6 (3.9)	73.4 (5.1)	76.7 (3.0)
	M	57.3 (7.9)	69.5 (7.8)	71.3 (6.0)	76.9 (2.1)
Late	F	59.4 (14.1)	60.9 (14.0)	62.5 (12.5)	74.1 (4.1)
Intervention	M	58.7 (14.0)	63.1 (9.9)	60.0 (11.9)	72.6 (4.9)
Edinburgh Reading Test Raw Scores					
Intervention	F	29.6 (18.9)	46.7 (17.3)	46.1 (23.2)	48.6 (24)
	M	21.6 (13.0)	37.6 (6.8)	21.1 (16.7)	29.8 (19.2)
Late	F	25.9 (24.7)	37.5 (18.6)	35.7 (19.1)	38.1 (13.7)
Intervention	M	18.2 (22.2)	17.0 (20.4)	19.0 (18.7)	25.6 (21.2)
Meadow and Kendall Social and Emotional Assessment Index (Social Adjustment)					
Intervention	F	3.02 (0.71)	3.18 (0.59)	3.45 (0.53)	3.11 (0.74)
	M	2.76 (0.45)	3.01 (0.58)	3.43 (0.29)	3.08 (0.31)
Late	F	3.00 (0.65)	2.91 (0.49)	2.82 (0.83)	2.80 (1.00)
Intervention	M	2.70 (0.64)	2.67 (0.60)	2.86 (0.68)	2.46 (0.69)
Meadow and Kendall Social and Emotional Assessment Index (Self-image)					
Intervention	F	2.99 (0.44)	3.18 (0.47)	3.36 (0.45)	3.03 (0.52)
	M	2.90 (0.35)	3.06 (0.45)	3.22 (0.34)	3.16 (0.41)
Late	F	3.07 (0.32)	3.03 (0.40)	2.75 (0.59)	2.97 (0.44)
Intervention	M	2.87 (0.37)	3.22 (0.33)	2.96 (0.39)	2.70 (0.37)
Meadow and Kendall Social and Emotional Assessment Index (Emotional Adjustment)					
Intervention	F	3.18 (0.50)	3.30 (0.38)	3.60 (0.28)	3.45 (0.39)
	M	3.23 (0.36)	3.34 (0.40)	3.42 (0.25)	3.11 (0.42)
Late	F	3.32 (0.57)	2.99 (0.50)	3.03 (0.47)	3.38 (0.47)
Intervention	M	3.09 (0.55)	3.22 (0.38)	3.09 (0.49)	3.18 (0.25)

are more difficult to interpret. The children in the early intervention group showed more rapid rates of change in mean scores for all three subscales (social, emotional and self-image), although mean scores fell back towards baseline means at 21 months. In contrast, mean scores on all three subscales fell in the late intervention group at 21 months. However, only 1 of the late intervention schools returned SEAIs for 21 months.

The hypothesis that the curriculum would significantly reduce levels of impulsivity, as measured by the Maze sub-test, was not confirmed. Finally, with respect to the children's scores on the Edinburgh Reading Test, the reading skills of the children in the early intervention group appear to have developed more rapidly than those of the children in the late intervention group.

Following data collection, the authors learnt that the upper age range for scaled scores was 10 years. The older children in the study passed their tenth birthdays during the study and, as a result, raw rather than scaled scores were used. However, the scatter of the children's raw scores was so wide that any statistical significance was lost.

NOTE

For further information please contact Helen Reed at:

National Deaf Children's Society
15 Dufferin Street
London EC1Y 8PD
Tel: 0171 490 8656
Fax: 0171 251 5020
e-mail: helenr@ndcs.org.uk

REFERENCES

Goodman, R. (1997) The strengths and difficulties questionnaire: a research note. *Journal of Child Psychology and Psychiatry*, 38, 581–6.

Greenberg, M. and Kusché, C. (1988) Cognitive, personal and social development in deaf children and adolescents. In M. Wang and M. Reynolds (eds) *Handbook of Special Education: Research and Practice*. Oxford: Pergamon.

Greenberg, M. and Kusché, C. (1993) *Promoting Social and Emotional Development in Deaf Children: The PATHS Project*. Seattle: Washington University Press.

Gregory, S. (1995) *Deaf Children and Their Families*. Cambridge: Cambridge University Press.

Gregory, S., Bishop, J. and Sheldon, L. (1995) *Deaf Young People and Their Families: Developing Understanding*. Cambridge: Cambridge University Press.

Hindley, P. A., Hill, P. D., McGuigan, S. and Kitson, K. (1994) Psychiatric disorder in deaf and hard of hearing children and adolescents: a prevalance study. *Journal of Child Psychology and Psychiatry,* 35, 917–34.

Meadow-Orlans, K. (1983) *Manual for the Meadow-Kendall Social-Emotional Assessment Inventories for Deaf and Hearing-Impaired Students*. Washington, DC: Gallandet University Press.

University of Edinburgh (1981) *Edinburgh Reading Test: Manual of Instruction*. London: Hodder and Stoughton.

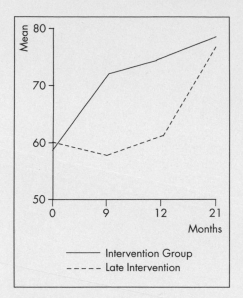

Figure 7.5 Recognition: Kusché Emotional Inventory

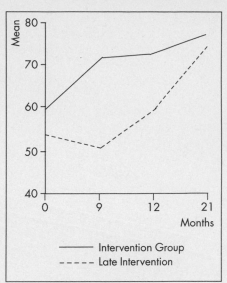

Figure 7.6 Labelling: Kusché Emotional Inventory

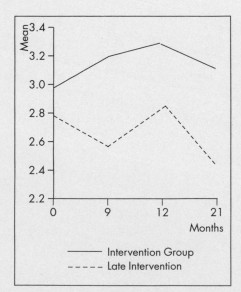

Figure 7.7 Social and Emotional Assessment (Self-image): Meadow and Kendall

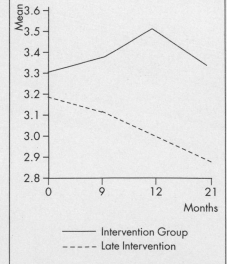

Figure 7.8 Social and Emotional Assessment (Emotional Adjustment): Meadow and Kendall

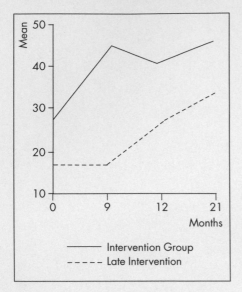

Figure 7.9 Edinburgh Reading Test: Raw Scores

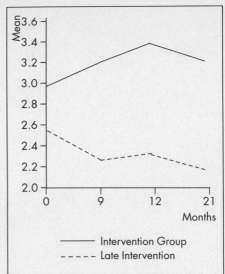

Figure 7.10 Social and Emotional Assessment (Social Adjustment): Meadow and Kendall

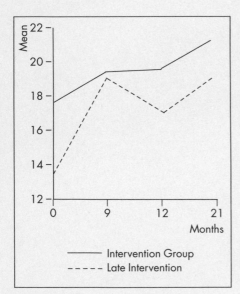

Figure 7.11 Maze Test

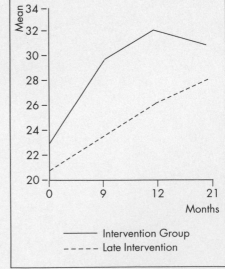

Figure 7.12 Recognition of Faces with Photos

Taking Groups Seriously

'The meeting of . . . personalities is like the contact of . . . chemical substances: if there is any reaction, both are transformed.'
C. G. Jung

Part III: Groups

Therapeutic group work has unrealized potential in education.

- How can a specialized group setting be used to help disturbed children work through difficult feelings?
- How can the circle-time approach be used to foster the group spirit in the classroom?

CHAPTER 8

Splits and hurts: an account of therapeutic group work in mainstream schools

Heather Geddes and Michael Green

This chapter describes group work we did in schools as teachers working in multi-disciplinary teams in local authority Child Guidance Units. We consider the value of group work in schools and we also look at the process of working with schools and staff groups – a key aspect of the work. This leads us to comment about the role of teachers in bringing about change, and on the concept of the 'good enough school' able to meet its pupils needs in the same way that Winnicott's 'good enough mother' (1971) is able to provide an adequate nurturing environment for her child's development.

The children referred to the groups had two characteristics in common: they were underachieving in school and were causing concern to their teachers because of their challenging or puzzling behaviour. Underlying their behaviour was a wide range of problems: physical trauma, sexual abuse, domestic violence, parental depression, twin dependence and rivalry, other sibling rivalry. They varied in their response to learning from being totally silent to having a deafening voice.

The title of this chapter, 'Splits and hurts', comes out of our direct experience of the work. It reflects how we felt at times under the psychic barrage we faced from the children and our understanding of processes we observed occurring during the group work: between ourselves as workers, in the children as they formed various alliances in the groups and hurt each other verbally and physically, and sometimes in the professional network around the groups. Working with split-off feelings and with painful experiences was the key element of the groups. These split-off, hurt parts of themselves were what we believed was causing these children's difficulties.

When feelings are too painful to be experienced or acknowledged directly, a primitive defence system in the psyche comes into play which distances us from uncomfortable feelings by locating them in somebody else; this can then lead to that person being attacked, criticized or hurt, the classic scapegoat, carrying the guilt and pain that we cannot bear. Thus a child who is feeling wounded and vulnerable may bully another child so they 'carry' the hurt. (It doesn't actually work in the long term because at an unconscious level, guilt, fear and anxiety are actually increased.) Similarly, as we experienced, a staff group experiencing communication difficulties and a lack of support from their senior management team may unconsciously create a situation where they can blame and attack outside support staff, rather than confront the painful inner reality of the school itself. Working with disturbed and damaged children is itself painful, and unsupported or unaware teachers can easily find themselves distancing themselves from this hurt that can become so easily located in themselves, by mirroring in staff dynamics the children's conflicts. We had to watch carefully for this happening between ourselves, as it inevitably did.

WHY DO IT?

A lot of children who get referred to child guidance never get there, or never finish off their assessments. Many children are not referred because their parents won't even consider it. In every school there are such children who desperately need help, for whom a relatively short intervention might be all they need, but who don't get it. Their problems can become deeply entrenched and seriously affect their educational opportunities and their whole lives as a result. We became interested in seeing if there were ways of taking therapeutic work into schools.

We had both employed therapeutic thinking in our work with individual children in the child guidance units as well as in consultation work with teachers in schools, and we were confident that the approach could transfer to a school setting. Our interest was supported by the findings described in the book *Help Starts Here* (Kolvin et al. 1981). This describes a major research project carried out over several years in the 1970s in schools in the Newcastle area. The team of researchers set out to assess the value of different approaches with children who were underachieving in schools. The project involved using techniques in counselling, consultation, nurture groups, behaviour modification groups and therapeutic groups and concluded that short-term therapeutic groups can have significant long-term effects for children with emotional and behavioural difficulties. The project team recommended that 'mental health programmes in schools be extended, with a particular emphasis on psychodynamically based group therapy and behaviour modification'. As regards working therapeutically in schools the team stated,

> Taking treatment techniques into the school, rather than taking the child out of school to a clinic setting, has enormous advantages in that it allows study of the effect of therapy in its social context. It also has the advantage of avoiding labelling the child as a psychiatric patient.

We have since discovered that many people have run therapeutic groups in schools. Child psychotherapy trainees from the Tavistock Institute in London have been doing this from the late 1960s (Reid, Fry and Rhode 1977) and there is a long tradition of such work at William Tyndale School in London. More recently, The Place To Be (an organization based in London) has been providing therapeutic support to children in primary schools in various imaginative ways. Regrettably though, Kolvin's recommendations have not, to our knowledge, been taken up in a systematic way by any education authority.

METHOD

Groups ran for 10 sessions over a school term. Sessions lasted approximately one hour. We worked with a maximum of 6 children, the same 6 each week. If children left for any reason, they were not replaced. We needed a room safe from interruption, ideally soundproof or isolated from the main school, as empty of cupboards and other non-essential items as was possible, with some tables to work at and enough chairs for the children and us to sit down. We tried to start and finish each session sitting around the joined-together tables. At the beginning of our first session with the children we introduced ourselves, told them how many times we would be meeting, and said they could use this time each week as they chose. We introduced group rules as necessary.

In 1947 Virginia Axline set out in her book *Play Therapy* the basic principles for this type of work. She stated that the therapist must:

Develop a warm, friendly relationship with the children;
Accept the children exactly as they are;
Establish a feeling of permissiveness in the relationship so that the children feel free to express their feelings completely;
Be alert to the expression of feelings in the children and reflect those feelings back to the children in such a way that they gain insight into their behaviour;
Maintain a deep respect for the children's abilities to solve their own problems if given an opportunity to do so – the responsibility to make choices and to institute change is the individual child's;
Not attempt to direct the children's actions or conversation in any manner;
Not attempt to hurry the therapy along;
Establish only those limitations that are necessary to anchor the therapy in the real world.

Axline believed that all children have an urge towards growth and, given the opportunity, will actively seek positive change for themselves. Attempting to direct this process was, she believed, counter-productive. Our main task was to keep things 'safe' and feed back to the children our understanding of what was happening in the room.

Winnicott knew of and valued Axline's work, and with regard to the value of play, he wrote in *Playing and Reality* (1971): 'It is good to remember that playing is itself a psychotherapy. To arrange for children to be able to play is itself a psychotherapy that has immediate and universal application.'

EQUIPMENT

Our basic equipment kit was intended to provide scope for a wide range of expressive play. We abandoned the use of paint after the first group we ran together! This kit was compact enough to fit in one car. A safe storage cupboard in the school made life easier.

The basic kit comprised:

- creative materials – felt pens, pencils, rulers, Pritstick, safety scissors, plasticine, Sellotape, white A4 paper, A3 sugar paper
- play materials – toy soldiers, cars, planes, two telephones, glove puppets (one must have teeth), tea set, gun, black and white baby dolls, a doll's house and pipe cleaner people to go in it, wild and farm animals, fences, a bag of dressing-up clothes including various hats (soldier, policeman, fireman)

- other materials – a giant teddy bear and two large bean bags, used for a number of purposes but provided especially to provide a safe outlet for aggression

The furniture in the room was used extremely creatively by the children. Chairs and tables were turned into camps, empty cupboards became bunks, private places to hide away or a focus for group activities. All the objects in the room were drawn into the children's imaginative worlds.

THEORY

According to Melanie Klein, splitting is a primitive defence mechanism used by the developing infant to protect itself from the overwhelming anxiety produced by its aggressive feelings. The 'all good mummy' who feeds and looks after the infant is separated in the infant's mind from the 'all bad mummy' who isn't there when it is hungry and causes it frustration. Under normal circumstances, with a good enough mother able to cope with infantile rages, and a reasonable understanding building up between the mother and infant, less primitive splitting occurs and more complex mental functioning can begin (Klein 1946). The mother contains the infant's anxiety and, in so doing, enables the infant to develop a capacity to contain and understand its own feelings and start the process of thinking about experience from which all complex mental functioning develops (Bion 1970).

Michael Fordham, a Jungian analyst, proposed a rather different model in which violence, pain and suffering could take place in the course of normal healthy 'deintegration–reintegration sequences', and contribute to development. He reserved the use of the word 'splitting' solely for those occasions when 'pain is excessive and intolerably prolonged' (Fordham 1993). See Figure 8.1.

For the children we worked with in the groups, some event or situation or thought or feeling had been experienced by them as too unbearably painful or dangerous or bad to assimilate in a normal way, and the only way they had felt able to deal with it had been to use this primitive defence and split off that awareness from the rest of their thinking. They made the situation go away in their mind, as if by magic. Klein wrote that this

> Omnipotent denial of the existence of the bad object [internalized person] and of the painful situation is in the unconscious equal to annihilation by the destructive impulse . . . and therefore a part of the ego is denied and annihilated as well.

The unbearable external situation becomes internalized deep in the psyche where it can wreak havoc, like an internal terrorist that hinders and disturbs development (Jung 1960, Williams 1997). Jung (1940) compared it to a 'possession' of the mind:

> when a part of the psyche is split off from consciousness it is only *apparently* inactivated; in actual fact it brings about a possession of the personality, with the result that the individual's aims are falsified in the interests of the split-off part.

Winnicott (1960) described a similar 'false self' organization which cuts an individual off from true spontaneity and creativity.

Figure 8.1   Ripped up crying head

The drawing (Figure 8.2) produced by a child from one of the groups illustrates the psychic process we have described. The figure's head is breaking open like an egg and a smaller sub-self is separating out at the top of the drawing. Another drawing (Figure 8.3), by a younger child, shows a similar 'escape' taking place. There is nobody at the wheel now; the car is out of control, and the driver has no means of getting where he needs to go.

For a child this means that they will be unable to utilize all their mental resources in the demanding task of growing up, unable to apply themselves to learning new skills, unable in the most severe cases to think at all. Jung (1958) proposed that split-off parts of the psyche came together to form a kind of sub-personality, a shadow self:

> Everyone carries a shadow, and the less it is embodied in the individual's conscious life, the blacker and denser it is . . . if it is repressed and isolated from consciousness, it never gets corrected, and is liable to burst forth suddenly in a moment of unawareness.

This division in the psyche is graphically illustrated by the following drawing (Figure 8.4) by a boy whose major problem was his inability to control his violent outbursts.

Segal (1957) writes that 'something like a pocket of schizophrenia exists isolated in the ego and is a constant threat to stability.' Violent acting out can be the result. Thinking itself can seem dangerous because you might risk coming into contact with the painful or dangerous part of yourself that you've hidden away. As mentioned earlier, the split-off parts can be projected on to other children and lead to bully/victim ways of relating. Such children are terribly handicapped. When they say, 'I didn't do it', they are often telling the truth. They did not consciously choose to do something; it happened, it erupted, it spilled out.

The intention of the groups is to provide a safe place for the children to play out the hurts and fears and split-off parts of themselves that are causing them so much difficulty, to get back in touch with the energy they have lost, to come to terms with their shadow. It is not easy. It requires great courage. They will have reverted to this defence under extreme circumstances and for good reasons. Now though, they are stuck, unable to move on, and it is time to face what they couldn't previously. At some level these children know what work they have to do and quickly sense the opportunity that the group provides. Once the group mechanism gets activated, the old hurts and pain and anger will start to surface. It can feel at times like being in a war zone, but out of the chaos new life can emerge. The description of a session that follows will make clearer what the experience is like for us and the children involved.

GROUP SESSION

The session described is the third in a series with a mixed group of 5 children. Six had started the group, but one had left the school suddenly. There are 2 girls and 3 boys, 1 girl is black. The ages range from 6 to 10 years. The facilities are good, the escort is reliable, but the relationships within the staff group of the school are quite poor. We are uncertain about the containment of the children in their classes

Figure 8.2   Split head

Figure 8.3 Escape/out of it

Figure 8.4 Good boys/bad boys

between the sessions. Despite that anxiety, which we are trying to address through the reviews with the classteachers, the children have begun to use the group very effectively. (The names of the children are changed, as throughout.)

The children are at the door, brought by the escort, four of them charged through, clamouring to get into the room, leaving behind Steven, a quite tall, mature-looking boy, who was hiding in the corner of the doorway. He said he didn't want to come to the group. He looked furious and determined as we took some minutes to persuade him to come into the room and discuss it. The others were in the room and had 'begun'. Gemma, who was quite little, was yelling and screaming about having a cushion of her own, trying to hold onto one by lying on it. The other cushion was also being fought over. Sharlene, a much larger and stronger girl, the biggest child in the group, joined in as well. She occupied Gemma's cushion giving Gemma elbow jabs and finger pokes telling her to, 'Stop yelling! . . . shut up! . . . you're spoilt! . . . selfish! . . .'

We entered into this noisy scene with Steven who was saying that the group was useless: he didn't learn anything . . . he wanted to be in science . . . doing proper work. We reflected how hard it was to share and that everyone seemed to want a cushion of their own. As Steven fought to escape from the group, trying to get past us out of the door, we tried to keep him in the room to talk to us about how he was feeling, at the same time trying to encourage everyone to sit around the table. John was busy at the table with the plasticine, saying he wanted to play, Jason was planted on a cushion. Sharlene responded to our request by trying to lift/force Gemma to the table. Gemma screamed in protest that she didn't want to, she wanted her cushion. As she was being dragged away by Sharlene, passing the dressing-up bag Gemma grabbed the sequined (elastic tube) skirt and white high heels. She struggled free and put them on, becoming it seemed more 'grown up', as if wearing the 'adult' clothes made her feel more her age. We commented on this. For the rest of the session, Sharlene and Gemma more or less played 'mums'. They made plasticine food for picnics, gallons of tea (water), dolls were dressed and undressed and giggled over. Sharlene made some excursions into the ongoing 'cushion frenzy' (see later) and also went to the toilet, but otherwise had a lower key presence.

Steven, with occasional attempts to escape from the room, became involved in cushion grabbing or fighting over them with John and Jason. Jason seemed unable to shift his attention away from the cushions. Steven invented a game of jumping into the cushions from the (two-drawer) filing cabinet. All three boys loved this. Shoes came off and they played increasingly riskily. We warned/reminded them of danger, keeping safe, being careful. It went on a long time, three boys diving into two cushions. (The 'attack' on the cushions seemed relentless and HG was beginning to feel sorry for the 'cushions'.) We pointed out the two different types of play that seemed to be taking place in the room.

Steven appeared to bump his knee on the hard floor during one leap. He withdrew from the game with a pained expression, rolling up his jeans to display his sore knee. In this manner he sat at the tables where the girls played industriously. We began to reflect on the danger of this play, talking to each other, and decided that jumping from the cupboard was too high. We gave them five more goes, then stopped them. They tried to persist and Steven invented a different cushion diving game, running from the far end of the room then leaping onto them. The other two boys joined in with this. Then, led by Steven, they used the table and next the chairs as jumping-off points to try to reassert the diving game and continue challenging us. As this petered out, both of us working hard to restrain the boys from their dangerous antics, John became angry with Steven who had jumped on him and hurt him. We had to separate them at first and hold the furious John back (he was probably relieved to be held back as he was smaller than Steven). John took a large sheet of paper and drew a figure which he said was Steven, then punched and ripped up the paper. We commented on how he'd found a way of expressing his anger without anyone getting physically hurt. However, Steven became angry and we had to hold him back. John then made another picture and turned it into a 'puppet' which he pretended to rip. Other creative ideas followed from this. Jason and John began play fighting and Jason began jumping on John and the cushions. Inevitably this got a bit serious at one point and we had to calm things down again. Sharlene came into the play for a while, getting jumped on, then behaving in what seemed to us afterwards a rather disturbing, sadistic way, a fixed expression on her face, holding John down so he couldn't breathe, until we intervened.

John retired to quiet play with the plasticine and appropriated the 'food' the girls had made, putting a trayful carefully into the 'safe' box (where the things they made and their drawing folders were kept) as if it was his. We talked about this, and Sharlene said he could have it. As the session drew to an end, Jason joined Steven in a return to trying to escape from the room. When we mentioned it was nearly time to leave now, Gemma became furious. She made a 'love card' for her mum, with big red hearts on it, that she carefully put into her folder, then swept everything off the drawing table and stamped on the paper, yelling, 'I want to stay here! . . . I don't want to go!' Steven was saying the group was 'rubbish', then 'acted' being very sad and hurt and vulnerable. All except Gemma left to join the escort who was now waiting. When told it was time to go now, even though she really didn't want to go, she grabbed the gun and hurled it across the room before stomping out to join the others; all then left peacefully with our wonderful, calming escort.

All surfaces had been swept clean of their contents, and toys were everywhere in a jumbled mess. We hadn't managed to get them round the table either at the beginning or at the end. It was a long time before we could function. We lay crashed out on beanbags amidst the mess, overwhelmed and despairing. Finally, we pulled ourselves together, cleared up, put the toys away, scribbled some brief notes and made our way to the teacher review meeting that was scheduled – it turned out to be a re-enactment of the attacks we'd experienced in the group.

We had experienced this before, the third session being the end of the 'honeymoon period' with an eruption of activity to do with looking for and challenging boundaries. However many groups we ran, even though we could see patterns like this, each session felt like new, unexplored territory. Reflecting on this session in supervision helped us to make sense of the children's actions and our feelings, and enabled us to move on to the next session. Despite the difficulties we experienced working in this school, our follow-up meetings showed that all the children had benefited from the group work, and we found a more positive attitude towards us from the teaching staff.

HOW WE COPED: MAKING IT SAFE

It is very evident from this description that, even with relatively small numbers of children, the potential emotional experience is enormous. It can be extremely difficult to contain the powerful emotions present in the room and bring sufficient understanding to the experience. At least once in every group we would wonder why on earth we had chosen to work like this. Something akin to a chemical reaction takes place, generating the emotional equivalents of heat and light. Old stuck patterns of relating get burned away. The impact of all this on us was considerable.

We had to make it safe enough for the children to be in touch with difficult and painful feelings, and safe enough for ourselves to work like this. We had to be able to cope with and contain all the pain and hurt in the room. The extensive *setting up procedures* we describe next were designed to make the school a safe container for the work. Clear, consistent *limit setting* was vital in enabling the children to feel safe during the groups, and this we describe in detail later on. But the most important element in our coping was the already mentioned weekly supervision/consultation session we set up for each piece of group work. This role was provided by various members of our multi-disciplinary teams, from consultant child psychiatrist to child psychotherapists. The discipline of writing up notes after each session in preparation for supervision was a containing task in itself. As we recalled events and placed incidents in the right order, it restored our capacity to think together after the emotional onslaught of the group session.

Supervision provided us with the thinking and objectivity of an outside person who could help to interpret confusion, contain anxiety and reflect upon meaning. Within these weekly sessions, we used our feelings and reactions to individuals and events to make sense of what had happened. We experienced our own differences of perception and of opinion, and thinking about these differences within supervision was valuable in enabling us to better understand the children's experiences which we were at times reflecting. It was possible with the support of supervision to remain an intact thinking couple who could resist the attacks on our 'marriage' that we constantly experienced. This was another aspect of the meaning of our chapter title, 'Splits and hurts' – attempts to split us as a couple and to destroy our capacity to think together. We were occasionally idealized, but were more frequently attacked and abused. The cry of 'I wonder what Mr Green/Mrs Geddes thinks about what is happening' helped us to reach out to each other and maintain our partnership in a maelstrom of conflict and need.

The work was difficult and challenging, but we derived satisfaction from seeing children working through difficult feelings. Hearing from their teachers about exciting changes taking place in the children gave us much needed encouragement during those times when we doubted the method and ourselves. Sometimes it was fun. The experience was overall highly rewarding for us personally and professionally.

Setting up procedures

We were aware that working in schools could be fraught with potential mistrust, misunderstanding and conflict. For this reason we developed a very thorough setting-up process to try to iron out as many problems as we could beforehand. The establishment of a contract with the school and the process of negotiations about time and place and referral of pupils took as long as the group work. This was accompanied and paralleled by reviews with the classteachers and meetings with parents. Groups were followed up with termly reviews for a year afterwards. The actual group was the core of the work, but it was also part of a collaborative association with the school that lasted a year and a half. We could not work in isolation even though what happened within the group sessions was confidential. There were many boundaries to clarify, negotiate and maintain.

In any negotiation with a school system it is imperative to take the expectations of the institution into account. These expectations represent the needs and challenges that the school is facing and need to be heard and understood rather than displaced by the requirements of group work. Listening to the headteacher, the Special Educational Needs Co-ordinator (SENCO) and the classteachers put us in touch with the perceptions and difficulties of the teachers and gave us some insight into the ethos and the system which the children experienced.

First steps

We began each piece of work by meeting with the head of the school and the SENCO to describe the way we worked and to see if they were interested. Without the clear support of senior management all kinds of problems can arise. At this first meeting we made it clear what our requirements were. We presented a typed list of 'Necessary Conditions for Successful Group Work in School' and asked for the head to sign a contract agreeing to them before beginning any further work. This meeting was followed by a presentation to the whole staff group setting out the therapeutic approach, the level of collaboration planned with classteachers of the pupils referred, and discussion about the kind of pupils who were most likely to benefit.

If no member of the staff questioned our approach, we learned to our cost that this was a bad sign, and likely to lead to criticisms and doubts surfacing later. Hard-pressed teachers are bound to be sceptical of what can seem a very different way of understanding children. The more vigorous our initial discussion, the more likely we were to be able to develop a solid working relationship.

Following our discussion a request for children's names to be put forward was left with the staff. At a subsequent meeting with the head and the SENCO we discussed these children in detail to reach a final short list of six pupils. The school negotiated permission from parents and let them know that we would be available to meet with them at a later date if they wished.

The practical arrangements for the group then had to be negotiated: dates, times and an escort to bring the pupils from class to the room. Ending the group at the beginning of break was helpful as this helped to mark the boundary between the group experience and the classroom, and gave the children some time to run around a bit and work off individual tension if they needed to. Possible disruption to their classes after a child had been in the group was a worry frequently expressed by teachers. This caused far less difficulty than we had expected. With clear reminders, the children were able to move quite easily from the intense experience of the group, with its relative freedom of choice and action, to the more orderly setting of the classroom, with their teacher's different expectations of them. This is not to say that children will not try to stretch the boundary between the group and the school.

On one memorable occasion Wayne, a boy with some serious behavioural difficulties, stood in the open doorway at the beginning of a group and shouted down the corridor, 'Isn't it true we're allowed to fucking swear in these groups, sir?' Whilst our therapeutic stance was to think about the meaning of the children's communications, including swearing, we would always make it clear to children that we were in a school and that certain expectations and clear rules applied outside the group and at points of transition. We also had clear rules that applied within the groups, about which we'll say more later.

The room

Finding an appropriate space in a school was extremely difficult and on one occasion we were unable to work in an open plan school because of a lack of suitable space. For one group we accepted a room that was too small and this contributed to difficulties during the sessions. Whilst running another group we found ourselves always having to clear up the boxes belonging to the parent-teacher association. In one school we assumed that the head of the Early Years Unit had been informed about us being in her part of the building. At our first group session we were met by her, understandably irate at having not been consulted about the arrangements. Having worked hard to create a secure, cosy environment, she did not want a group of 'disturbed' older children near her younger and vulnerable infants. In the end she became supportive of our work, but issues like this indicate the disasters that can result from poor communication within a school – something we encountered in other ways whilst working in this same school.

The group mix

Group work is most effective with a mixed group, mixed in age, gender, race and behaviour. A mix of behaviour and response offers a wider choice of options and experience to all the children in the group and the extremes can help to modify each other. Our intention was to help all of them to move towards a more thoughtful and self-aware position and to do this they needed to experience other ways of responding to challenges, not just from the adults but also amongst their peers. Most of the children in the groups were from 7 to 10 years old and at an age when peers are becoming increasingly important. Again and again we had to work hard to resist the pressure put on us to work with the six most difficult boys in a school and had to push for staff to identify the very withdrawn pupils as well. One school persisted in referring six boys and were completely unable to think of a single girl who might need such a resource. This was also a school in which there was a football culture which was used as the metaphor for the rules and regulations that governed much of the behaviour. It was a very male culture and we, to our amusement, became affected by it. After one of the sessions in which one boy, Jerry, had made a particularly significant shift from his painfully withdrawn, near-mute state, and become outwardly assertive and positive in expressing himself, Michael commented gleefully that 'Jerry played a blinder!' After this group we regretted not standing our ground and insisting on at least two girls to be put forward.

The classteacher

A further factor in the choice of referral was the reliability of the teacher. It was important that, after a group, pupils returned to stable and reliable classrooms. This kind of group work is necessarily chaotic, seemingly anarchic at times, and children need security and clear boundaries afterwards to enable the insights gained in the different setting of the group to be internalized. For this reason it was important to identify classes where a teacher was struggling, or where a change of teacher was imminent and likely to unsettle the children. We ruled out probationary teachers for the same reasons. Such uncertainty would have undermined opportunities to use the group effectively. There need to be clear, easily identifiable differences between the world of the group and the world of the classroom.

These initial discussions and negotiations were lengthy, but they meant that the group sessions, once begun, could proceed with as little unexpected interruption as possible.

Before the sessions began we asked the classteachers of the referred pupils to describe four hoped-for changes in their pupils, and we used these as base lines for the exchange of reports and observations in regular reviews, and for our evaluation following the group. Classteachers agreed to submit a weekly written comment on the pupils in their class so that we could anticipate difficulties and monitor what happened in between the sessions. Times of reviews were arranged in advance, and also included one of the senior staff with whom the original contract was made. Termly reviews were arranged for the year following the group with the same senior manager, to ensure continuity.

The good enough school

This detailed and careful process of setting up evolved out of experience. It was soon our belief that the school system within which the group took place was the basis for the safety and success of the group work. The outcome for the pupils was directly linked to the school staff's capacity to develop the thinking process about the children. Some children made dramatic and conspicuous changes that could not pass unnoticed, but most made small but significant changes which required the teacher to be observant and perceptive and aware of the child. Without the teacher's awareness, these small changes could be disregarded and the opportunity to build on them would be lost.

We developed a sense of schools as being 'good enough schools', using Winnicott's sense of the 'good enough parent'. The 'good enough school' was one in which pupils experienced sufficient care and thought to enable them to make the best of their opportunities. An important aspect of this was the school's capacity to think about difficult and challenging issues in a way that was not blaming or persecuting and in which change could be tolerated and supported. If the senior management could do this for the teachers, then the teachers could do this for the pupils. Within such a regime, we could then work safely. We were building the professional partnership within which we could work safely and which would be the container for the therapeutic experience of the children.

The challenge of the work within the groups required a very high level of safety and containment. In a school setting this requires close collaboration, both practical and reflective, between the teaching staff and the group workers, within strongly held boundaries, the foundations of which are laid down by the negotiations before the work begins.

Limit setting

Axline's principles, which we tried to stick to, emphasize the importance of 'permissiveness', of the children feeling free to express all sides of themselves. With this in mind we did not set any rules up in the groups at the beginning. Also, rules can in themselves be seen as a provocation. As soon as it became necessary though, we made it clear that they were not to hurt us or each other, and the room and the equipment in it were not to be damaged. They were also not allowed to leave the room without consulting with us. To maintain these limits we used a combination of techniques recommended by Bixler (1949) and Ginott (1959). This involves using a series of graded steps:

1. Reflecting the desire or attitude of the child. ('You're so cross with Anthony because of what he said/did that you'd like to hit him.')
2. Stating the limits of a particular act while acknowledging that the feeling is acceptable. ('You feel like hitting Anthony because you're angry about what he said/did, it's OK to be angry with him, but you know that hitting is not allowed in the group.')
3. Pointing out other channels through which the feelings or wishes can be expressed. ('You can hit the bear or the bean bags to show how cross you feel if you want, draw a picture, tell them, etc.')
4. Helping the child bring out the feelings of resentment bound to arise when restrictions are invoked. ('You wish there weren't any rules in the group, that you could do everything you feel like doing.')
5. Control by physical means of the child's behaviour. ('We won't let you hit/hurt/break Anthony/the toys, it's important to keep everyone safe here, even though you feel like . . .' – repeat steps 1–4.)

Actually physically restraining children is obviously the last resort, and also a controversial issue in schools. We see no alternative but to be able to safely hold children in situations where otherwise they could lose control of themselves. Gentle holding, with one of us on each side, was what we found to be the least threatening and therefore most effective way of calming down a very angry child, whilst firmly but gently interpreting their behaviour and stating the rules as above. Often it was enough to show that we understood and accepted the desire to break the limits and this removed the need to act out the feeling.

There were times though when we would have to take the further step of excluding a child from the group for the rest of a session, when they consistently refused to keep to the limits. Having gone through all the steps several times, we'd warn the child that if they carried on we would have to take them to whichever member of the school staff we'd arranged to be available in this eventuality (part of our setting up). We stressed it wasn't a punishment and they would be welcome back in the group the following week.

Jack, an 8-year-old boy who was referred because he got into fights a lot, ripped up his work, and some days sat in the classroom in tears saying he wanted to die, began really testing our limits in one group. He climbed on top of a high cupboard, refused to come down, hurled felt marker pens about, stamped on toys and then began to draw on the walls. Again and again we stopped him and finally warned him that if it was too difficult for him to be in the group today and keep to the rules, he would have to go to Miss X's room. He continued his behaviour, then refused to go when we asked him. We reassured him that he would not be told off, Miss X would understand (she had been carefully briefed beforehand), but he now had to go. He refused and threw more pens. MG carefully picked him up and carried him struggling out of the room to Miss X. The other children were subdued when MG returned and we talked to them about what had happened. One of the girls who had little trust in adults seemed convinced that something awful would have happened to him. Would he actually get into trouble? Were we telling the truth? Was the group really confidential? Could we be trusted?

Seeing Jack in the playground afterwards, apparently unscathed, was a relief to the children. They heard from him that he hadn't been told off. Maybe we could be trusted. The following week Jack announced at the beginning of the session that he was not going to be taken out of the group this week. He proceeded to loudly and energetically and *safely* express his angry feelings, stamping his feet, jumping up and down, making swift, violent drawings with the marker pens. He had been contained by the experience, as had all the others in the group, and the extra feeling of trust created enabled deeper work to go on in that group.

Seeing us responding thoughtfully to extreme emotions and behaviour (sometimes with difficulty!), not becoming angry or violent ourselves, able to keep things safe, opened up for these children the possibility of understanding and controlling their own violent feelings.

The effect on children

As we said earlier, many of the changes brought about by this experience were apparently small. With classteachers alert to change, the small change could have an impact on the child's ability to use the opportunities of the classroom, their relationship with the teacher and peers, and they could begin to make significant progress in their learning. This was proved over and over again, and reflected changes also occurring at home. One parent told the classteacher that they found their child 'easier to get on with', another that their daughter seemed 'more likeable'. In one touching review a parent told us that they now understood just how unhappy their son had been. This suggested to us that some kind of reparation was going on and that relationships were being affected beyond the boundaries of group and school.

For some children the changes were more dramatic. This is demonstrated by the case of Louise, an 8-year-old girl. When she was chosen for the group, we were told that she wasn't reading and that she was withdrawn and uncommunicative in class. She seemed to hide behind a veil of hair. If an adult touched her she went rigid. Following a change of teacher, she hadn't spoken to her new teacher for six months. In her past was an unsubstantiated allegation of sexual abuse.

When she started the group, Louise wouldn't talk to us. Gradually she opened up and involved herself in play with the other children and began to communicate a little more with us. About half way through the series of sessions, she began to play with puppets and other materials to work through something that we struggled to follow, in which issues of trust were paramount. This material seemed to have a sexual content. Finding the right words for what we thought she was showing us was hard. A breakthrough seemed to come in one powerful session which involved sexualized behaviour and resulted in Louise using the crocodile puppet in a miming activity with MG. The crocodile first bit off his ears, then his eyes, then his mouth and finally his brain. We suggested that someone wouldn't be able to hear or see or talk or think if that happened to them. She then attacked us both with the puppet. We suggested that she had shown us something she had been through, how she had felt at the time and how angry she was about it.

In the following sessions Louise began to talk to us more, awkwardly at first, words tumbling out of her, sometimes jumbled up. We began to get reports from her teacher of a new confidence in class. At our final evaluation session with the teachers, we heard that Louise had sought out the teacher she knew she was going to have next term and introduced herself. All the hoped-for changes were realized and her mother was reported to be 'delighted' with the changes in her daughter.

A year later, Louise was, in her teacher's words, 'a totally different child'. She was now reading, and valued her time with the reading helper. Her classmates were being surprised by her contributions to class discussions. Whilst academically still below the class average, she was making tremendous progress. She had used the opportunity of the group to communicate something about her past experience and to begin to free herself from its impact on her.

This case gives some sense of the effect that traumatic experiences can have on children's capacities to learn, and demonstrates the importance of providing a safe but relatively unconstrained place where powerful feelings can be safely re-experienced and resolution can begin.

REFLECTIONS ON THE PROCESSES OF THE GROUPS

The original intention was to try to transport therapeutic group work directly into the mainstream system. In this respect we feel that the project was successful. In particular, annual reviews indicated that the benefits to the children were long term and for some very significant. With the teachers, it was possible to note a change in perception about the meaning of some children's behaviour, a lessening of their sense of confusion and helplessness and a development of their use of their own skills as teachers. This was based on the greater awareness of the child and observation of their behaviour so that small but significant changes could be built on. No doubt the increased focus on thinking about the emotional needs of the children in class had an effect on the child, perhaps in some cases as much as the awareness of being thought about in the groups.

What became immediately apparent was something we had taken for granted in working within our clinic teams. An important aspect of working therapeutically is that the situation and the worker are sufficiently safe – safe from being disturbed while working, and properly looked after and supported whilst carrying out professional tasks. This applies as much to the teachers as to the therapists. The guidelines and procedures for setting up the groups were evolved from a sense that some schools were not very safe places. At times we were let down, forgotten, abused and in one school our reviews were forgotten and not attended. There could be 'splits and hurts' within the school system that made communication and consistency difficult to maintain. This inevitably affects the teachers' ability to work effectively with challenging and needy children. Thankfully, this was not always the case and mostly our relationships with schools were constructive and productive.

During the work we experienced situations that challenged us as adults and teachers and as a 'thinking couple'. We experienced enormous attacks on our capacity to think and experienced first-hand the importance of keeping safe. We concluded that 'limits and boundaries' played an enormously important part in establishing a setting safe enough to permit feelings to be explored rather than just acted out. In every group the children seemed driven to finding this limit. Once this was found and experienced then other responses were possible, thinking could take place, and emotional and intellectual development could proceed.

The experience of this relationship between safety and learning made us think not only about our own practice but also about the significance of the setting and keeping of boundaries within the school system. We see this as the basis for a functioning learning environment, as important for teachers as for their pupils. Children's behaviour may be a symptom of their need to experience such boundaries. Once this could happen then thinking could be restored, and emotional development and learning could proceed.

Other features, such as absences and endings, poor self-esteem, subtle racial pressures and unresolved traumas, reminded us of the complexity of children's experiences at school, and of the value of therapeutic thinking in the mainstream setting that can help to make sense of such complex situations. It was also made clear that this thinking could work within and alongside the teaching task to bring about a more successful outcome for the more challenged and challenging children.

CONCLUSION

In the present climate of concern and anxiety about children who are failing in school and presenting behaviour that feels overwhelmingly challenging, it is easy to despair and feel hopeless and deskilled. In the groups that we experienced, the teaching staff were able to identify children at an early age who were likely to be at risk of exclusion or who were not responding to remedial interventions. It was made clear to us, and to the teachers and the schools we worked with, that it was possible to affect this situation significantly and with a relatively small allocation of resources. Over the years this form of intervention has been practised in many schools and in many forms. The 'nurture group' was a common practice at one time which aimed at similar goals. Our conclusion from this work is that therapeutic practice can work within a mainstream setting whether as a rigorously therapeutic model or in other guises. The commitment to work with the most challenging children has been waylaid for some time by the demands and new priorities of recent legislation and change, but we would encourage schools to recall their histories and skills in this field, to look at all the work that has been done in schools, and to make available the help that some children need in order to overcome their difficulties and have an equal opportunity to learn.

REFERENCES

Axline, V. M. (1947) *Play Therapy*. Boston: Houghton Mifflin.

Bion, W. (1970) *Attention and Interpretation*. London: Tavistock.

Bixler, R. H. (1949) Limits are therapy. *Journal of Consulting Psychology* 13, 1–11. In Schaefer, C. (ed.) *The Therapeutic Use of Child's Play* (1976), New York: Aronson.

Fordham, M. (1993) Notes for the formation of a model of infant development. *Journal of Analytical Psychology*, 38, 5–12.

Ginott, H. G. (1959) The theory and practice of therapeutic intervention in child treatment. *Journal of Consulting Psychology* 23, 160–6. In Schaefer, C. (ed.) *The Therapeutic Use of Child's Play* (1976), New York: Aronson.

Jung, C. G. (1940) The psychology of the child archetype. In *Collected Works, Volume 9, Part 1, The Archetypes and the Collective Unconscious* (1959), London: Routledge and Kegan Paul.

Jung, C. G. (1958) *Collected Works, Volume 11, Psychology and Religion: East and West*. London: Routledge and Kegan Paul.

Jung, C. G. (1960) The feeling toned complex and its general effects on the psyche. In *Collected Works, Volume 3, The Psychogenesis of Mental Disease*, London: Routledge and Kegan Paul.

Klein, M. (1946) Notes on some schizoid mechanisms. *International Journal of Psycho-Analysis*. In *Envy and Gratitude and Other Works* (1975), London: Hogarth.

Kolvin, I. et al. (1981) *Help Starts Here: The Maladjusted Child in the Ordinary School*. London: Tavistock.

Reid, S., Fry, E. and Rhode, M. (1977) Working with small groups of children in primary schools. In Daws, D. and Boston, B. (eds) *The Child Psychotherapist* (1977), London: Wildwood House.

Segal, H. (1957) Notes on symbol formation. *International Journal of Psycho-Analysis*, 38, 391–7. In *The Work of Hanna Segal* (1981), New York: Jason Aronion; and in Spillius, E. B. (ed.) *Melanie Klein Today, Volume 1, Mainly Theory* (1988), London: Routledge.

Williams G. (1997) On introjective processes. In *Internal Landscapes and Foreign Bodies: Eating Disorders and Other Pathologies*, London: Duckworth.

Winnicott, D.W. (1960) Ego distortion in terms of true and false self. In *The Maturational Processes and the Facilitating Environment*, New York: International Universities Press.

Winnicott, D. W. (1971) *Playing and Reality*. London: Tavistock.

CHAPTER 9

Therapeutic group work in an inner-city primary school

Gill Ingall and Margaret Lush

For many years therapeutic groups have been run within the setting of the inner city primary school where we worked. In writing this chapter, we aim to record the way in which the groups were organized and what we feel they offered to the children, the staff and the ethos of the school. We think that this model of working with children, whose emotional difficulties restrict their access to the curriculum and to being part of the school, could be adapted elsewhere. Our experience is that schools are places that can promote healthy developmental growth in children, and that this process is helped when schools are able to acknowledge the different needs of their children whilst understanding what is and what is not possible to address within the classroom.

We were fortunate to be working within a school where groups had taken place for almost thirty years, each groups teacher bringing his or her own particular way of working within an established setting. This allowed us, as new workers, to gradually discover the nature of our task and to be open to learning from the children. A new headteacher of the school started shortly before we began to work in our posts. The established tradition of groups allowed us some breathing space to discover what becoming a group worker entailed and allowed the head to suspend his disbelief and to wait until it became clearer what groups could offer the school. These factors made our situation unique and we are aware that the experience of teachers setting up provision in another school may well be completely different.

Appointments to the post of groups teacher were made with the co-operation of the tutors on the course named 'Observational Studies and the Application of Psycho-Analytic Concepts to Work with Children, Young People and Families' at the Tavistock Clinic. This meant that our work was known by the staff of the course and could be supported through the Work Discussion seminars on the course and by private supervision.

The Observational Studies course, as the name suggests, gave us a grounding in how to observe what the babies and young children we regularly visited were actually doing and then think about the meaning of that behaviour in the context of that observation. We were then gradually able to see what the children were making of their experiences and what was the quality of their earliest relationships with the important people in their lives. This detailed observation of behaviour, together with thinking about our emotional responses to it, was the basis of our work in the groups.

Through studying Freud's case material in our theoretical seminars, we were able to discover how his contribution to psychoanalytical theory was firmly based in his observation of behaviour, a skill developed through his early work as a research scientist. The theoretical component of the course showed us how Melanie Klein's work developed from Freud's, concentrating on the psychic mechanisms that she understood were operating as the infant developed. She showed that these infantile mechanisms and preoccupations continue to influence emotional experience throughout life. The concepts and theoretical formulations the two of them developed helped us both to understand the processes that were taking place in the groups and to identify how a group was developing.

The Groups Workshop of the Tavistock Clinic provided a framework within which to think about our work, as well as a chance to learn about psychoanalytically orientated group work taking place in other settings. The Foundation Course in Group Therapy also provided similar support. The approach of these courses at the Tavistock Clinic was to help us understand the meaning of behaviour as well as the unconscious processes and feelings that underlie behaviour. This was very useful in understanding the meaning of what was going on in the groups. However, this kind of group work does not need the leader to make overt psychoanalytical interpretations to the children and indeed, in a school setting, this would not be desirable. It was important to be careful not to involve the children in a dependent relationship of the kind that would expose them to unnecessarily painful and disturbing feelings when we were seen with other children or staff around the school.

Looking back on our experience of being groups teachers we can see how children can be helped to begin to think about their emotional difficulties within the umbrella of thinking together about the group's experience of beginnings and endings, new and lost members, and the relationship to the group teacher. The challenge for us was to enable each group of children the opportunity to discover aspects of themselves and others hitherto unknown or underused. The fact that the groups took place within the setting of a school meant that many children who otherwise might not have been able to make use of other external provision were able to benefit. We were also extremely well supported by the teachers, parents and governors of the school. The high quality of the educational provision and teaching in the school meant that we returned children to classrooms which allowed them to make the most of what we could offer them and build on it. Our aim was therefore to help the children attending groups to benefit fully from being a member of a class and a school.

In this chapter we shall first describe the structure and setting of the groups and the referral process. Following this, using material from several different groups, we shall discuss in detail the processes and work that took place within the groups. Finally, we shall explore the implications of working within a school, some beneficial outcomes that could be identified, and our work with parents.

DESCRIPTION OF THE GROUPS AND THE REFERRAL PROCESS

The groups described here were set up within an inner city primary school to provide a space in which children with a variety of emotional difficulties could be thought about. There was no directly educational input from the adult group worker and the children's time was undirected. What was available to them was the physical equipment in the room and the worker's attention, and this was different from what was on offer in the rest of their school lives.There was one adult worker and usually three or four children in a group, although we did work with groups of two, particularly in the beginning. Reid and Kolvin (1993) discuss the suitability of different size groups for different ages. Reid, Fry and Rhode (1988) illustrate the possibilities of working with just two children in a group. Most of the groups met once weekly for about forty-five minutes. Some groups met twice weekly, but it is debatable whether twice weekly offered significantly more benefit than once weekly. Obviously, more children could be accommodated if each group met only once a week.

We were fortunate in having a specially designated room, used exclusively by us for the groups, which was set apart from the school at the side of the playground. Although it did at times feel isolated, it had the advantage that a group did not disturb the rest of the school when behaviour became boisterous and noisy. The room was full of toys and equipment – there was a cupboard full of pens, pencils, crayons, stencils, glue, Sellotape, farm animals, etc. Paper and paints were available. In one corner there was a box full of junk boxes which could be made into models. There were three shelves full of board games and jigsaws, Lego and Duplo. At one side of the room there was a doll's cot with dolls, a doll's house with furniture and little people, dressing-up clothes and a small bed that a child could get into. There was a small cooker with saucepans and a sink with running cold water. There were also a few guns. Most of these things had been collected in the room over the many years that groups had been running, but experience showed us that those that were most useful were the ones that encouraged or allowed group activities. The Duplo train set and cars, for example, always proved popular and lent themselves to co-operative play.

This physical setting provided the most basic level of containment. There was a space, which was apart from the school but enclosed by its four walls, and a once weekly regular time with the same adult leader. In this context we are using the concept of 'containment' put forward by the psychoanalyst W. R. Bion in *Learning from Experience* (1962). He considered an experience of containment to be an essential prerequisite for mental growth, which, in healthy circumstances, the mother provides through the psychic capacities she brings to the care of her infant. The essence of containment is that the personality is held. In therapeutic work this holding can be provided both through the correct management of the setting and through the psychic qualities the worker brings through her closely focused attention, her thinking and her memory. A contained setting in this case was provided by giving the group a regular appointment time, which was firmly held to, and a designated space enclosed by the four walls in which the equipment was set out in the same place each time ready for the group. It was also made clear that the group membership would be stable – if one child was absent he was held in the worker's mind as an absent member rather than being replaced by another child. The management of breaks was also important, and any changes, for example school holidays or a class trip, were prepared for in advance. Thus we tried to demonstrate predictability and reliability in our behaviour. This was particularly important for those children whose difficulties may have been bound up with having the experience of unreliability in their early lives.

Another important aspect of the management of the groups was how long each group ran for. While we were undertaking this work, we did not initially have a set length of time in mind for each group, although groups tended to run for 18 months to 2 years. We found, however, the uncertainty about how long the group would go on, in both the leader's and the children's minds, could be unhelpful and cause anxiety. It led to anxious questions such as 'Will we be here next week?' followed by 'Will we be here next month?'. A child in Year 2 who had been attending for some time and who was feeling quite involved asked 'Will I still be here in Year 4?' and then '. . . in Year 6?'. These questions were difficult to answer, if no set time had been decided on at the outset. One possible way of approaching the problem if a group was to start off with an indefinite length was to set a review date when progress to date could be reviewed and the future possibilities discussed. When this was put into practice, it did create some feeling of a boundary. We felt it was important that the children should not be left in doubt unnecessarily.

Towards the end of our time we decided that setting a time limit of one year was probably the most appropriate in this setting, although we found it necessary to be flexible rather than to adhere to this as a strict rule. When a group finished, we were often left with the problem of how to provide more help for any child who still needed it. We had to decide whether to bring the provision to end, whether to start her in a new group, or whether to refer her to a child guidance clinic, knowing that the resources there were already overstretched. Usually none of these options was ideal and the problem of re-forming groups could be fraught with difficulties. Although we always aimed to keep the numbers of a group the same throughout its life, there were some children who left the school, sometimes quite suddenly, and occasionally a parent wanted to bring their child's involvement to an end. These situations led to groups having to be re-formed.

THE REFERRAL PROCESS

The groups in this school had started many years earlier when some teachers felt that it was not possible to address the emotional needs of the large numbers of emotionally disturbed children they were teaching in the classroom situation. However, our experience was that the reasons for referral were varied and we considered seriously any child who was brought to our attention. We took children who were disruptive and acting out in the classroom, those who were withdrawn and anxious, those who were suffering in very adverse home situations, as well as those who came from stable homes and who might be doing well academically but who had not yet made the same progress in making friends. If a child provoked a strong emotional reaction in the teacher, e.g. if the teacher was enraged by a child who was behaving in an extremely passive and apparently non-provocative way or, conversely, if a teacher found that a child in his class was constantly slipping out of his mind, this might also be an indication that the child might benefit from group work. We were much helped by the teachers in our school being very experienced at spotting a child who would benefit from groups and they did not just refer overtly disruptive children.

Some referrals were very detailed and precise in describing a child's difficulties. One teacher wrote of a 5-year-old girl, Sarah:

Sarah likes to be the centre of attention, tell other children what to do and be everyone's best friend if possible. She cannot cope with failure, cannot tolerate injustice or rejection and will sometimes lose her temper dramatically, or become extremely upset, crying and screaming and stamping her feet. She never seems to be really happy and seems insecure about her own abilities and friendships. I am concerned about her general unhappiness and insecurity and the unhappiness she causes the other children by bossiness, spite and an inability to co-operate in games, etc.

Other referrals were more vague, and such referrals could be a good indication of the nature of the feelings aroused by the child in those around him. We found this often gave us an insight into the way the child was experiencing things. Particularly, if a referral was vague, we often did a classroom observation, as this might reveal more specific problems. The referral process itself and the discussion that went on alongside it acted as an umbrella, under which a child could be thought about, classroom strategies could be discussed and the teacher could share her concerns. Specifically for younger teachers we hoped to introduce different ways of thinking about a child, especially if they were feeling overwhelmed by difficult behaviour. Some children did just remain within that thinking process. Obviously there were instances where we didn't take a child into a group, e.g. if the family moved around a lot and it was uncertain how long that child would remain at our school. It sometimes happened that a child had to wait until a suitable group was starting. If a very difficult child arrived new to the school, a panic reaction sometimes set in, with the responsibility to do something about it falling on us. We learnt that it did not help very much to put such a child into a mismatched group immediately because we felt pressurized to do something. It was much better to wait until there was a suitable mix of personalities to start a group, for reasons that will be explained later in the chapter.

GROUP PROCESSES: THE LEADER'S ROLE AND AIMS OF THE GROUP WORK

We have decided to focus on the beginning, middle and end stages of a number of groups we ran, describing the predominant features at these periods, as a framework for illustrating aspects of our work. This way of looking at the developments within a group was introduced to us by Susan Reid and her colleagues at the Tavistock Clinic. We found this framework a useful way of understanding the material presented in the groups as well as for evaluating progress.

GROUP PROCESSES: BEGINNING

Each group has a beginning and, in a children's group, the most beneficial way to begin was found to be for the worker to meet each child individually in an initial interview. This took place after a discussion between the classteacher or headteacher and the parents about the groups provision in the school, and why the child was thought to be likely to benefit from attending. This was followed by a meeting between the parents and the groups teacher to explain further about groups, to give a chance for the parents to think about allowing their child to participate in a group, and for us to learn about the parents' concerns and hopes for the future.

In the initial meeting with the child, the worker would explain that she would be meeting all the potential group members individually, and would give practical details of how many children would be attending the group and when and where the group would be held. At this point it was found to be useful if the worker could think about how that child might initially be seen by the others. For example, one child may lend himself to being labelled as the bad one, one as the stupid one, another as the posh one, etc. The worker might also gain some idea of how the child might respond to thoughtful attention and how much capacity he might have to think about himself and his own behaviour.

When a group met together for the first time, although the children often had an intuitive feel for why they were there, there was also anxiety about taking part in a group experience. There was often also an air of hesitancy and questioning about why they had been sent there and what it might mean to them, sometimes with the assumption among particularly disruptive children that they had been naughty and had possibly been sent out for punishment. Each child's previous experiences coloured the expectation of what was on offer for them within the group. As well as these common anxieties, a marked feature of a beginning group is that projective processes and stereotyping quickly become apparent. Projection means attributing feelings and unwanted parts of the personality to others and manifests itself in easily observable ways. For example, in the first session, Sarah, whose referral was described earlier, took on a superior air, looked on with horror at what the naughty boy was doing, and tried to get the groups teacher to agree with her view that she was so good and he was so naughty. She spent a lot of time and effort in attributing all the 'bad' things to others, leaving herself rather brittle and seemingly very anxious that she might be tainted by having anything to do with the feelings she was projecting. This little girl, who had recently been joined by a younger brother, made many superior comments, such as 'Oh yes, boys like guns, don't they?', when it was clear she was very keen to play with the guns and have an aggressive shoot with them herself. As well as aggression and destructiveness, she was also projecting her own neediness, incompetence and fear. As a result, she was was left quite im-poverished and, as her referral suggested, precarious in maintaining relationships with other children.

The feeling at the beginning of the group was of a collection of individuals gathered together. They were sometimes rather wary of each other, there was not much connection between the children, and it was from this point that they started their journey towards becoming a group. In describing psychoanalytical group work with children, Reid (1987) said that 'becoming a group' is the therapy and through a schematic view of the beginning, middle and ending periods of a group it can be seen how the thinking processes that are involved bring about this development from a collection of individuals to a group.

THE GROUPS TEACHER'S ROLE

As already discussed, there is much containment inherent in a well-managed setting, but equally, or perhaps more importantly, is the containment that the groups teacher's mind offers. A fundamental anxiety at the beginning is whether the group will be a safe place, and these unconscious fears come to the fore particularly if the time is undirected and the group is not specifically task oriented. Most importantly, the groups teacher's role is to provide safety both by maintaining firm boundaries in the setting and behaviour, and by showing that she is able to think about the group and the meaning of the behaviour going on within it. At the beginning she is starting this thinking process and introducing it to the children, some of whom may be rather surprized that they are being thought about seriously, rather than being told off.

We would like to consider the manner in which we attempted to verbalize our understanding of what was happening in any group session. Some of the comments we made were along the lines of describing what children were doing, thereby bringing things to their attention and telling the story of the session as it evolved. Other comments would be closer to interpretations in that they would imply an understanding of something unconscious, although this would not be made explicit.We also often put a name to a feeling and we agree with Muir (1985) that it was usually helpful to put the feeling in a wider context in order to avoid heightening anxiety. In practice this often meant waiting to comment on a current concern which was expressed by or shown in the behaviour of one child, until it appeared somewhere else within the group, and then making it explicit as a shared concern thereby bringing relief to all. Often demonstration is what is needed rather than interpretation (Reid 1987). This means also that the work can be done by teachers and social workers without specialized psychoanalytical knowledge or experience, although we feel it would be necessary to have supervision to lead the worker to have a deeper understanding of the meaning of behaviour.

In our school we gave each child a tray with his name on in the first session. This tray was kept safely in a cupboard from week to week and the child could keep in it anything he made during the session. It often became for the child a symbol of being kept in the worker's mind and, if the child was very destructive, the tray might be greeted with slight surprise when it appeared the following week with its contents intact.

In order for the group to be successful, children must feel safe and the following extract is an example of how Sarah showed, through her play, that she was beginning to feel safe, that her feelings were containable and also that she was beginning to feel that she was being kept in mind. It also shows both the way in which we wrote up each session, a process which in itself helped our thinking, and how we were thinking about the meaning of the children's play, not only during the sessions but also after work.

Sarah had missed her previous session and, when she returned, she argued with the little boy Hanif over a box which they both wanted to make something with. After a considerable build-up of frustration, Sarah had a huge tantrum, whining aggressively and desperately, 'I want it, I had it first.' Even though the groups teacher was talking about the emotional significance of the box (that what the children were really fighting over was having to share the groups teacher and that Sarah was feeling very hard done by just at the moment, because she thought the teacher had given everything to Hanif when Sarah had been away the previous week), Sarah became more and more desperate, screaming in an out-of-control way, 'I want it', and completely beside herself with distress. In the report of that session the groups teacher wrote:

When they started fighting I felt that I had to step in and took the box from them, saying that I was going to hold it. I went on talking and said that we needed to think whether they were really fighting over the box and what the other things were that made it seem so important to them. I said more about Sarah possibly being more upset than she thought about missing coming here the previous week and talked also about the difficulties of sharing me, being disappointed and thinking that the other person was getting a better deal. Sarah was calming down and began to listen quietly. She had taken a piece of paper off the side and had begun to make something . . . She was making what she called a bag (more like an envelope) out of paper and asked me to cut out four little cards with rounded corners to go in it. I did that and she was satisfied. While they were calmly occupied, I reminded them about next week's break (for half term) and Hanif said, 'I know.' Sarah did not respond immediately but then said that she had made a bag by herself yesterday so she knew how to do it already. I said that it sounded as if she was saying she did not need me, she could manage by herself, particularly if it seemed to her that I was going to go away . . . Then she made another little bag for the four cards that I had cut out for her. She wrote on each one Sarah . . . put a picture of a boat, a car or a house on each one and tucked them anxiously inside the bag.

The groups teacher felt that Sarah was showing that she had felt helped with the very strong feelings that had threatened to go out of control in the tantrum, and this was because the groups teacher had not been overwhelmed by the strength of her feelings, nor had she become retaliatory or vindictive. The groups teacher had been able to go on thinking about what the emotional significance really was without being overwhelmed, and this provided something that was needed at that moment. As a result of that experience of containment, Sarah's subsequent play with the cards inside the envelope/bag seemed to be asking, 'Will you be able to keep me in your mind over the break as well?' This experience of the continuity of being kept in mind is very valuable to someone such as Sarah who has experienced several changes of carer in quick succession in the past. Such experiences were now needed to help strengthen her feelings of security.

There are certain ways in which the worker can promote the group 'gelling' process right from the start, and one way of doing this is by picking up any links that the children might make between themselves and by building on them. This can be done very simply by noticing what the children are doing in relation to each other and saying something about it. For example, child B might be playing with a toy, while child A looks on interestedly. The worker could point out that A looks interested in what B is doing and this might lead to the two children getting together. Later on, there may well be opportunities to link in another child with A and B, or different constellations may suggest themselves. At the same time, if the worker is able to see links in the different activities of the group members, this is then a clear indication of a group anxiety that needs to be addressed. The demonstration by the worker of a shared anxiety brings relief to all group members, and promotes a sense of group cohesion and lessens the need to project anxieties into vulnerable members of the group.

Throughout the life of the group the worker needs to be able to hold in her mind not only the group but also each individual within it. To let people slip out of mind would create dangerous anxieties in all group members.

THE 'HERE AND NOW' EXPERIENCE AND THE MIDDLE PERIOD

A common misconception when this sort of work is discussed is that the children came to the groups to talk about their problems. Although children were always free to talk about any problems at home or at school if they wished, it was the underlying anxieties that we sought to address. The benefit of the group work was not gained through a verbal offloading of problems, but in a much more dynamic 'here and now' experience of discovering themselves and different parts of themselves in relation to other chidren and the group leader. This is where it is vital to have a mix of ages and, more particularly, of personalities. It has been discovered that a group consisting of similar personalities will probably have difficulties making progress. For example, a group of three disruptive boys may well spend the whole session charging around with guns and behaving like stereotypical boys with the result that no work is done. A group of withdrawn or timid children will probably be equally unsuccessful, as there may well be an emotionally flat atmosphere with no experimentation with other parts of their personalities. However, a group consisting of a mix of acting-out and withdrawn children will offer the greatest potential for progress (Reid and Kolvin 1993, Reid 1987).

An example of a well-balanced group might be one acting-out boy aged 7, one shy boy aged 9, one acting-out girl aged 10, and one withdrawn younger girl, something akin to the ages of possible siblings within a family. It is also good to have a mix in the level of disturbance. As we said before, some children might be very disturbed and making very little academic progress, and others might be doing very well generally but having difficulties making friends. This mix of personalities is what leads to emotional fluidity, as children project parts of themselves on to others, and then have a chance to see that these aspects are tolerated and accepted in the others. This makes it possible for them to experiment with these aspects of themselves more freely and not be afraid to acknowledge them as parts of themselves.

So, in the middle period of a group, if a good mix has led to emotional fluidity the children will both be able to learn from how others react to situations and experience some freeing up of their own personalities, as they discover that what they felt previously was unacceptable is in fact accepted. This can lead to a 'mellowing' of the personality and, in the case of the brittle little girl Sarah, she began to relax and seem warmer as she was able to take back into herself some of the aggression, naughtiness and messiness which she had earlier attributed to the little boy. So the groups teacher's role at this time is to describe the mechanisms of projection as they occur within the group, thereby facilitating change.

It seems necessary here to explain what we mean by accepting all parts of the personality. It might imply that all sorts of dangerous behaviour was tolerated, but this was not the case. It was important to keep firm boundaries around the behaviour. The children were not allowed to hurt themselves or to damage anything in the room. So, although much of the behaviour could be frightening to the children and sometimes to the groups teacher as well, the sessions were not to be used totally freely if that meant outright mindless destructiveness. Obviously, in practice it was difficult to maintain the boundaries, as most groups tested them to the limits after the initial honeymoon period. We kept the ultimate sanction that a session would be stopped if things got out of control and it was very useful in our situation that we knew that the headteacher would always back us up appropriately and sensitively if needed. For the adult in the room he represented the other half of the parental couple, and his support was essential for running the groups with one worker.

One of the groups teacher's tasks throughout the group, as well as keeping all the group members in mind, is to give an equal space to each member. This may mean at times that it is necessary to deny the immediate gratification of the individual's needs for the good of the group (much like the experience of being in a family that is working well). If one member is seen to be favoured at any one time, the groups teacher will become a bad figure to all the children, including the one who is favoured, because she is seen unconsciously as an unreliable mother who is unable to cater for the needs of all her children and in future might neglect also the one who is currently favoured. It is easy for the groups teacher to fall into the trap of attending exclusively to the child who is behaving in the noisiest and most demanding way, but this needs to be avoided.

In one group, Tony found it unbearable for the group worker's attention to be given to the other children in the group. He experienced this as being completely dropped from the worker's mind into a terrifying unprotected place. In order to avoid such anxieties, Tony sought out dangerous pursuits such as switching on and attempting to touch the high, wall-mounted electric fire. This would necessitate the physical removal of the worker from the other children and the certainty of feeling her physical holding as she removed him from the cupboard he was standing on. After some time and interpretation, Tony was able to contain these anxieties within games of hide and seek which involved the other older members of the group looking out for him while the groups teacher's eyes were shut. It was important to limit the number of times this game was played and to offer turns to the other children who occasionally tried it out for themselves. The other children also gained from feeling that Tony's inability to share the groups teacher's attention was being tackled and contained, and from being offered a benign role in the process. This also reflects how older children can benefit from seeing a younger sibling being cared for in a more adequate way than their parents were able to care for them.

In summary, the middle period is one in which the children are discovering new dimensions of their personalities as there is a move towards introjective processes from projective processes. This means that, as well as attributing unwanted parts of themselves to others, the children are taking back some of these aspects into themselves and this leads to a warmer and more tolerant feel in the group.

Before leaving the middle period, we would like to give an example of a group in the process of facing a changing composition. The experience of this particular group helped us to see a potential value in going through the difficult process of joining together depleted groups. With the help of the Groups Workshop, we were able to see that this often mirrored many of the children's experiences within their own families, as parents separated and found new partners bringing with them children from previous relationships. For the existing children, the newly formed parental couple brought with it the concern or the reality of babies being born.

In one group, Matthew and Yolanda had lost the two other group members recently and were about to join up with another group which had also lost a member. In the first group, Robert had been put into a nearby school after a holiday without prior warning being given to the school. He had returned for a day to say goodbye and was able to attend a final session. He told the group in a disorientated and painful way how he felt only his computer was now available for him. Albertina, the second member to leave, just disappeared from the school when her family left for another city, after one of her parents had had a traumatic accident. Our efforts to trace her, so that the group could send a goodbye letter, completely failed. Albertina had shown the group the confused and agitated state she was in while her family were in such turmoil, and this had elicited considerable concern in the other children.

Matthew and Yolanda, therefore, were in the process of experiencing the traumatic loss of Robert and Albertina, whilst knowing that in a matter of weeks they were to join up with the remaining members of the other group.

In the session the children were showing the group worker, through their play, that they were remembering the earliest days at the beginning of the group. This led on to a sharing of equipment, with Matthew using a box brought by Yolanda as a container for his felt tip pens.

Matthew began to draw a picture, putting two felt tip pens in his hand and drawing a wavy line along the bottom of his page. Yolanda had selected a big and a little tray, taking the one Matthew's pens were in, with no protests from him, and was joining them together along one side with pieces of masking tape.

Matthew now took four pens and holding them together drew a yacht shape made from several triangular shapes drawn in a continuous movement. He showed me his ship. Yolanda now introduced two identical cardboard lids and put them in a line with the other two plastic trays. The sense of twoness and fourness coming from the children's work was very striking. I mentioned this and wondered whether the forthcoming change from being two of them to being four, when they joined with the other two children, was on their minds. Yolanda said, 'No.' Yolanda's big tray was Robert and the little one was Albertina. Matthew added that the big tray was a boat and the little one was a lifeboat. He then suggested that the lifeboat might sink and Yolanda started to pile on the other little lids, Matthew declaring it still to be sinking each time. Yolanda looked at the pile of lifeboats and said that there was a problem that if there were too many boats, they might all sink. She took out some lids leaving just one lid inside the smaller tray.

Yolanda now started to join up the cardboard lids in the line. Looking at Matthew's work, she said that they were both joining things today. The conversation returned to Robert and Albertina and I said that they seemed concerned that they were all right. We went over where they were and what I knew and did not know of how they were.

Matthew's ship became called a 'rainbow ship' and both children worked on colouring it. Matthew later stated several times that he did not want any new children to join their group.

This extract shows some of the opportunities offered to children to share working through traumatic and more ordinary experiences of loss and change as a group. While the process was difficult for these children, a new group was successfully re-formed. It managed to retain for a time the memories of the missing children from each of the original groups and the loss of the original groups, whilst allowing also for the establishment of a new group which became important to all the children.

MATURE GROUPS AND ENDING

In a mature group or a group approaching the end of its time, there will be a different atmosphere from how it was at the beginning. The relationships between group members show features akin to normal personality developmental processes described by Melanie Klein as the 'Depressive Position' (Klein 1935). Features such as an increase in concern towards others, greater toleration of conflicting feelings towards loved people and a desire to make appropriate reparation for harm done to others characterize Klein's description of this capacity which develops in normal circumstances. Klein used the term 'Depressive Position' to show that these capacities were not permanently fixed in the personality, but were available at times oscillating with more primitive ways of relating to others.

Within a group these features come to the fore in various ways and affect the general atmosphere of the group as a whole. If the group had been successful, there was generally much more of a cohesive feel. The fact that the group had gelled was apparent often from the beginning of the sessions when the children would greet each other warmly as they were being collected, and might often refer immediately to something they had been doing in the group the previous week. They seemed to 'get together' more quickly each week, helped by the groups teacher's comments, while more of the session was spent in calm, co-operative relaxed activities. There was often a feeling that the children really knew each other and accepted aspects of themselves which were not previously known or denied. We noticed that children talked less in terms of 'I' or 'she' and more often started a sentence with 'we', e.g. a group member might say, 'Do you remember when we did . . . ?' In this way they were not only expressing their feelings about being part of a group but also reviewing their life in the group, looking back at some of the things that had happened with more understanding now, and a recognition that if behaviour had been unruly or frightening it did still have meaning and had been thought about. This looking back could also be seen as sharing a development of memory; things that did not seem so unmanageable could be remembered.

Towards the end there were also more group activities. Sometimes a group might start on a project or activity which they might all think about and contribute to, possibly over several weeks. There was a camaraderie in this, a sense of belonging and a feeling that they were all investing in the group experience and gaining strength from it. Hopeful feelings were expressed as well, and there was generally a feeling that it is possible to overcome difficulties. Particularly when a child was coming up to secondary transfer, he might look at the outside world with trepidation, but also with optimism and a degree of confidence which led us to believe that the benefits inherent in the group experience would extend to some extent into the rest of the children's lives.

Perhaps one of the surest signs of success was whether a group generally could tolerate the sadness of ending without rubbishing. Obviously individuals will vary in this capacity, but if one member by the end was still only rubbishing it was suggested to us that she may well be suffering from ongoing abuse. Otherwise there will have been developments towards tolerating the sadness in all the members and in the group generally.

Gerald had the difficult experience of missing the last session of the group in order to accompany his grandfather on a special day out, for which the latter had previously bought tickets. Gerald felt torn as to what to do. The disappointment for the other group members was very great and they sought to deny the significance of having a missing member for the last session. Despite invitations to accept that he was lucky and that the last session did not matter, Gerald managed to say how sad he felt and how he wished he could have been able to do both things. The very last session of this group did feel as if the group was depleted, but also that Gerald could be thought about and the other members of the group had not been left on their own with all the difficult feelings to manage or deny.

Interestingly, Gerald had had to miss a session a couple of weeks earlier, without the groups teacher's prior knowledge. The other two members of the group had very much wanted not to wait or to try to find Gerald. The subsequent session started off in a fractious way. However, when the groups teacher helped the children to think about why this might be happening, all three children were then able to work on different projects that symbolically represented the forthcoming ending. Gerald made three paper areoplanes which parted when thrown into the air. It was then possible to think with the group about their different futures once the group had finished.

While the theoretical structure of development within a group has been described above, groups did not proceed in a steady way through the three phases which have been featured. As groups teachers we had to learn what kind of comments and remarks best promoted a feeling of containment within the group for a working ethos to develop. The composition of a particular group also probably influenced the course of its development. A great deal of our time was spent trying to understand what the children showed us, and learning to keep hold of all the children in our minds. In some groups, a lot of time was spent at the beginning setting limits to keep the group feeling safe enough for the children to benefit from being with each other and allowing the groups worker time to think with the children. Sometimes our experience was of groups that were only able to start establishing a coherence when the ending was in sight.

In one group, the sense of a group identity was almost prematurely fostered when the group learned about a session having to be cancelled because the school was closed for staff training. A kind of pseudo-independence appeared to have been fostered, a subject often catching the imagination of writers of children's literature.

Tom had been away the week before on a school journey. It was the sixth session of the group and there had already been another break for half term. As the groups teacher talked about the forthcoming cancelled session the following week, the three children went together to the car cube for the first time. Tom and Joshua had played there before, but Serena had never joined them. Serena, usually quiet and rather passive in the group, took the 'steering wheel' of the 'car' and asserted she would be the driver. 'Look,' said Tom, 'Gill's left out.' Here the groups teacher was to know what it felt like for Tom to have known he was missing a session the week before. The three children clung together, showing their sense of being deserted by the groups teacher, while Serena demonstrated her determination to banish all feelings of dependency on an unreliable adult. She did not want to risk just being a passenger in the car cube.

WORKING WITHIN THE SCHOOL SETTING AND BENEFICIAL OUTCOMES OF THE GROUP WORK

Working within the school setting

While we do think that the experience of groups was beneficial to the children concerned, it is important to acknowledge the extra demands that we had to make on the staff for groups to be successfully accommodated within the school. In order for groups to have the necessary boundaries to build up trust in the children, we had to ask teachers to tolerate not knowing about the content of the sessions, although we did try to share our understanding of the children where appropriate, and particularly at the termly reviews with parents and with classteachers.

We had to be excused from routine break duties in the playground and school, and from tackling children's bad behaviour around the school. We tried to generally keep a low profile so that the children we worked with were not constantly having to see us with other children. A duty was done in the school's nursery class, and a close and valuable link with the nursery staff was made as a result. This also offered an opportunity to observe how the children adjusted to school life when they first arrived.

We also tended to keep a slight distance from the rest of the staff, only attending staff meetings if they directly concerned us or if they provided, for example, information about possible changes to the timetable, which might affect our groups. This distance meant that we were then more available to all of the staff, but it also potentially made us seem in a privileged position not having to deal with the day-to-day committments of teaching in large, busy classrooms with the numerous curriculum and administrative demands placed on teachers. This situation could potentially lead to conscious or unconscious lack of co-operation in a school without an established tradition or when a groups teacher was not sensitive enough to the impact of her different position on the rest of the staff. Woods (1993) looks at this point when he considers the impact of a children's group on the rest of the staff in a clinic setting.

We needed the assistance and tolerance of the staff when bringing children to and from their groups. These were sometimes difficult transitions for the children and the focus of many feelings for them, e.g. about which child was returned first to a classroom and who was left to last. We also asked classroom teachers to give their classes as much notice as possible about any planned absences they might have and to think about acknowledging the absence and return of children in their class.

In return, the existence of a groups provision seemed to symbolize the possibility of thinking together about children whom staff were anxious about. Occasionally this paid enormous dividends when it was adopted by the staff as a working method. On one memorable occasion, a child who had attended a group for some time, continued to concern staff about his lack of literacy despite many resources being offered. A meeting was held and it was concluded that no one understood or really knew why this child failed to progress, but that we would meet again to share the difficult sense of failing the child and of having to wait for longer to see if any progress emerged. Everyone felt supported by each other but none the wiser. Within a very few weeks, the child's work blossomed and the sense of the staff bearing together the 'not knowing' and fear of failure seemed to offer the child the necessary atmosphere within which to risk developing.

With other children who puzzled staff, detailed observations of the child in the classroom, as well as thinking about what it felt like to be observing the child, could sometimes throw light on the difficulties the child was having. On one occasion, a girl was causing enormous concern to the nursery teachers through not being able to settle and conform to the basic requirements of the nursery setting. She attacked other children, played alone and could not sit on the carpet with the other children. During a morning's observation it became clear that although she was having severe difficulties in adjusting to a school environment, these problems were being compounded by the other children being only too ready to blame her for problems she had nothing to do with. This knowledge enabled the nursery teachers to protect this little girl from being the recipient of all the bad projections of the group.

Some children received enough help through being thought about in discussions with classteachers, or by observations being shared, so attendance at a group was thought inappropriate. The school's careful system of classteachers reviewing each child on a termly basis with the head, or latterly the SENCO, provided a very valuable structure within which children could be safely kept in mind without further provision being necessary.

When it was thought to be appropriate for a child to become a member of a group, this often offered relief to the classteacher who was then free to concentrate on developing strategies to use in the classroom to promote the child's learning, once the burden of concern about a child's emotional difficulties had been found a more appropriate setting. It was frequently our experience that the teachers of new children in a group would come to us with successes in the classroom from fresh ways of working with the child which they had tried.

Perhaps because of the long-established tradition of groups in the school, all members of staff, including those who were ancillary, would approach us with their concerns about individual children, giving us valuable information, for example, about difficulties a particular one might be having in the dining room, playground or with creative work. The staff were also generous in sharing their joy in any signs of progress within the children we worked with.

New staff found groups particularly difficult and we needed to take considerable care to acknowledge their concerns about handing over their children into our care, when they knew so little about how we worked. It was our experience that regular staff in-service training sessions about our work were essential and helped new staff in particular. We did not manage to run these every year, which we regretted.

Beneficial outcomes of the group work

Although group cohesion took some time to develop, we found that children often managed to make some noticeable progress in their lives outside the group quite rapidly. With some children there was a marked reduction in symptoms quite early on. One of the reasons Hanif had been referred was that he had a very high profile around the school because he was always causing trouble and was repeatedly being sent to the head's office as a result. When the groups teacher concerned enquired how Hanif was getting on, after he had been in a group for one term, the head was surprised to realize that Hanif's profile had diminished so much that he had not come to his attention for several weeks.

Group work did not exist in isolation. Each child's home situation was important in determining whether progress was being sustained outside the group. After one year in a group Sarah's mother said she was a 'different child', meaning that she was generally more relaxed and happy. This could not be attributed solely to our work in the group as there had been many improvements in the family's home situation; the family now had a permanent home and Sarah's mother's state of mind was much improved. However, the groups teacher felt the group work had enabled Sarah to benefit from these improvements by being able to take in more of the good things that were on offer to her within the family. Sarah managed not to stay stuck in old ways of behaving which had been developed in earlier times when she had less support and security. In contrast, after initial progress, Thomas was unable to continue making progress, which puzzled the groups teacher. It was difficult to engage Thomas' parents in any thinking process about him. This may have contributed to Thomas' lack of progress.

Sometimes taking up some help within the school could assist in making therapy accessible to some families. One family in great difficulties, who were initially adamant in not accepting help from anyone, agreed to their child being in a group at school. This led eventually to the child being taken into therapy for more intensive help. For a small number of children, taking part in a group seemed to contribute to stable placements in good foster homes, offering the possibility of thinking about the child with the foster parents.

Another child, whose behaviour would have led to exclusion in many other schools, never actually took part in a group, but was worked with individually with the view to including him in a group when his placement in the school was no longer at risk. It is interesting to note that during the time we worked in the school there were no exclusions. We wonder whether a contributory factor to this was the tradition in the school that difficulties and emotional distress could be thought about.

WORK WITH THE PARENTS

We are now going to turn to discussing the parental involvement in groups. During our time as groups teachers, we became increasingly interested in how best to involve parents in our work with their children and at the same time maintain the confidentiality of the setting.

All parents were involved from the beginning when the classteachers, the SENCO or the headteacher discussed the possibility of groups for their children. This would normally follow on from concerns about their children having been expressed by the school or by the parents. Reactions were varied to the suggestion of groups being an appropriate provision for their child. In all cases, the next stage would be to meet with one of us before a final decision was made and permission asked for from the parents. At this initial meeting we welcomed any knowledge of the child or family situation that the parents could give us. Some parents welcomed this chance to think about their child, whilst others were much more reserved and wary. This meeting also gave the parents a chance to assess us.

The initial meeting set the pattern for the regular termly reviews, and occasionally for more frequent meetings with some parents. Our aim was to reach a shared view of the child. In some cases, our meetings helped the parents focus more on their child when they were in the midst of instability and turmoil at home.

Provisional plans were drawn up for setting up a parents' group within the school. Although this has not yet happened, we do feel it would be an additional valuable support for a small number of the parents whose children we worked with.

We were not by any means always able to achieve a sustainable working relationship with parents. Very occasionally, difficulties resulted in a child being removed from a group at short notice. When this happened a great deal of insecurity and unhappiness followed for the remaining members of the group who could lose trust in the groups teacher's capacity to offer a safe and secure place.

CONCLUSION

In conclusion, we would like to summarize some of the possibilities that working within an educational setting offers as well as the limits it imposes. One of the main advantages is the accessibility of the resource. As long as a particular child is attending school regularly and parents are happy about their child's involvement, the child is able to take part in a group without having to rely upon a parent being available for transport for regular appointments at an outside clinic. It was often more acceptable to the parent when some therapeutic provision was offered within the educational setting and offered with the aim of enabling the child to make better use of the eduactional provision available in the school. The acceptability to parents was helped by the fact that groups were generally held in high esteem by the staff and governors. Attendance at a school-based group is also far less disruptive for a child's timetable than attending an outside clinic and we were certainly referred children who would not have been considered for referral elsewhere. Usually we could offer something reasonably quickly for a child who was in crisis, e.g. where there had been a sudden death in the family, even if it was not immediate attendance in a group.

The accessibility of the provision to children with varying degrees of disturbance and coming from different backgrounds and in different circumstances meant that we were usually able to form workable and well-balanced groups which could possibily be more varied than groups run in other clinical settings.

In considering the limitations of therapeutic group work within an educational setting, we were aware of the slightly uncomfortable nature of a therapeutic endeavour, with its need for boundaries of confidentiality, taking place within an educational establishment. One way that this would show was in the greater need for trust when we were not open to inspection in the same way as the educational aspects of the school would be. Another constraint was that, whilst the responsibility for the management and funding was in the school, our supervision and training came from outside the school within the field of mental health. This meant that we did not have psychiatric backup or psychoanalytical supervisory support available on site.

From the school's viewpoint, the funding of groups provision, not being part of the National Curriculum, was competing with other valuable provisions such as art, music and additional classroom support. This meant that groups provision was consistently eroded and its future funding remains precarious. We would argue that the cost to the school was relatively small when compared to the benefits both to the children in the groups and to the wider life of the school. Within the context of the current debate about school exclusions, we feel that it is significant that this school had established a tradition of thinking about children with difficulties whilst containing them within the school, and had high expectations of resolving difficulties over time, sometimes in conjunction with outside agencies, without resorting to exclusion.

REFERENCES

Bion, W. R. (1962) *Learning from Experience*. London: Heinemann.

Klein, M. A. (1935) Contribution to the psychogenesis of manic-depressive states. In *Love, Guilt and Reparation and Other Works 1921–1945* (1975), London: Hogarth.

Muir, E. (1985) The Kleinian concept of position and group therapeutic process: an experience in group psychotherapy with emotionally disturbed boys aged 6 to 9½ years. *Journal of Child Psychotherapy,* 2(2).

Reid, S. (1987) The use of groups for therapeutic interventions. In Thacker, V. J. (ed.) *Prevention and Intervention: Working with Groups*, Division of Educational and Child Psychology, British Psychological Society, Leicester. Occasional Papers 3 and 4.

Reid, S. and Kolvin, I. (1993) Group psychotherapy for children and adolescents. *Archives of Disease in Childhood,* 69(2).

Reid, S., Fry, E. and Rhode, M. (1988) Working with small groups of children in primary schools. In Daws, D. and Boston, M. (eds) *The Child Psychotherapist*, London: Karnac.

Woods, J. (1993) Limits and structure in child group psychotherapy. *Journal of Child Psychotherapy,* 19(1).

ACKNOWLEDGEMENT

We would like to acknowledge and express our gratitude for the guidance given to us in our work and in writing the chapter by Lisa Miller and Sue Reid, Consultant Child Psychotherapists at the Tavistock Clinic. Along with Katherine Arnold, Trudy Klauber, Dolly Lush and Sheila Miller, they introduced us to many of the ways of thinking about group work with children that we discuss in this chapter.

CHAPTER 10

Circle time: a whole class peer support model

Jenny Mosley

Over twenty years ago I was very lucky. I was working in a school in Clapham Junction, South London for emotionally and behaviourally disturbed children under the guidance of an inspiring headteacher, Jack Wood, who had this great belief that all people were equal and that everyone must be listened to. I remember one of his first assemblies where he brought the cook on to the stage and he said: 'This is a very important member of our staff. Let us treat her with the greatest of respect. Without her wonderful food none of us would be able to work as hard as we are doing!' He continually used to praise all the staff so that we each felt valued and special. To pursue his belief further he introduced us to a form of 'Circle Time' meetings. An agenda went around during the week, and all the children and adults were encouraged to put any items of interest on it. These were then prioritized, and because we were a small school we were able to meet on a weekly basis in the hall and sort through the issues together. I was fascinated by the potential of circle time, and continued in my own career in mainstream and in special education to develop structures and strategies in order to make circle time an even more powerful and purposeful forum for adults and children. Early on I realized that it was no good creating oases of respect in the classroom through circle-time meetings if the other policies did not also foster and ensure respect for both children and adults. Subsequently, I have spent many years working with teachers to devise a series of systems that would help bring order, calm and wellbeing into their schools. I have now devised a 'Whole School Circle Time Model' which aims to meet the needs of all individuals within a school (Mosley 1996).

This chapter focuses on the importance of initiating circle time as a whole class team-building model which enhances children's self-esteem. Through circle time, children are encouraged to participate as partners in the process of developing responsibility for their own behaviour and learning. Thousands of primary schools now timetable circle time. Teachers claim that circle time boosts interpersonal skills, strengthens relationships and helps children to develop self-control and confidence, at the same time as allowing all participants (including teachers) to have fun together. This chapter describes my approach to circle time and includes practical scenarios and contributions from teachers currently using circle time within their classrooms.

BACKGROUND

In my experience, teachers, working in an increasingly stressful profession, forever trying to meet deadlines whilst responding to 30 unique individuals at a time, often feel unable to meet the personal, social, emotional and behavioural needs of children. It is also my experience that the circle-time model, once incorporated into a whole school policy for raising self-esteem and promoting positive behaviour in both children and adults, has the potential to meet the needs of both teachers and children, as it can act as a respectful forum through which individuals can express themselves honestly. It is not only exciting to sit back and allow children to take responsibility for meeting their own and others' needs, but also rewarding to listen to a child, whom you may not have had a chance to engage with in any positive way during the week.

The self-discipline of practising the ground rules demanded by circle time is a gentle reminder to teachers of the skills we all need to build positive relationships. A half-hour circle session of talking quietly, using positive body language and 'taking a back seat' not only is extraordinarily refreshing, but also can challenge one's perception of individual children in a very positive way. Teachers often report that circle time has reminded them of the original idealism that prompted them into choosing the profession. It creates an oasis of harmony and shared enjoyment, which is vital for teachers to experience regularly if they are to face the escalating demands being made on them.

WHAT IS CIRCLE TIME?

Circle time is a group listening system that encourages children to support and learn from each other, by involving them in a circle framework integrating games, social skills, group problem-solving, 'counselling' opportunities, assertiveness training and a range of drama approaches. Timetabled weekly circle meetings from 30 to 40 minutes long offer children the opportunity to feel part of a trusted group, in which their feelings, views and unique strengths are acknowledged and valued. Mutually agreed ground rules for teachers and children based on the core conditions of respect, empathy and genuineness ensure emotional safety. These might include 'all contributions must be valued' and 'everyone, including the teacher, must take their turn'. In my particular circle-time model I also insist that no person may be named in a negative way – children may 'tell a tale' on themselves but not on others, and their honesty must always be accepted with thanks (Mosley 1996).

CIRCLE TIME AND GROUP COUNSELLING: SOME DIFFERENCES

Because circle time is a whole class model often involving up to 40 individuals, the above ground rules are important to ensure that children are protected from negativity or further labelling. This distinguishes the model from group counselling where individuals in small groups are encouraged to express all their feelings, prejudices and resentments in an immediate and direct way. In circle time, children may be encouraged if they have personal concerns or secret worries, to use two other supportive listening systems – Bubble Time and Think Books – to share these individually.

The structure of circle time pays rigorous attention to rituals, pace and activity. Fun, success, celebration, team building and the practice of pro-active social skills are emphasized during circle time, in contrast to the more fluid and unstructured approach in group counselling.

THE THEORETICAL BASIS OF CIRCLE TIME

Dr J. L. Moreno, the forefather of all active group-work approaches, talked of his own work with children in the early part of the twentieth century. He brought children into groups as 'a crusade of children for themselves for a society of their own ages and their own rights' (Moreno 1934). Moreno, who saw human beings as responsible for their own actions, stressed the importance of the 'group', and of social interaction, to the development of self. He evolved the methods of sociometry, psychodrama and sociodrama, which have greatly influenced experiential group-work programmes. My own circle-time model uses a variety of drama approaches as a means to self-discovery and empowerment.

Mead (1934) and Rogers (1951) both stressed the importance of enhancing self-concept through group work. Mead's Symbolic Interactionist Theory recognizes the contribution that others make towards a person's self-concept:

> At the first stage the individual self is constituted simply by an organization of the particular attitudes of other individuals toward himself – but at the second stage – also by an organization of the social attitudes of the generalized other or the social group as a whole to which he belongs. (Mead 1934)

The activities of circle time help the individual and the peer group to understand the effects of their actions, and the reactions of others which occur as a consequence. Great emphasis is placed on the importance of the whole group's responses towards an individual who wishes to change, for as Mead (1934) asserted, the self cannot be reorganized unless the social relations of the self to others are also altered.

Circle time promotes this condition in that respect and valuing are key elements in the ground rules, and negative comments such as put-downs are not permitted. Each participant is given equal worth, and experiences success through initiating, reflecting and contributing during circle-time activities, facilitating therefore the opportunity to create more empathic, controlled and powerful selves.

Carl Rogers' person-centred philosophy is based on the theory that people have the capacity for self-understanding and the ability to reorganize self-structure, if core conditions needed to facilitate this ability are present. Rogers (1951) stated these as genuineness, empathy and an unconditional positive regard – the core conditions of circle time's ground rules. Likewise, Burns (1982) showed that the academic and social performances of children will flourish if they experience respectful relationships and a caring, supportive ethos. Bandura (1977) and Michenbaum (1977) proposed a social learning theory based on observational learning through modelling. Circle time offers participants an opportunity to watch and consider positive behaviours and their consequences. It also gives children the chance to try out different responses in a safe environment, through role-play and games, and thereby understand and experience alternative ways of behaving which can bring more positive results.

Finally, Glasser (1967 and 1985) stressed the need to foster 'warm constructive relationships essential for success'. He proposed a classroom meeting model that was committed to enhancing interpersonal relationships by creating a non-competitive, honest and sharing atmosphere.

Circle time fulfils all these criteria. It provides a time for relaxation and fun away from academic pressures, where each child is an 'equal' in the field of human relationships. Of course, the actual concept of coming together in a circle has been used throughout history as a democratic process. More recently, it was introduced into Japanese industry during the 1960s in the form of Quality Circles from Total Quality Management, where representatives from all levels in the hierarchy could meet to discuss problems and find ways forward. It proved to be a highly motivational and successful strategy which gradually gained worldwide publicity and led people to consider its use in other areas, including education.

CIRCLE TIME: A WHOLE SCHOOL APPROACH

Circle time provides a firm foundation for promoting positive relationships within a school. My own model incorporates circle time into a whole school approach, as it is only through involving *all* the members of a school community in unified strategies that we can provide the consistency and firm boundaries that all children need. All the adults, including lunchtime supervisors and ancillary staff, have important roles to play in implementing and maintaining agreed standards of relating to each other in a school. Circle time for both adults and children provides a forum for maintaining the impetus of these agreed standards, and for solving any problems that may arise.

All policies are based on the Golden Rules, the moral values that inform and develop the culture of the school. These could be:

Do be gentle	Don't hurt anybody
Do be kind	Don't hurt people's feelings
Do be honest	Don't cover up the truth
Do work hard	Don't waste time
Do look after property	Don't waste or damage things
Do listen to people	Don't interrupt

The incentives and sanctions policies are designed to promote the Golden Rules with Golden Time, a set period for chosen extra-curricular activities, and a privilege to be enjoyed by all those individuals who keep the Golden Rules. Loss of Golden Time therefore becomes an important sanction in this model, although children are offered the opportunity to earn back any time lost by signing a contract in which they agree to certain behaviour/work targets.

My whole school model acknowledges lunchtimes as key areas for consideration, since these are often stressful times for adults and offer children opportunities to engage in destructive or anti-social behaviours, which can greatly affect the classroom climate. Lunchtime supervisors therefore need to have access to incentives and sanctions which are seen as having equal value to those used by teachers. I advocate that lunchtime supervisors hold their own circle-time meetings, and also attend and feed into occasional circle times involving children. This will not only raise their own profile, but also allow them to see the children in a different and perhaps more positive light.

BUBBLE TIME: A ONE-TO-ONE LISTENING SYSTEM

I evolved the idea of Bubble Time as an extra safety valve for children who may need to 'name' someone negatively, to expand on a private fear, or even to invite the teacher to enjoy a quiet celebration. For very young children we call this symbol of listening a 'bubble'.

The teacher makes a card or thin wooden bubble which is attached to a piece of wood so that it can be placed on a table. The teacher explains that the bubble symbolizes the privacy that can be achieved if two people were really conversing inside a large bubble. Any child can request Bubble Time with the teacher to discuss a private matter. However, it must be stressed that, because a teacher's time is limited, the children can only use Bubble Time for news or issues that could not be raised in the circle. Initially, as with all new ideas, children may be keen to experience Bubble Time often, and may want to use it for all sorts of trivial reasons. But once the novelty has worn off it will operate as a valuable private listening system between child and teacher. The teacher might decide to operate Bubble Time during break or lunchtimes to ensure complete privacy. However, if it takes place within lesson times, the teacher places the symbolic bubble at a table at which she and the pupil are seated to inform the rest of the class that a Bubble Time session is in progress. The class is instructed that Bubble Time sessions should not be interrupted. Once the children have become accustomed to Bubble Time they can request the 'bubble' to use with each other in order to resolve problems that may have arisen between them.

THINK BOOKS: A NON-VERBAL LISTENING SYSTEM

Another useful 'listening system' for busy teachers and children unable or not wishing to face personal contact is Think Books. Each child is provided with a small book in which to record private thoughts, anxieties, queries, etc. The books are confidential and kept in a designated 'safe' place, and only the classteacher is allowed to read them. Any child can request her Think Book to write a private message for the teacher. The teacher reads the message and writes a reply in the book or, if necessary, arranges a Bubble Time session with the child. Think Books provide another outlet children can use to communicate and express worrying things, and can be useful if a child is having difficulty broaching a subject verbally. They can also be used to record happy events and achievements, or just as an opportunity for children to maintain a quiet dialogue with the teacher. It can be very valuable for children to know that their concerns will be listened to and taken seriously, and that they can share them with their trusted teacher, although teachers should of course know the proper channels of referral for children who clearly need more time or skilled counselling, etc.

CIRCLE TIME: A GROUP LISTENING SYSTEM

Although ideally circle time is most effective within the context of a whole school approach, it can also play a very positive and important role simply as a class structure. Circle time involves the whole class, or sometimes a small group of children, and the teacher sitting in a circle. Using a range of strategies which include co-operative games, experiential approaches, rounds and discussions, the class or group are motivated and encouraged to share in the aim of promoting better caring relationships, responsibility for self and others, and reflection on whole school issues. A programme of carefully chosen circle-time activities is structured to help individuals within the group to develop self-esteem, and to feel more empowered in their daily choices. The role of the teacher within the circle is essentially facilitative rather than instructive. Of course, such a different role may take a while to achieve, but it is the ideal to work towards. It is sometimes not easy to wait while children struggle, or to stay with not knowing or with discomfort, until the children are ready to find their own way through a problem. In circle time particularly, the process is as important as the content of the sessions. Handing over responsibility and power within the circle to the children can have very far-reaching effects as the following example illustrates:

> About eighteen months ago, I was off work with flu for over a week. My Year 3/4 class had been in the hands of a supply teacher. When I returned, the children told me, 'Jonathan started being really silly in the dining room every lunchtime last week. He was pulling faces and making funny noises and the dinner lady got really cross.'
> I expressed concern.
> 'Oh, it's all right now,' they assured me. 'Andrew made a chart and he put a tick in it every time Jonathan was good, because you weren't here and we couldn't find the stars. When Jonathan got three ticks we let him have extra time on the computer. He's good again now.'
> The supply teacher didn't know a thing about it. It was one of my proudest moments!
>
> Sheelagh Wurr, Year 3 teacher

Many of the activities, especially those involving role-play, are also chosen to encourage the development of empathy, which helps the children to become not only more self-aware but also more able to achieve insight into the complexities of social interaction. Teachers are often amazed at the depth of understanding of complex moral issues that children reveal once they have been provided with a suitable forum in which they feel safe to express themselves. Several things contribute towards making the circle a safe forum for the children. The teacher's calm, containing, but unobtrusive presence both as a facilitator of the games and processes, and as an equal member of the circle is important, while the strong structure of the agreed Golden Rules, which ensure everyone is taken seriously and no one is hurt, is equally vital.

Once circle time is up and running it can become a powerful forum for drawing upon the inner resources of the group to help others, and it can also give the children a chance to focus on and improve their own ways of responding to academic or to social challenges. Because there are 30 individuals within a circle, they can offer a wide range of help and understanding. The games and activities help refine children's natural 'counselling' skills. They learn to offer positive body language, to treat all contributors with great respect, and to empathize with other people's worlds. The structures and patterns of circle time are designed to help children talk and listen to others with warmth, acceptance and praise. Too often, adults feel that only they have the therapeutic skills necessary to empower others. In my own and many other teachers' experience, a class full of children offers a far wider range of skills than those available from one stressed adult.

The structures used within the Circle Time Model encourage children to think about their own responses and their interpersonal relationships, and to feel more confident about their own role in being able to change these situations. Moreover, as the group becomes more cohesive and the group identity becomes stronger, this in itself provides a strong support system and an important sense of belonging.

Many of the games and activities help bond the group together by emphasizing the intrinsic value of each of the participants. Every child is made to feel unique and special through self-affirmation exercises and strategies which are chosen to enhance self-esteem. A reception teacher explained how one affirmation idea worked with her class:

A useful assessment task that I introduced once the children had settled into school life was a treasure chest with a mirror inside. The children were told that there was a very special person inside the chest, and that there was no one else in the whole world like this person. Individuals had to peep inside and pass on the chest without saying anything. As I watched, it became clear who the children were with low self-esteem. I then carried over this knowledge into the rest of classroom life to help positive image-building; where possible involving those parents whom I knew would be interested and helpful!

Gish Hobbs, Reception and Head of Infant Department

Many teachers have endorsed the value of circle time to enhance children's self-esteem:

The introduction of regular circle-time games produces excitement and anticipation. It also helps us to share great fun, again easing the atmosphere caused by curriculum pressure. Nobody revels in these games and sessions more than I do, except perhaps those children in my care with lower than average self-esteem. They know that at these times everyone is valued equally, no matter how 'bright' or popular the child.

Circle time differs from the other 'quick fix' behaviour ideas because, whilst encouraging self-discipline, it allows the child to put herself proudly upon a pedestal, alongside, rather than above, others. The child is fully encouraged to value herself highly, and to respect and value others just as much, and so a stable social community can be developed. Schools hold the potential to help mould a society which is, as the phrase goes, 'at ease with itself'.

Richard Wyatt, Year 2 teacher

During the circle time, I did a round where the children had to say one thing they liked about themselves. One child 'passed' and said there was nothing he liked about himself. At the end of the round, I asked if he had thought of anything and again he said, 'No' – he really didn't like himself. I then asked the children in the class if they could raise their hands if there was something they liked about this child that they could share with him. A mass of hands went up and he chose several children, who commended him for such things as being fun to play with and being a good friend. At the end of the session, his face was beaming. It was a memory I will never forget.

Theresa Hoye

Robert is a large, easy-going, pleasant child, whose ambition is to get through life with the minimum of exertion. He doesn't like playing football, the all-consuming activity of nearly all the 8-year-old boys in our school, nor does he have a particular friend, although he seems to get on well with most children. Robert confided one day that he was 'being bullied'. Closer questioning revealed that there wasn't any actual bullying going on; although finding himself with nobody to play with, Robert had commandeered some of the younger boys and ordered them to play with him. They had appealed to other, older children who had launched a rescue operation which involved some name calling and other unpleasant behaviour directed at Robert. Robert was left feeling both aggrieved and lonely.

Robert was among the nine new children to enter my Year 3/4 class in September. Eighteen members of the class had been with me the previous year and were familiar with circle time. I suggested that we might discuss the problem during circle time and Robert agreed to this. Between us, Robert and I explained the problem and then we threw it open to suggestions. Jamie (who was on the special needs list, stage three, for academic problems) said we should give Robert a 'warm fuzzy'.

In our class from time to time when a child needs some extra encouragement, he or she sits in the middle of the circle holding a small piece of soft sheepskin. The children and adults in the circle each make a statement beginning, 'I like (Bobby) because . . .' The soft material that the child is holding provides a physical sensation which complements the 'warm, fuzzy' feeling he or she received from the statements of the circle.

So we did that. Then we hammered out an agreement whereby Robert agreed to leave the younger children alone and, in return, there would be no more verbal abuse from the class. The problem of loneliness was also addressed. One or two less fanatical footballers said they would be Robert's 'friend' and took on the temporary role of 'minders' so that Robert would have some company in the playground. Our circle times are fortnightly. At the following one, the situation was briefly reviewed and Robert reported that things were going well. Two weeks after that when we came to the 'anything to bring up' spot, Robert put his hand up and produced a packet of smarties from his pocket saying, 'I would like to give a present to Andrew to thank him for being a really good friend to me. I'm really happy at school now.'

We had never had 'presentations' during circle time before, other than stickers and compliments. After four weeks, Robert felt secure enough in his relationships within the class, both to make a statement about his friendship and to find for himself some way of expressing his gratitude.

Sheelagh Wurr, Year 3 teacher

When children feel more confident about their own self-image and worth, they will contribute more readily to the benefit of the whole group. They begin to accept responsibility for their actions and explore alternative ways of responding which have a more positive outcome. All children want approval from their group and confirmation that they are accepted as part of the team, as these children's circle-time comments illustrate:

'I didn't know it made him so sad.'
'I don't like some people to be frightened of me, I'd like to change.'
'I don't like having to say in the circle that I'm still doing that horrible teasing.'
'I'd like to be kind.'

One class group contained a very unhappy, angry child who could not be motivated to behave sensibly by any teacher-chosen strategies. During circle time it became clear both to this child and to the other children that his hurtful behaviour was a way of gaining their attention, and that what would really please and motivate him to change would be to win their approval and enjoy some friendship. The class and the child worked jointly on an action plan focusing on certain relationship targets they had chosen together, and on how they might help him to achieve them. 'Help each other to be good' became one of their Golden Rules.

Another teacher similarly reports the power of circle time to support a lonely, bullied child:

In my second year of teaching I had an extremely difficult Year 6 class who had continued to be very unsettled despite various management and positive behaviour techniques. Two children were permanently excluded in the first term (so much for my positive behaviour techniques!) and the 26 who remained were fragmented and confrontational, but nevertheless eager to try new things. One boy in particular was never included in the main group. He had a bed-wetting problem and he smelled. His home life was fairly inconsistent and generally his life at school was miserable. Most of of the class picked on him and consequently he became a victim who also instigated trouble. When I started doing circle time with the class at first, they interrupted each other constantly and did not take anything seriously. Slowly this changed. Children began to come up with problems of their own that they wanted to develop strategies for. Other children would share feelings and ideas and most importantly come up with solutions. The bullied child found circle time very difficult to deal with and initially he would leave the circle or the room because he could not cope. Slowly, however, he began to stay and share his feelings with the others. After a time he plucked up the courage to explain to them how they made him feel when they treated him badly. I remember listening to this and becoming aware that the whole class was hanging on his every word. After that his class life changed. He was accepted and, although there were still flare-ups, it was never so bad. I would never have believed that circle time could have changed the nature and dynamics of a class – but it did. It got to the point that if a problem arose they would ask for a circle time to resolve it. It was the best time of the week, even if we just sat in a circle and told jokes.

Alice Witherow

Many children with low self-esteem have difficulty forming relationships with other children. Their lack of friends can increase their feelings of low self-worth and further isolate them, encouraging them to use tried and tested forms of negative behaviour to gain attention. They lack the normal friendship skills children need to create positive relationships with their peers, having never had the opportunity to practise them.

Circle time offers the ideal forum for promoting and enhancing the skills necessary for forming positive relationships. Through circle time, children are able to explore the qualities which make for friendship, and think about their own emotional needs in relationships, like trust, caring, sharing, co-operation, being included, and being listened and talked to. The children can discuss which behaviours are seen as being friendly and which are not, and then practise positive approaches and attitudes through role-play. Circle time also offers the opportunity for the whole class to acknowledge and praise any child who is making a specific effort to change a negative behaviour into a more positive one. One way of doing this is to have a Golden Nomination Board. During circle time, any child can nominate another to go on to the board. If, at the next circle-time session, all the children, staff and dinner ladies can vouch for the nominee's good behaviour, then the nominator can award her a sticker (or another agreed reward). Public acclaim from both the teacher and a child's peers is important for two reasons. Not only does it enhance the child's self-esteem, but it also allows other children to view the child, perhaps for the first time, in a positive light. Helping a child to change negative behavioural responses will also require a change in the attitudes and expectations of that child's peers. Both these can be thought about and fostered through circle time. In fact, children themselves often come up with suggestions which enable a child to move towards a new class identity. An excellent example of this was related by a teacher who had a child in her class who continuously disrupted lessons by making car noises. He had adopted a 'car persona' in preference to his own 'self' as it gave him a more powerful, attention-gaining identity. Both the teacher and the children were tense and exasperated by the boy's behaviour, and it came as a great relief to them when, one circle time during the Open Forum, suggestions were proffered to this child by his classmates offering various incentives in return for a cessation of car noises. It happened that the boy's obsession with cars extended to his stylized drawings which were much admired by the other children. One of the suggestions was to offer him the opportunity to teach his classmates in turn how to draw these cars, during a brief afternoon 'art session', if he remained quiet during the morning work period. This proved to be a very powerful and successful incentive, as it offered the new and more fulfilling identity of 'artist in residence', which greatly improved his status from class 'weirdo'.

Another strategy, having already focused on positive relationships in circle time, is to create small groups (4 or 5, at random) of children who are not normally close friends. The children are asked to try to be positive both in words and in actions towards every other member of their group for a week. Every time they think they have achieved this they can tick their own chart. By discussing the chart with other children they can assess their performance, and try to ensure that they are equally positive towards all the other members of the group. At the next circle-time session the children can discuss their progress and sort out any problems that may have arisen. This strategy can be repeated several times with changing groups.

As the children see how they can resolve issues amongst themselves in circle time, they gain increased confidence in their abilities to sort out problems for themselves. One class found circle time so useful for sorting out problems that they decided to invite the dinner ladies, so they could do some thinking about dinnertimes together. During this time, with the dinner ladies contributing, they decided on all the unacceptable behaviours they wanted to stop, e.g. hitting each other, swearing, spitting, and the behaviours they wanted to encourage, e.g. playing together, being kind, asking people to join in games. Having decided on and written down these standards they then agreed on incentives to encourage them, e.g. dinner ladies would award 'smiley' badges whenever they spotted the good behaviours. If they spotted any bad behaviour, the name of that child would be entered on to a small pad which listed all the unacceptable behaviours – the relevant one was then ticked and the slip of paper given to the teacher at the end of playtime. The teacher would then ensure that that child was excluded for a short time from certain privileges already specified by the children themselves.

When children are motivated to think about solutions to the problems that their behaviour causes both to themselves and to their peers, they can devise many inventive systems to support their goals. One group decided that they talked too much in class and consequently were not working as well as they would like. They arrived at the solution of making 'do not disturb' signs which they could put on their tables to signify that they wished to work uninterrupted. If any other child attempted to disturb them or if any child did not stick to their own 'do not disturb' ruling, then the teacher would remove a previously specified and agreed privilege. Other class groups proved equally inventive in their ideas for promoting 'working harder' with such suggestions as a designation 'work table' or particular privileges for reaching work targets.

Many of the relationship problems which the children bring forward in circle time can be explored through role-play. This gives children the opportunity to learn how they appear to others and to understand others' responses to them. Role-play offers the children a chance to 'try out' alternative modes of behaviour and discover ways of behaving which will bring them positive responses from their peers.

Role-plays can also give all children, even those usually seen as naughty or anti-social, the opportunity to play the 'hero' or 'expert' empowered to dispense benefits to others. Some role-play exercises require co-operation from the participants, and subsequent discussion can highlight the value to the whole group of being co-operative and considerate to others. Many people underestimate the ability of children to understand and be able to act upon moral precepts, and to share moral responsibilities. As one teacher wrote:

Whilst there are other whole school development and discipline programmes available to schools, I believe the circle-time approach is the most valid because rather than aiming to invoke the authority of the adult, it begins with the child and places the responsibilities upon children themselves, rather than on some all-knowing and all-seeing teacher. It is essentially a democratic process, not an authoritarian one.

Once children have seen how acting as a team benefits them all, they are more willing to work together and help the more unhappy children overcome their problems instead of excluding them.

Circle time is for many children the first time they will have been asked to consider their own behaviour and its effect on others, and they very quickly realize how it can help them, as their comments illustrate:

'Circle time is to teach people to get on in life and have good fun.'
'It can solve problems for you about other people and yourself.'
'It helps with name calling and bullying and other horrible things that happen.'
'I think it is to have everybody's views on something.'
'To learn and to think things over and to think things out.'

In order that circle time is able to realize its full potential it should be given a regular weekly slot on the timetable. If held infrequently, e.g. 'when time allows', it will lose its power as an ongoing and therapeutic force. There is also the danger that it can degenerate into merely a fun and games session. Whilst fun is the initial motivating and involving factor of circle time, it should not be allowed to become the overriding force.

It is useful to plan circle time sessions in themes, each theme having an underlying moral value (Mosley 1996). The activities for each session can lead the children into a discussion of the moral value involved. Generally, I include an opening activity which is fun and relaxes the children, and helps bond the group together for the subsequent, co-operative activities. As well as role-play and reflection exercises, an 'open forum' phase (which includes discussion) can be an important opportunity for children to bring their problems and concerns to the attention of the circle. However, it is vital when addressing any issues raised that the children's responses are non-contentious and non-threatening. I therefore advocate that suggestions to children with problems are phrased in the following manner: 'Would it help if I . . . ?' or 'Would it help if you . . . ?' The child who has brought forward a concern then has the freedom to make a personal choice regarding the suggestion, after due deliberation. Once a suggestion has been taken up, other circle members can help a child work out an action plan which incorporates this idea, and consider a suitable incentive if required.

The children are encouraged to show respect for all contributions, even if they are not used, by thanking the contributor. This is very important, if all children are to feel equally valued. An example of this in practice is shown below:

Ellie: Sam, would it help if you had a 'do not disturb' sign on your desk?
Sam: Thank you Ellie, but I don't think I would take any notice of that.
Ahmed: Sam, would it help if you sat at a table in the corner by yourself?
Sam: I wouldn't like that but thanks Ahmed.
James: Sam, would it help if I was your special helper and sat by you to remind you to work. I could give you a sticker every day that you managed to work hard.
Sam: I would like to try that, thanks James.

Though this is a shortened and simplified version of the process, it will give a basic idea of how it works. In order to further enhance the chances of any action plan succeeding, it is sometimes useful to fully engage the co-operation and goodwill of all the children by offering a group incentive when a child achieves an agreed target.

Thus, in the example used, the whole class were offered a session of parachute games if they all helped Sam to achieve five ticks in the following week. This gave Sam the opportunity of providing a benefit for his classmates and lessen the chance of other children deliberately sabotaging his efforts.

The 'open forum' phase can also be very useful for the classteacher. Not only can it take away the teacher's burden of being solely responsible for helping children with their behaviour and enforcing discipline in the classroom, but it can also provide a greater knowledge of individual children and more insight into their behaviour. As much as possible, the teacher should try to lessen her role as leader during 'open forum' and become an ordinary participant. Especially over 'home-grown' concerns, children often have insider information and a greater knowledge of the issues concerned than their teachers.

Because 'open forum' is at times a thought provoking and emotional experience, I like to ensure that circle-time sessions always include a closing activity that lightens the mood, so that everyone leaves the circle with a positive feeling.

Since circle time was developed to help teachers and pupils create more positive relationships within their schools, I will leave the final words to them:

> The children are much more aware of the needs of their peers and so value their peers much more highly. They are given the time and space to reflect upon their thoughts and actions alongside their privileged teacher.

REFERENCES

Bandura, A. (1977) *Social Learning Theory.* New York: Prentice Hall.

Burns, R. (1982) *Self-Concept Development and Education.* New York: Holt, Rinehart and Winston.

Glasser, W. (1967) Classroom meetings. In Joyce, B. and Weil, M. (eds) *Models of Teaching* (1986), New York: Prentice Hall.

Glasser, W. (1985) Reality therapy. *Theory into Practice*, 24 (4), 241–6.

Mead, G. H. (1934) *Mind, Self and Society.* Chicago: University of Chicago Press.

Michenbaum, P. (1977) *Cognitive Behaviour Modification.* New York: Plenum.

Moreno, J. L. (1934) *Psychodrama,* second revised edition. New York: Plenum.

Rogers, C. R. (1951) *Client-Centred Therapy.* Boston: Houghton Mifflin.

RESOURCES

Mosley, J. (1989) *All Round Success.* Trowbridge: WEST.

Mosley, J. (1993) *Turn Your School Round.* Wisbech: LDA.

Mosley, J. (1996) *Quality Circle Time in the Primary Classroom.* Wisbech: LDA.

Mosley, J. (1997) *The Jenny Mosley Photocopiable Resource Pack.* Available from the author.

CHAPTER 11

Danielle: a class teacher's account of circle time and beyond

Kate Ashby

In this chapter I will be sharing some of my experiences and thoughts on using circle time (see Chapter 10) with my class during a particularly difficult time. As an infant teacher in a suburban primary school, I have found circle time to be a very valuable opportunity and whole class experience. Through circle-time activities and 'rounds', individuals can develop the courage to share their thoughts and feelings openly, and experience being listened to and taken seriously. A round is a way of taking turns to speak, using a precious object (in our case a painted egg), which is passed around the circle. When someone is holding the egg, they can speak and everyone else has to concentrate and look at them and listen to them and think about what they are saying; later they can have the egg and say what they want to say. Listening to each other can foster understanding and empathy. Circle time can also encourage the class as a whole to grow into a caring, sharing community, thinking about and solving problems together. I have found circle time to be both a helpful regular practice and a springboard into a way of relating and thinking about feelings and about others, which can become part of the whole classroom atmosphere and relationships.

The year before I had Danielle was when I first heard about circle time. That year there were considerably more difficulties than usual in the Year 2 class. In the beginning it felt as if I couldn't even think about doing any work with the children because their attitude was so bad. As individuals they were lively and interesting, very bright too, but as a class the dynamics were awful. They argued. They couldn't get on with each other. They had all sorts of social problems, and they were easily distracted. They had lots of problems in the playground as well. I really needed some way to help them get together, to get them behaving acceptably, before they would begin to learn properly. So I decided to try the circle-time approach. I made a tremendous input that first term. We did circle time twice a week, and we used the language every day. We would talk about the skills – 'the listening skills, and the looking and thinking and the concentrating skills'. When they heard those words, they would clue in, and I would stop them almost every 10 minutes that first month or so because they couldn't last more than a few minutes before their behaviour would start to deteriorate. For me the language is crucial, but they also need the experience to know what the language is all about.

Once you've done that – and they clue into what you mean when you say, for example, 'Are you *looking* at so and so while she is speaking?' – you can start to use it with them in a regular and a meaningful way. It's not just giving them the labels, 'looking skills, listening skills etc', it's actually showing them and observing how they're using them. With that class it was very much all through the day picking up on those skills as they were happening: 'Will, it feels like you're not really thinking about what I am saying, it seems as if you're thinking of something else.' It was all tied in, and circle time was a place where we practised this process of looking and listening and thinking and concentrating – and respecting each other too, and how it felt not to be respected.

The next year, Danielle's year, was a very different class. I'd had them in reception and I knew them well, and they knew me. When we started the year, the children were already aware that Danielle was very ill. She had come into the class the previous September. Her brain cancer had been diagnosed in May, and we could all see that she was very poorly. She was 6 at the time. I don't know that the children thought in terms of death, at least until the very end, but they knew that she was seriously ill – much more ill than they had ever been. I think that they almost realized it at an intuitive level. The previous teacher had told them about Danielle's illness as she had been away since May having treatment. They had been told that Danielle had a very bad lump in her head; and when she came back in September and they saw that she had lost her hair, they knew that she was different and special in some way.

The personalities in the class were a lot calmer than in the previous year and they got on very well as a group. We began, as usual, with weekly circle-time sessions, but after 2 or 3 weeks they were well into it, and we didn't have to keep reinforcing things. Generally in circle time I would start off with a sentence such as 'I feel happy when . . .' or 'Sometimes I need some help with . . .', but with this class we had got beyond that and we could do it any time with or without the egg. After the first half term they no longer needed to sit in a circle to use the skills, although I would still do a formal circle sometimes because they loved all the games. Formal circles were good also when we wanted to talk about something serious, or if there was some problem I really wanted them to think about. We'd get the odd occasion when they had some problems in the playground and we would have a circle to talk things through. I can remember one day when Juliet (a very expressive child) came up to me and said:

> I've had the most awful time in the playground. I didn't have anyone to play with and when I asked them to play with me they just looked at me as though I was a piece of dirt under their feet. So please can I have the egg to sort this out with them. We'll go outside to sort it out now.

I was really taken aback and I gave her the egg. They came back in, and I said, 'Is it OK now?' and they said, 'Yes, fine now', and they put the egg back on the desk. This time with Juliet was the first time anyone said, 'Can I go outside and resolve it myself?' – without me being there – and they were only six! Soon, if there were any little problems in twos, threes or fours they would use the egg.

In the class that term we had four adults. Danielle's mother came in for the whole term. Then there was a welfare assistant allocated, because Danielle needed a lot of help with drinking, etc; and I also had another mother who had been coming in regularly to help for two years. All the children knew all the adults and there was a really good supportive atmosphere in the class. Danielle was a little bit the focus of attention and, because she was a fun child, we giggled and laughed a lot. It was as supportive for us adults as for the children. We all benefited, both from the caring, supportive atmosphere and from all the extra help. The adults were all very caring and accepting of all the children – each with their own strengths and difficulties. There was no labelling or competitive behaviour, which you can sometimes get in classrooms where there are several adults. They were possibly quite exceptional adults, as they all had the capacity to bear the pain which was increasingly around. So this soft atmosphere filtered through to the children. The humour was helpful too. We had a very gifted child in the class that year, and he would say such funny things, which would make us laugh as adults. Although his comments were usually way over the top of the others, they would see the connections between him and us and they would laugh too, and that would release something for all of us. The whole thing had all sorts of odd little dimensions. You could almost feel the atmosphere. I had never before been in a classroom where there's an atmosphere like it – and probably never will be again. In a way we had a very cosy secure place together. It probably wasn't so easy for the rest of the school or for other parents to cope with Danielle's obvious deterioration, because they weren't involved; they could only feel the distress, whereas for us, involved on a daily basis with all this support and care, it was, in a way, a very positive experience.

Danielle was getting to the stage where she couldn't talk, and it was becoming difficult for her to write. Then, when she started walking quite a bit slower than the others, and her vulnerability became dangerous, she would stay in with her friends at playtimes. Soon she needed a wheelchair, because walking became just too difficult. One day when Danielle was really poorly, I realized I would need to prepare the children somehow. I decided I needed to do some thinking with the children about Danielle, but I didn't feel I could be specific at that stage about the possibility of her death, as her mother still had a lot of hope. I suppose I took my cue from Jill, Danielle's mother. If Jill had mentioned it, or said she wanted to talk about it, I would have talked then and there with the children, because then they would have been prepared for it. In fact maybe I would have preferred to have done that, but I felt I needed to go slowly, because Jill was still needing to be hopeful. But I knew I had to do something, because Danielle could die suddenly, and the children might think, 'Hey, you never mentioned she was that sick – that she was dying – hey, you never mentioned death.'

Although I wasn't going to focus specifically on Danielle, I decided we needed to use the circle to think about sadness. So one day when Danielle was off feeling very poorly and arranging for a wheelchair, I took the opportunity to have a 'sadness' circle time. I said: 'I want you to think about sadness, and about the saddest thing that has ever happened to you.' It was a very moving circle time, although the children didn't seem unduly distressed. While they were a very sensitive class, and there did come a time when they began to develop little worries about health, at that time perhaps they needed to some extent to keep the more unbearable feelings at bay. I started off the circle by saying that I had been very sad when my dog had died, and how I'd felt. The children seemed to pick up on that and lots of their experiences were about dying, e.g. 'My gran died' or 'My rabbit died'. So we had a very moving circle time where we talked about death and dying and, looking back on it now, I think that although nobody said: 'Is Danielle dying?' it was something they must have realized or sensed. Maybe they instinctively felt, with the heaviness of the atmosphere and the deterioration of Danielle, that I wasn't doing this just as a sentence to talk about. They were used anyway to the sentence stems being quite topical. For example, if somebody was struggling with something, I might start off a sentence with: 'I really don't like it when Mrs K (the headteacher) wants this form filled in and I can't do it very well . . .' and this would free them to share their own experiences of difficult things. So they were already used to experiencing connections between circle-time themes and what was happening in class.

A few days later we did another circle time on what you could *do* if you were very sad. They all had different things they would do, such as curl up in a blanket, go and cuddle a teddy, or talk to mummy. I started with the sentence: 'When I felt sad, I listened to Pachelbel's *Canon*' – and we all sat and listened to it in the circle, and it became the music of the year if you like. As we listened, they passed the egg around and they could say how they felt listening to it. Of course it's a very moving piece of music, and at any level it can reach you, especially if the atmosphere is one of sadness anyway.

The time came when we heard the sad news that Danielle had died that morning. I told the children as we sat together on the carpet and we talked about death and dying. We didn't need a circle to talk together about things by this time. We would just sense who wanted to speak, and the children would just look and listen to them when they spoke, and wait their turn. It seemed important on this day for us to be close to each other, and for them all to be close to me. They were shocked of course, but I suppose that in a way we had all expected it. At first they were all a bit stunned to silence. It was helpful that we had Hindu children in the class because they were much more comfortable with the experience of death than most of the others. In Hinduism, death seems much more like a part of life, and so the Hindus naturally talked about what they believed. And then lots of the children talked about what they believed about death, and all sorts of thing came up – things that you would never normally talk about, even with adults. For some children perhaps, this more intellectual exercise might have made the heartbreaking sadness more bearable, especially on that first day, but we did think about sadness too. A little Hindu boy, Gopal, had recently lost a friend. He had obviously talked a lot about this at home and he seemed very comfortable sharing his feelings. Then, as we had done so much work on sadness, it became very easy to feel sad about what had happened and they could support each other. Then we listened to Pachelbel's *Canon* again and talked together. One or two girls cried and hugged each other. Some of them seemed to want to split up into little groups. I suggested they could respond in whichever way suited them:

You might want to write a letter to Danielle's mummy. You might want to write down your thoughts. You might want to draw a picture. Or you might just want to talk about it with your friends for a little while.

One or two wrote letters, a few wrote poems and most of them drew pictures. Some drew pictures of how they remembered Danielle. Some drew pictures of graveyards with Danielle lying under the ground. A lot of them just talked about it. The only child in the class who didn't want to think about it was the gifted child who said: 'Can I go and finish my IT work now?' Perhaps he was stunned to silence in more of an adult way at first; or perhaps experiencing and sharing his feelings was just too uncomfortable for him. Certainly he was much more of a thinker than a feeler about things.

That week we talked a lot about Danielle's death, and we actually did have a formal circle time. I felt perhaps they needed the security of doing something they were familiar with, and maybe they needed the ritual of a more formal circle, to mark her passing. And then they needed the fun of the games as well. You can't carry a load that heavy all week – so the circle time included other things. Then there was the funeral, which I went to, and I came back and told the children about it. It was a Jewish funeral – so we couldn't send flowers. It was hard not to be able to send anything to express our feelings. So we did another circle time soon after the funeral when we talked about 'I remember when . . .' We drew pictures and wrote down our memories and we made them into a book, which we gave to Danielle's mother. Jill then sent us a book back about Danielle's life and illness, which she illustrated with drawings; at the end she put: 'And I remember when . . .', and she wrote a list of all *her* memories. She explained how one day they had found a lump on Danielle's head, and they had gone to the hospital, and the doctors had said that Danielle needed this special treatment, which would cause her to lose her hair amongst other things.

Danielle died just a few weeks before Christmas and, although by this time she wasn't able to do much, in the Christmas play she was to have sat in a chair playing the part of the 'modest teacher'. When she died, her friend was chosen to play the part for her, but the children were very keen that we mention in the play somehow that Danielle was to have played the part. So one child volunteered to stand up at the beginning of the play and say this – and so, in a way, she was included.

The next term came and we started seeing little after-effects. Because we had done so much thinking and talking throughout the year, these were perhaps quite mild compared to what they could have been. But one or two children were getting upset, and it was obvious that we needed to talk again about Danielle and all that had happened, and about the thoughts and feelings which were coming up. That was a much more practical circle. One child had developed a very bad cough, and she thought she was going to be like Danielle. We needed to think about the physical side of illness. I explained that it really was very unusual for someone to get an illness which was life-threatening like Danielle's. Bringing these very understandable fears out into the open, and giving the children such practical information, seemed helpful and they appeared to settle down a lot. But then after the anxiety of the Standard Assessment Tasks (SATS) some of the parents came in and said that their children had been mentioning Danielle again and getting upset. Maybe the stress of SATS had brought things to the surface again. I remember saying to one parent that we hadn't had an opportunity to think about Danielle for a while because of SATS, but we would be doing a circle again soon because the Stone Setting was coming up, and we would be making time to think about that together.

In June they had the Stone Setting. In Judaism you don't take flowers to the grave, but you can take a pebble or a rock later, as a mark of respect and remembering, and to show that you have visited. The Stone Setting was a very special experience for me. We had sat in a circle in class before the ceremony, and I had taken in a selection of pebbles which I spread out in the middle of the circle. As we listened to Pachelbel's *Canon*, we took turns to choose a pebble and give a message to Danielle while holding the pebble in our hands. We put the pebbles into a beautiful, decorated box. When I went to the Stone Setting I took the 30 pebbles in the beautiful box and laid them along the edge of the gravestone. That experience was very moving, because it almost felt as if Danielle was there receiving the messages from the children. After the ceremony I came back and told the children about it, and we formed another circle to think about it. That time it became a circle about hope, because I told them how when I was at the Stone Setting the sky had been grey, and as I laid out the stones I looked up and there was a tiny little rip of blue in the sky, and that had made it seem like a very special moment – and it had made me think about hope. Then they started saying things about hope in their childlike ways.

At the Christmas concert it had been decided to collect some money in memory of Danielle, and so after Christmas we had another circle to think about how we would use the money for a memorial to her. We thought about benches and trees and garden things. The children drew plans of benches and layouts and memorials, and that was all very useful, making another way of dealing with our loss. After that, and towards the end of the year, no parents came in again to say that their children had been distressed or anxious about symptoms, although I am sure that Danielle's dying will be something they will carry with them always and something special that we have been through together as well. In fact, I now go back into this class once a week to do circle time with them and it is so good – it's like slipping my hand into a glove. I think they have gained what a lot of adults probably won't even gain in a lifetime. I can sense it in that they are a class that seem to go beyond words. They pick up very easily on looks, on gestures. There is like a silent language somehow between them and me. Sometimes it is almost like they don't need to say things. Things happen which feel common to all of them and they seem to understand each other. Their new teacher has commented on their being a special class. They have so few friendship problems, if any. The new teacher said: 'They do things automatically without me having to ask them. They respond helpfully and thoughtfully to each other almost instinctively.'

Another spin-off related to Marcus, the child who was gifted. He often had problems relating to his peers and could be quite lonely. He had a very sophisticated sense of humour which the others couldn't quite pick up on, but in the circle the other children would see the adults laughing and that would make them laugh too. The circle was very good for Marcus, because when you speak in the circle everyone looks at you and you have to look at everyone, and Marcus normally found looking people in the eye acutely difficult. One of the games we played in the circle was called Purple Frogs. In Purple Frogs you took turns to go round the circle and ask everyone a question and they had to answer, 'Purple Frogs', and you weren't allowed to laugh. Most children would ask questions such as 'What did you have for breakfast?' The obligatory reply of 'Purple Frogs' made it quite funny, but Marcus's questions were *really* funny, often reflecting on the characters of the adults in the room. We were in stitches, and it was very good for Marcus, because he realized he could actually say things which would make everyone laugh. Whereas often he would be a bit isolated from the others, here he was the centre of attention in a nice way, and they came to appreciate him more. So in the 'I remember when . . .' circle after Danielle's death, as well as the memories of Danielle, one of the memories was: 'I remember when Marcus made me say 'Purple Frogs' in the circle!' Another thing we did in the circle which was really good for Marcus was when a child had to talk with the person next to them, trying to find something which they both liked. Normally Marcus would either dominate or go totally quiet in a social situation, but in this activity he had to think with the other person at *their* level, and he had to look at and talk to one person, and have them do the same for him.

Circle time is also very good for quiet children who would normally find it hard to say anything in a group, because, when they have got used to it, circle time can be a safe situation in which to speak just a little sentence, and of course they can 'pass' (choose to say nothing). It can take time, but I remember a little Japanese girl who said virtually nothing in class, and by the end of the term she was not passing. For such children, saying sentences in the circle which were based on their own experiences or feelings was particularly helpful because their contributions would not be something that someone else might know more about, so they wouldn't feel they were being tested in any way – as they might in other situations. They were also guaranteed good listening and respect while they talked. Of course, respect for others is an important part of the circle-time philosophy.

We would often talk, especially at the beginning of a year, about respecting others and about the value of making mistakes. Children are often nervous of making mistakes. Sometimes I would switch things around and say: 'Thank you for making that mistake. I have learnt now that . . .'; and we would think about how if you're not making any mistakes you may not be learning very much, because you're not trying out anything new, and we can learn such a lot through trial and error. I remember the first time I had an opportunity to bring up the subject of mistakes. It was in the first week of term, and a girl called Juliette answered a maths question and she got it wrong – and everyone laughed. I stopped them immediately and we talked for nearly half an hour about how Juliette must have felt, and how we feel when people laugh at us. I said that I was really pleased that Juliette had made a mistake, because she had given us this very valuable opportunity to think about how people felt, and about how much we could all learn from mistakes – which we wouldn't have thought about otherwise. I remember I gave Juliette a house point and, although she wasn't very good at maths, she was never shy to have a go after that. No one laughed at other people's mistakes after that either! Of course with many classes it would take longer, but they would get there. One problem with 'Danielle's' class was that they would sometimes become oversensitized to feelings, and they could hesitate to laugh when someone had said something which really was funny, or they might comment when there had been laughing that they weren't keeping their feelings safe. But with maturity they became able to distinguish between things which were really funny, and the sort of laughter which might hurt.

And so for me it's not just the circle times themselves which are important, but the language of, for example, 'listening skills, looking skills, concentrating skills and thinking skills, respecting people, keeping safe' and the little phrases such as 'thank you for making that mistake' and 'I wonder what happened there?'. I would use the language every day, particularly at the beginning of a year, so they would become steeped in it. 'What happened there?' or 'I felt uncomfortable then . . . what happened?' would open up an opportunity for everyone to *think*. They would pick up on what had happened and think about it, and we would think about how we could make it different. Sometimes, particularly with this class, it seemed as if the whole class had become a *thinking* class and a *thinking* space. Perhaps this is a kind of parallel with the situation of therapy, where the room and the relationship become a *thinking space* where difficult things and feelings which come up are taken seriously and thought about, in a safe way.

Although, as I have said, Danielle's class had in many ways moved beyond circle time, I do think it is important for it to be practised regularly. It is a very good grounding, which children can take away with them. On open days I used to get parents coming up and saying what is this 'circle time' which the children had been talking about, and I would have to explain it to them. I remember one parent saying how her son had been telling her about something which had happened to him at school one day while she was doing the ironing, and suddenly he had broken off and said: 'Mum, you're not using your looking skills and your listening skills when I am talking to you!' Of course there are times in classes when teachers need to set very firm boundaries, and many classes need much firmer handling a lot of the time. But being able to relate to a class in this way, being a facilitator rather than an authority figure, can really encourage children's abilities to think about feelings and consequences, and to take responsibility and develop self-discipline. This is certainly something to work towards with a class. Maybe there are levels of approaches with classes which change over time. Initially, children may need an authoritarian approach to set the firm, secure boundaries which enable everyone to feel safe. Later one might use a more assertive approach of stopping the class and saying: 'Hey, I'm not feeling comfortable with that – I wonder why?' Still later, and perhaps with more exceptional classes, the children might start noticing things themselves, which might have caused people to feel hurt. The relationship then becomes much more equal and mutual. They might, for example, ask for the egg to go and solve a conflict by themselves. They might use the skills themselves in the playground. Then they would have internalized the approach and the thinking, and it would become theirs. This is obviously what had happened with Danielle's class, although none of us would have wished for that so very painful path into maturity.

PART IV

Taking Schools Seriously

'Genuine beginnings begin within us, even when they are brought
to our attention by external opportunities.'
William Bridges

Part IV: Schools

The benefits of individual and group work can be enhanced significantly by a thoughtful approach to emotional issues at the institutional level.

- How can children develop skills to help each other reduce conflicts?
- How can teachers help each other deal with emotional issues?
- How can Special Needs be approached therapeutically?

CHAPTER 12

Creative conflict resolution: a workshop approach in schools

Ruth Musgrave

'Conflict and Change' started in 1984 in Newham, east London at a time when deeply felt changes had been happening in the area. In the south of the borough the docks had been closed and many families were moving to the new docks located at Tilbury, leaving those who remained behind feeling bereft of community. At the same time, in the north of the borough, many new communities were growing, mainly Asian and Caribbean, bringing a new vibrancy to those areas. The community was undergoing great change and old patterns of dealing with conflict seemed to be breaking down.

Consultation over a six-month period with local community groups confirmed the need for an organization which could be a resource for the people of Newham in finding creative ways of dealing with conflict and change. The aim was not to import ideas from outside but to draw on the experiences of handling conflict already there amongst people living in the borough, and see whether some models would emerge.

Eric Miller of the Tavistock Institute was initially the consultant to the project. Training for volunteer members and staff involved inter-group role-play activities aimed at helping people learn about how they individually react to conflict in groups. One area of work was to be a neighbour mediation service run by local volunteers trained by the project. Another was to be work in schools with both young people and their teachers exploring creative ways of dealing with conflict.

Initially the schools' work focused mainly on conflict resolution training with children and young people, but more recently there has been a growing interest nationally in peer mediation schemes in schools. Peer mediation involves training selected students to mediate in disputes between other students, which may range from name calling through friends falling out to playground fights. It is a method of conflict resolution which enables young people themselves to take responsibility for working through conflicts. The project has directed some of its resources into running peer mediation training in schools wishing to set up such schemes, as well as continuing to run workshops in conflict resolution with young people, teachers, lunchtime supervisors and parents.

THE NEED FOR CONFLICT RESOLUTION WORK

Emphasis on academic achievement in schools in recent years has relegated 'emotional literacy' to the sidelines of the curriculum. Not much time is given to developing an awareness of feelings and the ability to be in control of them, and to developing empathy towards others. This is producing lopsided development in young people at a time when the social and emotional skills of resilience, co-operation, creativity and adaptability are being more and more valued and needed in the world of work.

Social pressures which concentrate on gratification of artificially created wants by a consumer market do not encourage self-awareness or concern for others, qualities which are necessary for successful conflict resolution. Factors like high inner city unemployment leave many young people with a sense of hopelessness. When conflicts occur, they look for someone or something to blame. Conflict and Change is one of the growing number of groups, in both the voluntary and the statutory sectors, working with young people in this context.

Schools represent one of the only genuinely civic institutions left to which virtually all members of society relate at some point in their lives, so they are strategically a good focus for our work. The project works with all age ranges and whole classes, rather than only with those with special needs. The aim is that, through the conflict resolution and peer mediation workshops, all the children will develop confidence in themselves and trust in the group so that they can work together to solve conflicts. We do not advocate that this work be done as a substitute for work with individual children with special needs, but we aim to help to create the kind of climate in a school where all children, including those with special needs, will feel nurtured, and will themselves be able to nurture and handle conflicts in creative and healing ways.

THE VALUES UNDERLYING OUR WORKSHOPS

Conflict as opportunity

Conflict is a key part of human experience and it is especially important in psychological development. Much growth and change happens through conflict, whether personally, socially or culturally. Most people, however, see conflict in negative terms, because their experience of it has often been destructive, escalating into violence or diverted by avoidance or scapegoating. We believe there are some processes which can lead to the healthy expression and resolution of conflict, though the shape of these processes varies from culture to culture (Augsberger 1991). Healthy conflict resolution processes have mutual respect as their source. This respect is possible because both parties have a sense of their own worth, of acceptance and of belonging, which gives them the capacity to trust their adversary.

Self-esteem and mutual respect as the basis for relationships

Our workshops reflect the principle of mutual respect as the basis for relationships. A strong emphasis is placed on self-esteem building and on developing the capacity to work together in order that young people may be open enough to risk change. We have benefited much from the work of Carl Rogers for our understanding of the importance of self-esteem building in this work. As Rogers has written, 'A person can change only when they accept themselves' (Rogers 1978). Building up a trust in oneself and in others is therefore the first building block for developing effective conflict resolution.

No-blame approach

People can easily become trapped in cycles of mutual blame when conflicts occur. Within our culture, the mutual blame, or 'win/lose', model of dealing with conflict is the one most widely used. The media polarize people and groups into 'winners' and 'losers'. Children watching a cartoon or an action adventure on TV are encouraged to identify with only one of the characters or groups in a story. The 'goodie' must win (in the end) and the 'baddie' must lose.

Similarly, if we listen in to the conversation between two people in conflict, we will very soon hear such statements as 'It's your fault' or 'You made me do it'. In conflicts the need to find a culprit and then give them punishment is very strong, and there are some pay-offs for it, as blaming the other means we can avoid looking at our own behaviour, a process which can be hard to do.

However, blaming (whether of others or of oneself) is not good for healing and growth in relationships. It does not encourage personal responsibility for resolving the problem, but rather it keeps people locked into cycles of recrimination.

The most effective way to preserve mutual respect and self-esteem in a conflict is to use a 'no-blame' or 'addressing needs' approach. Willingness to listen to each other and focus on the needs underlying a problem for both parties can often result in ways of moving on which are satisfactory to both.

SOME THEORETICAL MODELS WHICH HAVE HELPED US

Maslow: meeting needs approach

The ladder of needs developed by Maslow (1954) illustrates the way that all human beings are seeking to get their needs met, through their behaviour and their interactions. When needs are not met, conflict occurs so that underneath a conflict is usually an unmet need on both sides which is clashing with the needs of the other. In order to use the no-blame response to conflict, the basic need for personal safety and belonging for both parties has first to be met.

People who have confidence that their basic needs will be met can tolerate actions of others which might threaten this temporarily, but those who over long periods of time do not get their psychological needs met can be easily threatened by the actions of others, which take away what little they have. They are programmed by past experience to make certain reflex reactions in a conflict, even though they know that these responses have not been helpful in the past.

Through providing an experience of safety and trust, whether in the training group or by mediation, people can gain a different and more positive experience from what they have come to expect derived from their negative memories of the past. This new experience of trust makes it possible for people to find new, unexpected and freeing ways of responding in the conflict.

Freire: education for freedom

In the early 1960s Paulo Freire revolutionized learning theory with his book *Pedagogy of the Oppressed* (Freire 1972). The book had developed out of his work with literacy students in the slums of urban Brazil. He argued that all education is either to oppress (and imposed from above) or for freedom, and emanating from the learner's own experience. Education for freedom involves recognizing that feelings and motivation to act are directly connected, and as such are as important to learning as is critical thinking. Because of this, learning which aims to affect and become part of us requires that learners themselves set their own agenda starting from their own lives and experience of a problem.

A good facilitator recognizes all learners as thinking, creative people with the capacity to think and to act. She helps people to identify the issues which matter most to them. They share together their experiences of the problem, identify what new skills or resources are needed to change things, and then plan accordingly. Learning moves from action to reflection to action. It is a process through which the learner (and the facilitator!) can be transformed.

From Freire we have learned the importance of taking seriously the knowledge and experience of the learner. We have recognized that learning requires the engagement of feelings as well as critical thinking in order to be applied in action. We have also learned that the role of the facilitator is not to transmit a body of knowledge (in this case about conflict resolution), but rather to help people make sense of their own experiences and create models for new ways of behaving from this understanding.

The human relations movement

The human relations movement in the USA in the 1960s emphasized that the best conditions for learning occur when a climate of confidence and trust is built up between members of a group. Learning from the 'here and now' of the group has also become part of our practice, so our workshops always begin with a group-building activity, followed by an exercise which helps participants to think about aspects of their own behaviour, however simply this might be. An exercise might be to identify their preferred way of handling conflict with friends, through a role-play or tableau (i.e. a frozen image of a conflict made by one member of the group shaping others into the physical poses of people involved in a conflict). The variety of experiences shown in the tableaux and role-plays illustrate that there are many different ways of handling conflict. The group may then explore in depth one person's problem, offering creative ways forward, through acting out possible outcomes.

Left brain/right brain

A further influence on our work has been the discovery that there are two types of thinking: left brain, which is critical and analytical, and right brain, which is creative and artistic (Edwards 1979). For good quality learning to take place, both sides of the brain need to be engaged.

This insight has led us to balance creative, imaginative exercises with exercises needing critical thinking. This is particularly important in the field of conflict resolution, as conflicts very often sap creativity, leaving people feeling stuck in old, unhelpful patterns. Using creativity and imagination can unlock doors and open up new paths. A guided meditation using imagery, or a role-play using characters from a make-believe situation or a fairy story, can open blocked channels and facilitate identification with and empathy for people in different situations and with differing needs. We sometimes ask participants to think of a problem they have at the moment that feels stuck. We then ask them to imagine that they have some magic to help them get out of the problem; what sort of magic would it be? Ideas, such as a magic carpet, a huge bunch of balloons which would carry the person up into the sky and away, and a magic finger to freeze other people, are just three of the many images participants come up with. In pairs they then explore what it was that their magic gave them.Was it power over the situation, freedom, confidence . . . ? They then use their critical thinking capacities to explore other ways they might use to get what the magic gave to them.

CREATIVE WAYS OF DEALING WITH CONFLICT: THE WORKSHOP FORMAT AND CONTENT

Building trust

The creation of a climate of trust is the first task of the workshop facilitator. Trust between participants will open up opportunities for new ways of thinking and behaving in conflict situations.

Students working in a circle for the first time are often nervous. Lively introductory activities help to break the tension by allowing everyone to have fun. They also increase the energy level in a group.

Setting group ground rules is a further way of creating a shared code of behaviour in the group.

Reflection on experience of conflict up to the present

After trust-building activities, the group explores the different strategies the participants already use to deal with conflict. Dramatic techniques such as tableaux and role-plays allow them to visualize real-life situations of conflict they experience. Drama also means that those less confident in speaking English can fully participate.

Having identified the different ways that the participants handle conflict, we compare the 'win/lose' (blaming) approach to conflict, with the 'win/win' (or meeting needs) approach. Their own conflicts are the situations we work with, and they are encouraged to come up with their own 'win/win' solutions.

Expressing feelings

In order to use a no-blame approach children need to develop their ability to express their own feelings and listen to those of others, so we spend some time addressing this in the training. Awareness of and ability to express feelings are crucial if children are going to be able to empathize with the feelings of others. Work on feelings is therefore necessary at all stages of conflict resolution training.

In the workshops we spend time exploring how we deal with our feelings, particularly difficult feelings like anger. When asked what happens to their body when they are angry, children may reply that their leg feels as if it wants to kick, and it's hard to stop it. The first step for them is being aware of their characteristic response when angry and then developing strategies for more effective responses to the situation. (For an excellent manual with some helpful exercises, see Whitehouse and Pudney 1994.)

We first look for 'safe' strategies which group members already use to handle their feelings. The group may come up with as many as 30 different ideas. This is also an opportunity to introduce new techniques they can use when angry, techniques which give them time to respond effectively rather than with a 'gut' reaction to someone else's behaviour. Young people who have had problems controlling their reactions in the playground have quickly grasped the use of 'I' statements instead of 'you' statements when they find themselves in a conflict. 'I' statements help children to focus on their own feelings, rather than on blaming the other person. They also allow the opportunity for the children to make a request to the other person about the outcome they need, e.g. 'I feel frustrated when you won't let me play because I am your friend, and I don't like to be left out. I would like you to ask me to join in the game.'

Working together

Awareness of and increasing control over feelings needs to be accompanied by skills in working together. In our competitive society, children rarely have the chance to experience successful co-operation. Small group exercises involving co-operation provide opportunites for children to work together on a problem. These exercises counterbalance the individual development focus of self-esteem building work; they help participants not only to get their own needs met, but also to become more aware of the needs of others.

Listening

Once a child is able to own and express feelings in ways that do not blame others, it is relatively easy to develop skills in listening to others. Violence in a conflict often occurs because of poor communication, so a series of exercises to improve both observation and active listening skills are key elements of the training.

Listening carefully to both sides is a core skill for a mediator, and also a core communication skill for life, so learning to listen is a key part of the training. Speaking assertively but without judgement is also important in communication, so participants also learn how to cut out blaming language when they summarize a person's problem. They also learn the difference between closed and open questions, and how to use open questions to keep communication flowing when there is a conflict.

In exercises to practise these skills one student in a group of three will be the observer, and give feedback to the speaker and the listener on how they were doing in the exercise.

Valuing difference

Being able to value difference, whether cultural, religious or personal, is a fundamental part of the no-blame approach to conflict resolution which is also necessary in our increasingly multicultural society. Often people whose life experience has included living in two different cultures, as is the case with many of the children we work with, have already developed this capacity, and we can acknowledge this as a strength the group can build on in appreciating that there are at least two different points of view in every conflict.

We use the simulation game Ra Fa devised by Gary Shirts, which creates two cultures amongst participants (Shirts 1976). In the game everyone is first immersed in their own 'culture' and then visitors are sent between cultures to learn about what is going on in the other culture. Afterwards each 'culture' debriefs separately to analyse what they felt about the 'host' culture on their visit, and what assumptions they made about what was going on when they visited. This game invariably brings out a lot about participants' attitudes towards other cultures, and discomfort with moving into a strange, insecure situation.

One of the strengths of the training is the mix of the group, which always reflects the ethnic diversity of the school. With older groups (11 years upwards), we encourage participants to share their own experiences of being different, including experiences of discrimination. Sharing in this way can build bridges of understanding between the different cultures and backgrounds.

Finally, celebrating difference is linked to seeing both sides in a conflict. This is done by inviting participants to take the roles of different characters in familiar stories (Leimdorfer 1992). Through playing the role of the wolf in 'Little Red Riding Hood', the children learn to see the story from the point of view of the different characters and not from one side only.

Evaluating their own learning

Students are encouraged to evaluate their own development during the workshops through a variety of evaluation techniques.

We use paired interviews before and after the training, set homework tasks related to the training each evening, and ask students to evaluate the learning briefly at the end of each day and in a written form at the end of the training.

Peer mediation schemes

Children who have taken part in conflict resolution training, whether in our workshops or through circle-time activities, can use their skills by training to become mediators. In fact, running a peer mediation scheme is one way of practically monitoring how much students have learned from the conflict resolution training, and offering students a real-life opportunity to practise and develop their skills.

Mediation is a process which involves two impartial mediators helping two people in a conflict to find a way out of their problem in such a way that both parties' needs are met. Peer mediation schemes are run by young people themselves, and are not a part of the disciplinary structure of the school.

Peer mediation encourages young people to take responsibility for their own behaviour. The mediators do not take sides, but listen to both parties. By asking open-ended questions, they encourage the parties to come up with ways of solving the problems for themselves. They demonstrate to their peers that it is possible to solve problems together, rather than always needing to rely on an adult to arbitrate for them.

To set up a scheme, we initially arrange meetings with the head, or someone in the senior management team, and request that we then meet all the staff to explain the scheme and if possible do some training with them on the process of mediation. It is particularly important to have the active encouragement of both the teaching and the non-teaching staff since unsympathetic staff may perhaps unconsciously undermine the scheme, through using 'win/lose' strategies of dealing with conflict themselves. We have found that, before starting a scheme, a workshop with teaching staff, and another with lunchtime supervisory staff, allows anxieties to be aired, noted and addressed.

The co-ordinating teacher or the head recruits and selects potential mediators. Equal numbers of boys and girls are chosen so that mediators can work in pairs, demonstrating that it is possible for them to work together. Then training takes place. If the basic conflict resolution training has already been given, then mediation training can be completed in 1–2 days (depending on the age of the children and the time available).

Mediators are volunteers (usually from the upper school) who have also passed through an interview selection process, with the head or the co-ordinating teacher. Ideally they represent a cross-section of the pupils. Following the training, the children themselves make posters and plan a publicity campaign to launch the scheme, which ideally should be soon after the training has finished. Two mediators are available each lunchtime in a mediation room, and anyone who has an argument, fight or other problem with someone else can go there for a (voluntary) mediation.

Once the scheme is running, there is a regular weekly meeting for the mediators with the co-ordinating teacher to share problems and ways forward, and to plan ongoing publicity. The week's mediations are discussed and problems encountered by the mediators are used as material for continued learning.

Wherever possible, we keep in touch with the co-ordinating teacher so that any difficulties the scheme may be encountering can be discussed.

Conflicts suitable for mediation

The kinds of conflicts which mediators deal with usually focus on swearing, insulting or hitting. They are often between people who are friends, but have fallen out, and do not know how to make up. The disputants are usually of the same age, and relatively equal in power. This makes mediation an ideal process for helping them to restore their relationships.

Incidents of severe bullying are unlikely to come to the mediators because both parties must agree beforehand to the mediation. In the case of bullying, it is unlikely that this would be possible.

An anxiety sometimes expressed by teachers before a mediation scheme starts is that it will place an unfair burden on the mediators. We have not found this to be the case. So far we have never come across a problem which put the mediators out of their depth. Children know where to go for which kind of problem. Time is given in the training to explaining to mediators what to do if they feel a problem is serious. The first step is always reporting the problem to the co-ordinating teacher.

The mediation process

The mediation process begins by the mediators setting ground rules. This helps everyone to feel safe. The mediators then listen to both sides of the problem, summarizing and identifying the facts, feelings and the needs of each party. Mediators then encourage the two people to try to acknowledge the needs and feelings of the other person. Having got this far, the mediators then ask both parties what they would like to happen in order to make things better. They then encourage the people to come up with solutions which they can both accept. They agree to try one solution. They may agree to meet at a later date to review the situation.

The mediation bridge (Figure 12.1) shows how two people can find a way of meeting when previously they were on opposite sides. This visual demonstration of the concept of meeting is easily understood by trainee mediators. With younger children, the simple steps can be learned even before more complex conflict resolution skills are fully understood.

Figure 12.1 The mediation bridge. Reproduced with permission from *Changing Our School: Promoting Positive Behaviour*, Highfields Primary School, Plymouth.

The mediation process is described by Ali and Amelia, two mediators, as follows:

Ali explained that in mediation we have some ground rules. These are no swearing, or hitting or interrupting each other. He asked Mubiana and Nadra if they would agree to this.

Amelia asked Nadra to say what happened, and when she finished Amelia checked that she had understood what Nadra had said. Then she asked Nadra how she felt.

Ali asked Mubiana what had happened, and then checked he had understood. He asked her how she felt.

Then Amelia asked both of them how they thought the other one was feeling. (That part was quite hard.)

Amelia asked Nadra and Mubiana to say all the things they could do to make things better between them.

They gave some suggestions.

Ali thanked them and asked them to agree on what they would do to make sure the problem did not happen again.

At Manor Primary School in Newham, east London, 12 mediators were initially trained. They meet each week to discuss the mediations they have had. Shazia and Lobango had a difficult mediation. This is how they described it:

Shazia: Shana and Hasina are in my class. They kept fighting each other. They came for a mediation, but it was hard for me because they are my friends.

Lobango: We talked to each of them alone because they wouldn't talk together at first.

Shazia: In the end the mediation worked. When we asked them what they could do to make things better, they made cards to say sorry to each other.

Ali and Tosin told me this story:

Tosin: Charlotte and Bruce kept fighting, so they asked for a mediation.

Ali: We asked Bruce what was the problem. He said Charlotte slapped him.

Tosin: Charlotte said Bruce swore at her, that's why she slapped him.

Ali: We had a mediation with them, but then they started to fight again, so we had another mediation.

Tosin: This time we went to Mr Morton [the headteacher] and told him they kept on fighting. He said we should try again, and this time use his office. They didn't fight in the office. When we asked them what they could do to make the problem better, they made an agreement that Bruce would stop annoying Charlotte and Charlotte would stop hitting Bruce.

Ali: Mr Morton told us afterwards that he couldn't have sorted it out as well himself!

Mediators' meeting

At Manor Primary School, through their weekly meetings, the mediators noticed several problems through their experience on the job. The process of learning about conflict resolution continues through these opportunities. Below are a few examples of the problems they had encountered and their proposals for dealing with them.

The mediators noticed that only Years 4, 5 and 6 were using the mediation scheme. They thought this could be because younger children are either too young to understand mediation or too scared to go to the older children.

With their teachers' help they are each going to adopt a younger class and go to their circle-time session once a fortnight to play a trust-building game with the younger children. This way the younger children will get to know at least one mediator and learn more about what mediation is. This idea came from the children themselves.

As some of the mediators were going to move to secondary school in the autumn, they realized that in order to continue the scheme new mediators had to be found. The head was happy to release the children so that they could help to train a new set of mediators before they go.

Another problem the children noticed was that the playground supervisors did not seem to be encouraging children to go for mediation. The co-ordinating teacher agreed to talk with the lunchtime staff about this.

Difficulties had also come up in the actual process of mediation. Some children were bringing 4 or 5 'witnesses' along to back up their story! This was (not surprisingly) hard for the mediators as they sometimes did not feel that they had the authority to send these onlookers away. They discussed what to do, and decided to stick firmly to allowing only two parties in a mediation.

School structure

Conflict resolution workshops and peer mediation schemes are most effective when they are part of a whole school approach to developing open communication and healthy relationships. If this aim is held only by one teacher it will be hard to make much headway, as the children will be receiving contradictory messages about how to deal with conflict from the workshops compared with the approach of the rest of the staff and pupils; this may well lead to confusion.

Schools need to assess their own readiness to take part in peer mediation. Cohen (1995) developed a needs assessment form, which can be used initially to assess whether or not the school is willing to own the scheme.

Teachers' time

Because of increased pressures on teachers' time, it is sometimes difficult to find teachers who are willing to co-ordinate the programme within the schools. We always stress that the programme belongs to the school, not to us. Our role is to train and support. Although a peer mediation scheme is run by the children, the involvement of teachers is crucial, especially when setting up the programme initially. Teachers need to ensure the availability of a room, to encourage students to publicize the scheme, and to support the mediators by supervising them and helping them to further develop their skills.

The active involvement and support of senior management is also essential in order to give the programme and the approach credibility and to ensure its continuation after the initial honeymoon. Schools need to be able to offer a sustained commitment to the mediation programme; this needs to be long enough for it to become embedded in the school (at least 2 terms) in order for it to be effective.

Evaluation

Though little evaluation of peer mediation has been done nationally (Tyrell and Farrell 1995, Hayes and Saunders 1996), our own experience leads us to the conclusion that both conflict resolution training and peer mediation work best when part of a whole school policy for promoting mutual understanding. This has been demonstrated by Highfields Primary School in Plymouth, where a variety of complementary strategies (including mediation) have been used to create an atmosphere of mutual respect in the school (Highfields Primary School 1997).

We have also found that conflict resolution skills are far more likely to be reinforced when initial workshops in class are followed by a peer mediation scheme, as this gives a concrete opportunity for skills to be practised and developed.

In fact, when set up as part of a range of positive interventions, the benefits of mediation schemes far outweigh the problems. Schools report better relationships between children, less teacher time spent on disputes which young people could solve for themselves, and increased levels of maturity in students, especially in the mediators.

Parents comment favourably that their children are using mediation skills at home.

Evaluations of similar work in the USA have indicated that academic work also improves (Metis Associates 1990). The improvement in self-image which results from the training and practice of the process gives them the confidence to believe that they can do better academically, and they do!

APPENDIX

Organizations supporting peer mediation in schools:

ENCORE (European Network for Conflict Resolution in Education) is a European Network for teachers interested in developing the kind of work described in this chapter. It is co-ordinated by Marigold Bentley, Quaker Peace and Service Education Adviser, Friends House, Euston Road, London NW1 2BJ. Tel: 0171 387 3601.

Mediation UK is a national network of Community Mediation Projects. It can provide a list of organizations and individuals providing peer mediation and conflict resolution training in schools (Mediation UK, Alexander House, Telephone Avenue, Bristol BS1 4BS. Tel: 0117 904 6661).

REFERENCES

Augsberger, D. (1991) *Conflict Mediation across Cultures*. Philadelphia: Westminster Press.

Cohen, R. (1995) *Students Resolving Conflict*. Glenview, Illinois: Scott, Foresman (Goodyear Books).

Edwards, B. (1979) *Drawing on the Right Side of the Brain*. New York: St Martin's Press.

Freire, P. (1972) *Pedagogy of the Oppressed*. Harmondsworth: Penguin.

Hayes, R. and Saunders, L. (1996) *Preventing Bullying*. Kingston upon Thames: Kingston Friends Workshop Group.

Highfields Primary School (1997) *Changing Our School: Promoting Positive Behaviour*. London: Institute of Education.

Leimdorfer, T. (1992) *Once Upon a Conflict*. London: Quaker Peace and Service.

Maslow, A. (1954) *Motivation and Personality*. New York: Harper and Row.

Metis Associates (1990) *The Resolving Conflict Creatively Programme: Summary of Significant Findings of New York Site*. New York: Metis Associates.

Rogers, C. (1978) *On Personal Power*. London: Constable.

Shirts, G. (1976) *Ra Fa Game: Teachers Guide*. Del Mar, California: Simile 11.

Tyrell, J. and Farrell, S. (1995) *Peer Mediation in Primary Schools*. Belfast: University of Ulster.

RESOURCES

Kingston Friends Workshop Group (1996) *Ways and Means Today*. Kingston upon Thames: Kingston Friends.

LEAP (1997) *Promoting Positive Behaviour*. Leicester: Headstart.

LEAP Confronting Conflict (1995) *Playing with Fire*. Leicester: Youth Work Press.

Masheder, M. (1998) *Freedom from Bullying*. Woodbridge: Green Print.

Prutzman, P. (1988) *Friendly Classroom for a Small Planet*. London: New Society.

Whitehouse, E. and Pudney, W. (1994) *A Volcano in My Tummy*. New Zealand: Foundation for Peace Studies.

ACKNOWLEDGEMENTS

Thanks to the staff and mediators at Manor Primary school in Stratford, east London, for agreeing to share their stories.

CHAPTER 13

A systemic approach in a primary school

Stuart Livingstone

This chapter illustrates the use of a systemic approach as the foundation of pastoral care in a primary school, with particular reference to how systemics can aid responses to a range of problems in the education of a child with emotional and behavioural difficulties. Although the approach and responses described are based on my own experience with staff and children in a small primary school, much of the chapter is written as a story, with characters who are an amalgam of individuals and situations I have known and worked with over the last twenty years. The story centres around the arrival of Simon in the school and the way the various adults in the school think about and respond to the complex and problematic situations which ensue.

Systemics has its roots in family therapy. Ceccin and Stratton (1991) state that 'systemic expertise is in utilising whatever happens, and bringing it into the debate or conversation involving other people'. They continue: 'We are not offering solutions to problems, but facilitating a conversation which opens up their complexity . . . people indicate areas of trouble, and trouble like pain, is a pointer to the area in which new possibilities are needed.'

Much of a teacher's life is spent presenting the complex in an intellectually digestible way to her charges, using a range of strategies and skills which to an inexperienced practitioner can seem to be plucked from the ether. However, even for experienced teachers, challenging behaviour can provoke linear reactions and a desire for clear, instant cures and solutions.

The tensions created when such solutions are not lasting or forthcoming can be divisive and stressful, provoking feelings of defeat and humiliation, and a belief that the difficult child is only a problem in their class. Other teachers may exacerbate this feeling of failure by commenting or inferring that *they* have no problems with this child. Useful, open dialogue and creating a climate for positive change is thus stifled.

A more systemic approach can be less personally threatening as it can depersonalize the issue, offer a more sympathetic and yet not a maudlin view of the child, and legitimately share the problem collegiately. Just as marking work informs a teacher of a pupil's academic performance, so behaviour can be read, assessed, contextualized and responded to in a thoughtful way by teachers thinking together.

Within systemic disciplines it is the consideration of the individual within the context of wider systems and sub-systems which is important. A primary school is a sub-system of society, and within the confines of a local community it can have considerable influence over the lives of many individuals and families. Simon and his mother may be seen as a significant system within the system of school and the local community.

Primary schools are also unique systems with their own sets of expectations and mores. Where the sub-systems of family and school meet, there can sometimes be institutional and family norms which are at variance with one another. Ideally, a child's transition from home to school is facilitated by the parent's positive acknowledgement of the school, the support and transitional experience of playgroups and nurseries, and any induction processes the school may offer. Family and school are two clearly overlapping dynamic systems, with resistance to change as a common feature to both. In systemic thinking, homeostasis may be defined as the desire for stability and order in an ever-changing system.

The human body, for example, is a dynamic entity which maintains its healthy, constant temperature by endless minor adjustments and monitoring. Environmental changes provoke metabolic responses which in turn incur costs. Hunger leads to feeding, digestion and growth or, if good food is not available, to the utilization of less important resources such as muscle and, eventually, to starvation. The dynamics of school relationships could be seen as akin to regular feeding where hopefully there is safety and growth instead of dislocation and starvation.

Systems commonly resist change because of anticipated pain. Like physiological pain, uncomfortable emotions are avoided by a range of strategies. These can be most keenly observed during periods of great emotional change or transition, e.g. a child starting school, unemployment of a parent, divorce, marriage, remarriage or going to university. Hayes (1991) states: 'Typically, the family will respond to a disruption according to its traditional pattern of interacting and attempt to solve the problems in a similar way.' When family and school systems are healthy and compatible enough, 'a positive feedback loop can be fostered, but sometimes a vicious cycle may develop when a wrong solution is continually applied.' For some children and families then, the transition from home to school can feel quite traumatic.

Systemics is about breaking vicious circles. In schools, pupil/adult, pupil/pupil and adult/adult relationships can get stuck. The discipline of reflection and mindful intervention is central to the systemic approach. Some family therapists rely on working with whatever is present and attempt to take advantage of this. The view is that any positive change will prompt further change; that if relationships are perturbed or 'bumped' by some intervention then the creative process may continue. Rhodes and Ajmal (1995) use the term 'Ripple Effect'.

The fictional professionals within this story illustrate the benefits of such an approach which encourages collegiate sharing and reflection on problems, and which can lead to staff being less inclined to become bogged down in label giving, dismissive excuses and the scapegoating of individual pupils or their families. They are also less prone to wanting to rescue the troubled child single-handed, preferring calmly to ask questions relating to the possible needs of the individual and how each professional best fits into the systems of home, school and greater community. Rhodes and Ajmal (1995) see it as not being afraid to acknowledge problems and yet, with quiet persistent optimism, to set positive goals and look for new ways of moving on.

THE STORY OF SIMON AND HIS TEACHERS

Simon joined Mrs Edwards' class in the middle of the autumn term. He was 8 years old, and a short but handsome, slightly built child, crowned with a thick head of blond hair which rested on a face which ostensibly radiated sweetness and affection.

When not raising her own 3 children and being responsible for her 2 young stepchildren, Mrs Edwards was an experienced teacher who had taught in 4 other schools before being appointed as a classteacher and the school's special educational needs co-ordinator (SENCO) several years previously. She was 1 of 6 teachers in a partially open plan village primary school. The village was largely populated by owner-occupier families, with some council houses and a block of homes owned by a charitable trust.

Although Mrs Edwards was not one to make rapid value judgements, new children joining her established class always gave her a certain sense of foreboding. In Simon's case particularly, the omens were not good. The headteacher, Mrs Thrombosi, had already described her meeting with Mary Kelly, Simon's mother, as strained and unproductive. A telephone call to Simon's previous school had revealed a child with a history of disruptive and violent behaviour leading to a two-day exclusion. The detailed paper work had yet to arrive.

Mrs Edwards knew that potentially the fragile balance of her class was at risk, particularly as she already had two children with behavioural problems. These were two boys on the middle stages of the county's special needs programme. Neil and Dacre were both local boys and had a reputation for inappropriate behaviour which stretched back to playgroup. Mrs Edwards had just begun to get the measure of them. Her relationship with Neil, and Dacre's parents was warm and co-operative, although she soon came to realize that for these parents there was much by the way of good intentions, but little in effective support.

In keeping with all the other parents at the school, Mary Kelly delivered Simon to his class at the start of the school day. The early morning hustle and bustle of a classroom groaning with mothers, fathers and children still aggravated some of the more mature members of staff, whose views held that parents should not be heard or seen; but Mrs Edwards welcomed this arrangement because it gave a valuable five minutes for problems to be aired, and a chance for children to pass on any anxieties via their parents. Increasingly, Mrs Edwards was beginning to pride herself on being able to interpret objectively the interactions of parents and children and their body language. A simple, kind enquiry to any parent or child looking out of sorts would often save her hours of aggravation dealing with pupils who might have more on their minds than learning.

Mary Kelly was about thirty years old and like her son was crowned with blonde hair which had been cut close to her head. She exuded hostility, and a distancing, isolating animosity. She made no eye contact, but kept her head down and dragged Simon into class like a dead mouse, delivering him to his teacher's feet. This unconventional handover left Mrs Edwards bemused and speechless. Before turning to leave, Mary Kelly stooped over Simon and ordered him to give her a kiss. He did so dispassionately on her cheek. She bade him farewell, told him to be good and, without looking back, swept out of the class.

Mrs Edwards had decided that Simon should sit with Nathaniel and Sarah, two quiet, confident children who enjoyed school life. They did not suffer fools gladly, however, and, within 15 minutes and in a moment's exasperation, Nathaniel had pushed Simon, who in turn left his seat, ran around the classroom and kicked several children. Neil had received a particularly unpleasant blow. Their calm familiarity with school routine had obviously had no positive effect on Simon.

The day and the rest of the week saw no improvement. As the paperwork arrived from Simon's previous school, Mrs Edwards' assessment of the boy became increasingly pessimistic. His work was seldom complete and was of a poor standard. He made frequent verbally aggressive comments to his peers, as well as to Mrs Edwards.

Simon's attitude seemed in part to be governed by his mother's moods. As the days progressed, Mary Kelly's behaviour varied between distant aloofness and the now familiar hostility. There were some days when it looked to Mrs Edwards as if Simon and his mother were engaged in some dispute and Simon's time at school merely interfered with the battle's conclusion. On such days Simon was at his worst. Mrs Edwards consistently failed to engage Mary Kelly in conversation.

When Simon's behaviour was challenged (for example, if he was asked to be quiet during an exposition, or to complete a simple academic exercise), he was inclined to say 'No', roll on the floor under his table or run around the classroom. When gently apprehended by Mrs Edwards, he would throw a tantrum, screaming 'You hate me', 'I hate you', 'I don't love you any more', 'You don't love me' and worse. Soothing words and a cuddle could quickly allow his passions to subside, but the calm could be short-lived.

Before Simon's arrival, Mrs Edwards already had 35-year-old Mrs Atkliss, an able and committed teacher assistant, in her class every morning to support Neil and Dacre. However, when Simon arrived, his needs were so great that Mrs Atkliss' time had to be redirected to him.

Simon's papers gave a history of a previous school which had made considerable efforts to integrate and support a severely disaffected child. The school was a small, five-class urban primary school in an affluent part of a nearby town. His behaviour at playgroup had already led to his ultimate exclusion, and for this reason the school had funded an early entry to enable a gradual integration into the routine of classroom life. A scrawled note from Mary Kelly angrily acceded to the early admission, but it was laced with vitriolic statements about being picked on.

The headteacher, Mr Davencourt, had also recorded dates and times of conversations with the Social Services Child Protection Team. One day Simon had come to school with bruising and a scratch on his face which the school had reported. A social worker and a policeman visited Mary Kelly's home. A verdict of unreasonable chastisement was given and the scratch was accepted as an accident. Mary Kelly's view of the school was not enhanced by this event and, in another colourful missive, she declaimed Mr Davencourt and his staff as untrustworthy and vindictive.

With the patient tolerance of the reception teacher and the support of a teaching assistant, Simon had remained in the school. Clearly this was a budgetary expense, and a typed letter from a parent governor revealed a strength of feeling in the local community which viewed Simon's support as an unproductive extravagance. The criticism went on to say that Simon's support was provided because of his behaviour, and other needy, yet docile children received less. Mrs Edwards could find no copy of the headteacher's response, but imagined the growing atmosphere in the community. The school SENCO had tried to have Simon assessed for a Statement of Special Educational Needs.

Mary Kelly had reluctantly agreed to Simon being seen by the educational psychologist, but the resulting report showed her to be wholly unco-operative. The one-to-one interview was described as 'largely unsuccessful as Simon spent a lot of the time rolling on the floor and sweeping the materials from the table top'. The report continued:

At the post-visit interview Mrs Kelly remained oppugnant throughout. She held strongly to the notion that Simon was well adjusted and certainly not 'mad'. She claimed that he was perfectly behaved at home and his outbursts at school were due to insensitive teaching and the provocation of others.

The report concluded with Mary Kelly's refusal to have Simon statemented. To the educational psychologist's surprise, the suggestion of a home visit by a therapist from the child guidance clinic was accepted.

As Mrs Edwards turned the pages of Simon's history, she found a letter from the child guidance clinic thanking Mary Kelly for the useful first home visit and expressing disappointment at her absence for the second. Another letter expressed regret that, as Mary was consistently unavailable, the relationship with the child guidance clinic would have to be terminated.

The file revealed that, as the terms passed, the classteachers and the SENCO struggled on. Simon was put on a behaviour programme. Sitting in his own seat for more than five minutes seemed to be a target that ran for months. A number of the half-termly reports initially provided for parental rewards, but Mrs Edwards noted that these did not last for long. Simon sat alone away from the other children. He was given time out at the start of every session in order to allow the remainder of the class to settle and be quiet. Time for play was limited and adult supported. Mrs Edwards saw a very needy child who could not tolerate change. Perhaps inevitably his Key Stage One Standard Assessment Tasks (SATS) results were poor, all working towards level one, although the two teachers who had taught Simon and the SENCO were of the sincere opinion that he was quite bright and there were signs that his learning difficulties could be associated with dyslexia. Mrs Edwards allowed herself a wry smile, as if Simon did not have enough problems, she thought.

As she closed the file, Mrs Edwards glanced over a letter from Mary Kelly responding to Simon's two-day temporary exclusion for blacking the eye of a stooping midday assistant. Would there ever be a right time, she wondered, to tell Mary Kelly that there were not two r's in bastard!

Mrs Edward's headteacher, Mrs Thrombosi, was herself a former special needs teacher. Her support for children with emotional and behavioural difficulties seemed to tap a deep vein of stubborn and loving commitment for the children in her care. This deep concern plus a number of difficult 'Simons' had prompted her to undertake some training in psychodynamic methodology some years previously. So when Mrs Edwards subsequently made a whimsical request to attend a course on systemic psychology at the Tavistock Clinic in London, Mrs Thrombosi found the money. Over the previous three years Mrs Thrombosi and Mrs Edwards had created a philosophy of pastoral care and management in the school which used systemics to blend behaviourist, transactional and psychodynamic approaches. Under Mrs Thrombosi's leadership a culture of care and mindfulness had grown within the school, with each child being seen as an individual with their own needs and aspirations. For the most part the staff accepted these strictures and found the Thrombosi/Edwards model helpful, particularly in a changing world with parents applying more pressure on staff and some children displaying increasingly challenging behaviours.

Thus the staff acknowledged the concept of children or adults experiencing an Emotional Therapeutic Cycle (Figure 13.1): such that if life deals one of its many blows then the period of recovery is marked by a series of improvements and regressions until the pain is assimilated and gradually becomes part of an individual's psyche.

Mrs Edwards understood this well. She had found the acrimonious breakdown of her 20-year-old marriage caused her much pain. She described her gradual recovery as living with the loss of her marriage and lifestyle, rather than of being cured or being able to forget the pain. In Mrs Edwards' case, such personal experiences sharpened her powers of empathy rather than dulled them.

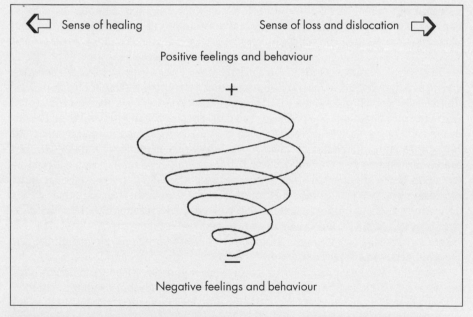

Figure 13.1 A model of an emotional therapeutic spiral. The diagram gives a view of individual growth and change. It shows this as a process rather than a linear progression. When learning new skills and concepts it is often necessary to revisit some point of prior learning. Although reinforcement is an integral part of effective teaching skills, the same principle is not always applied to the emotional development of children. Loss from death, divorce and other transitional experiences can result in dysfunctional behaviour. With a broad spectrum of support from home and school, healing and a greater sense of homeostasis and congruency can occur, but there will still be bad days.

Mrs Edwards knew herself that in the aftermath of a marital breakdown there were days when she felt less depressed and more competent than on others. She also appreciated that, devastating though family dislocation is, having her children and the support of her brother and parents, together with a profession, social status and a reasonable, regular income, helped offer some stability. As time passed, she recognized that she had revisited her pain as well as enjoyed increased healing. She also acknowledged that each period of dislocation was marginally less hurtful than the last.

Understanding this, Mrs Edwards wondered whether Simon and his mother enjoyed a network of support from family and friends. She suspected that, as Simon and Mary Kelly recovered from one catastrophe, life inflicted another. She had a vision of the Kellys being engaged in a giant game of snakes and ladders with rotten ladders and a plethora of snakes. She had seen it before with children in her care. It was time for a chat with Simon's old headteacher.

Mrs Thrombosi's acceptance of systemics gave teachers like Mrs Edwards considerable authority to take control of children in their care, although the emphasis was on teamwork, problem-solving discussion and consensus. In this, the classteacher was seen as a key worker with a child, sympathetic colleagues as part of the supportive team, and the headteacher as the supervisory figure. Following systemic discipline, Mrs Thrombosi seldom saw parents alone. She would ask how can an individual react, judge and make professional decisions all at once, particularly when dealing with emotionally complex issues. Thus one professional would talk, while another would listen, observe and reflect.

In systemic terms, schools are in a privileged and yet perilous interface between complex and dynamic agencies. Children attend school away from their families by dint of laws over a hundred years old. Most of these children value school and attend with little compunction. The police, the social services, the medical authorities and, most particularly, the philosophies of the incumbent government in part meet and find expression in school. Mrs Thrombosi often felt she walked a tightrope, her mandate swinging precariously with each child she dealt with. However, with a keen eye on her educational goals, and being careful not to fall off, or worse be knocked off, she would gently and carefully make her way forward. The assistance of her colleagues, their thoughts, reactions and reflections would help her keep balance with the more challenging cases.

So when Mrs Thrombosi telephoned Simon's previous headteacher, Mr Davencourt, Mrs Edwards was introduced on the other line, and listened in to the conversation. Mr Davencourt was a deeply caring and sensitive headteacher in his late fifties. He held traditional views about discipline and children's place within the school. Simon's behaviour had shaken him considerably. Both the chaos of the child and the hostility of the mother had seriously challenged him.

He spoke with regret about Simon's troubled life as if somehow he, Mr Davencourt, should have been able to make the boy whole or better. He sounded almost apologetic for inflicting Simon on Mrs Thrombosi, and kept saying that the boy needed to be in a special school or have counselling. If only I had had more time for him, he lamented. As he related Simon's history, Mrs Thrombosi and Mrs Edwards gained some unexpected insights. Simon was Mary Kelly's only living child, although a late termination of pregnancy had been rumoured some two years ago. Nigel, Simon's father, was unemployed and had been around periodically during Simon's life. Mary Kelly was a bully and was known to have a volatile temper which was directed at any suitable victim, most commonly Nigel. Simon was witness to these violent rows and on one occasion saw Nigel cut across the arm with a kitchen knife. It was this attack that led to Nigel leaving the family home for the sixth time, in an atmosphere of intense rancour. In all disputes Simon was expected to be the ally and confident of both sides, an impossible position. When unable to abuse each other at close quarters, Simon was used as an emotional pawn. On one particularly bad Saturday evening Nigel, in an attempt to see Simon, kicked in the door of the family home and tried to take Simon away. Mary Kelly screamed abuse at Nigel during a public dispute in which Simon's love for one, or the other, was at stake.

A restraining order on Nigel Kelly stopped any further spectacular arguments. However, Mary's animosity towards him continued in a custody dispute that required many visits to solicitors and an eventual settlement by the courts. Meanwhile, Mary continued a campaign of misinformation against him in order to draw Simon further in to her camp.

The courts deigned that Simon should see his father away from the family home once a week for an evening and a night. Departure times to be with his father became increasingly fraught for Simon. Mary tried a range of approaches to sabotage the contact visits from intimidation to tearful emotional blackmail. Nigel Kelly's access visits became more and more erratic. His predisposition to depression worsened with the ongoing battle. Simon's temporary exclusion precipitated individual visits to the school by both parents. Mary was virtually incoherent with rage and Nigel at his lowest ebb was quite maudlin. Mr Davencourt observed that Nigel smelt of drink. These interviews gave Mr Davencourt a tragic insight into Simon's unhappy life. He admitted that he felt impotent.

Later that evening Nigel Kelly arrived at the family home, although this was not the appointed access evening. Mary was, as usual, less than pleased to see him and was, according to the police report, baffled by Nigel's insistence on retrieving an unused tow rope from a cupboard. In order to make her disapproval as plain as possible, she sent Simon to find the rope. This he did and he handed it to his father, who appeared preoccupied until his point of departure, when he pulled out £400 and thrust the new notes into Simon's hand. Nigel hugged Simon fondly and said goodbye. Early the next morning at about 2.00 a.m. Nigel hanged himself from a beam in his mother's garage. This was three days after Simon's seventh birthday. Simon was not allowed to attend the funeral of his father. Mary said she could not face 'his lot' and besides Simon was too young for this sort of thing.

Mrs Thrombosi and Mrs Edwards put down their telephone receivers with a sense of numbness and foreboding. They felt great sympathy for all those who had dealt with Simon and admired Mr Davencourt and his staff for their sustained compassion. 'Well,' said Mrs Edwards, every inch a convert to systemics, 'let's press on.'

PROMOTING THOUGHTFUL CHANGE

With unpleasant and complex problems, starting to thoughtfully precipitate positive change is more important than worrying about where to start, or being intimidated by the size and irksome nature of the task ahead. Although they appreciated that incautious responses can make a situation worse, Mrs Edwards and Mrs Thrombosi knew that doing nothing is also a decision which has outcomes and consequences.

A group of interested professionals involved in the process of resolving a problem is described by Papp (1983) as a Greek Chorus or Consultation Group. Behind this process is the notion that truth is relative. Mason (1989) states:

> there are many ways of looking at the same thing, and if you look at something from a different perspective, it can have different meanings. We often get caught up with believing there is only one way of looking at something.

'Huddling' was an accurate, if sentimental, description of Consultation Groups within Mrs Thrombosi's school. Any group of professionals or para-professionals might decide to meet to discuss plans to move on a stuck problem; although within this culture of common intellectual property, problems and solutions were regarded as inextricably enmeshed, so that any solution – be it pro-active or passive – could in its turn create further problems. Hence the Therapeutic Cycle had to be seen over the longer term. So when Mrs Thrombosi organized a 'huddle' to discuss Simon, she found that Mrs Edwards (Simon's classteacher), Mrs Tube (the school welfare assistant) and Mrs Atkliss (classroom assistant) all expressed a keen desire to attend. Prior to the meeting, Mrs Edwards had collated a picture of Simon's academic profile. His responses to tasks reflected a child with poor self-esteem, although his performance at different times varied wildly, even when doing the same assignment. Mrs Thrombosi regarded 'huddling' as a process which can inform any problem or formal procedure, such as special educational needs (SEN) programmes, staff meetings and official contacts with other agencies. There was no bar on any individual calling such a meeting.

Mrs Thrombosi and Mrs Edwards had created a format for these meetings which was flexible, but directed the thoughts of those participating towards creating a picture of the child's present emotional and behavioural state. This sharing of information would ultimately lead to possible interventions, which could then be further discussed or reviewed in another 'huddle' or in a staff meeting later. The format for 'huddling' consisted of a series of open-ended questions which borrowed from behaviourist, transactional and psychodynamic philosophies, linked together with systemic ideas, with a view to implementing change in a thoughtful and strategic way. Prompt sheets (see below) helped direct the debate.

From the behaviourist perspective, a detailed picture of Simon's behaviour and the situations which provoked his unacceptable reactions would inform the creation of an effective behaviour modification programme.

From the psychodynamic perspective, staff would try to give some definition to the various feelings he evoked. Using this understanding of how he affected others, they would hope to gain insight into his needs, and how they might helpfully become part of his therapeutic cycle.

A disciple of transactional analysis would, with the systemisist, want to look at the nature of his relationships in and out of school to see if any individuals could be allied with the school to help support him.

The systemisist would also want to consider the overall situation objectively and strategically in order to select the most likely responses to implement change. Even if the next step was unclear, a systemisist would wish to perturb the existing situation sufficiently to give further information, which may later help in the development of a more effective intervention. Within the context of the school, consideration would also be given to cost and time effectiveness, particularly in light of the needs of other children.

The systemisist would also be looking for non-interventions on the 'if it ain't broke don't fix it' rule of thumb. This may be to allocate resources elsewhere, or perhaps to allow greater time for reflection.

Prompt Sheet 1: Family system and transactions

Those present at meeting: Mrs Thrombosi (head), Mrs Edwards (classteacher/ SENCO), Mrs Tube (welfare assistant), Mrs Atkliss (teaching assistant)

S1. Has the child suffered significant emotional dislocations during his life?
Simon has experienced death by suicide, separation by divorce and physical impoverishment.

S2. The function of the pupil's relationships:
How clear are the emotional boundaries?
Are the caring adults permissive with the child (allowing free rein), authoritarian or balanced?
Are they consistent, inconsistent or in conflict, e.g. permissive father authoritarian mother, or inconsistent and in conflict, etc.?
Unclear and variable mother–son relationship. Sometimes Simon is treated as a son who is expected to be wholly obedient and passive, then without warning his mother assumes him to be a natural confident and ally. Under these circumstances Simon is often treated as a quasi-adult partner. Simon's own feelings are often not acknowledged nor are his emotional needs met, e.g. not going to the funeral of his father.

Simon's mother is bullying, controlling and fickle. On many occasions she will quite unpredictably accede to Simon's wishes if this gives her pleasure, e.g. giving him his Christmas present in early December.

S3. Genogram (family tree showing relationships) (Figure 13.2)

S4. Known significant others in subject child's life at present

Elizabeth
In class Simon looks up to Elizabeth (age 8) who is considered by staff to be a self-assured and loving child and an excellent role model. She is academically very proficient, and has displayed tolerance and calm when dealing with Simon's outbursts. Elizabeth has a wide range of friends amongst both boys and girls. She deals amicably with all of them and is considered popular.

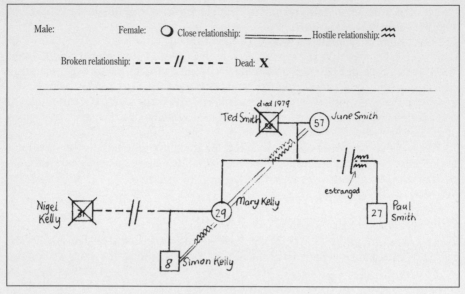

Figure 13.2   Genogram (family tree showing relationships)

Mrs Tube
Mrs Tube has a warm relationship with Simon. He has at least one minor injury or ailment a day in order to create an opportunity to see her.

Prompt Sheet 2: A behaviourist view

B1. Describe in behavioural terms what the child does in a given school environment, e.g. assembly, class, playground, hall periods. Describe an incident as if you were watching it on television.

16 December 1.45 p.m. Hall period for gym
Simon had spent the first 15 minutes of the afternoon session with Mrs Atkliss (teaching assistant) in the library quietly reading, to allow a calming end to the lunch period and promote a transition to the afternoon session.

Mrs Atkliss was committed to another class at 1.30 p.m., so Simon was left to cope on his own during the changing period and in the hall. When Mrs Atkliss handed Simon over to Mrs Edwards, he met her with a smile and allowed her to hold his hand. Mrs Edwards guided him to his seat at a desk away from the other children. She instructed the class to put away their reading books, and one group at a time to collect their PE bags. Standing in the doorway to the classroom, Mrs Edwards could supervise both the cloakroom and the imbroglio of children upending their PE bags and getting changed. Simon became particularly impatient to collect his PE bag when he saw Neil and Dacre get theirs. Mrs Edwards crouched before Simon, made eye contact and verbally rehearsed his expected behaviour.

'Simon, you may get your PE bag, but go straight to your peg, collect your bag and come straight back to me.' She made him verbally repeat the instruction, which he did returning her gaze.

He walked directly to his peg and, finding it empty, he turned to Dacre who was holding a bag with an identical logo and snatched it off him. Dacre offered minor resistance by pulling the bag to himself and protesting loudly, saying, 'Hey, Simon, this is my bag, you get off.' In less time than it took Mrs Edwards to walk the four paces to the scene of the incident Simon had called Dacre 'a fucking liar' and kicked him on the shin. Dacre burst into floods of tears. Mrs Edwards admonished Simon, comforted Dacre, found Simon's bag on the ground where he had left it last time, and placed the snivelling and struggling (albeit superficially) Simon on the class calming-down chair for five minutes.

Simon's bag only furnished him with a pair of shorts, a T-shirt, which was too small, and two left-footed plimsolls. After assuring Mrs Edwards he was calm, Simon took off his own shirt and started to walk without purpose around the class bare-chested. Mrs Edwards retrieved Simon and he held hands with Mrs Edwards as the class lined up and entered the hall. Upon the instruction to find a place and sit down, Mrs Edwards released her grip on Simon's hand. Simon left Mrs Edwards' side running as fast as he could, circumnavigated the hall in seconds, threw himself on a pile of mats, rolled on the floor accidentally knocking Neil off his feet, picked himself up, cast a fearful glance at Mrs Edwards and dived under a dining hall table.

B2. If all were well with this child, what would you see happening on the television?
Simon would enter the class at the end of lunchtime, collect a number of library books from the book trolley, and read the books silently. He would go straight to Mrs Edwards to have his reading listened to and assessed. He would put his books away when instructed and prepare for PE, go to his peg, ask another child to assist him in looking for his PE bag and, if unsuccessful, would inform Mrs Edwards. With the correct PE clothes in his bag, he would change quickly for PE and line up with the rest of the children. When instructed, he would walk into the hall and sit down in a suitable space alone, with his arms folded and legs crossed. He would look at the teacher and await further direction.

B3. If one thing improved, however small, what would that be?
Simon would get his PE bag and seek appropriate assistance if he failed to find it.

Prompt Sheet 3: A psychodynamic perspective

P1. What feelings does this child leave you with?
Confusion, anger, loss, frustration, emptiness, fear of losing control/need to control, concern.

P2. What chord does this strike in your own feelings and behaviour?

Mrs Edwards
Losing control, unreconciled loss, fear, disappointment, lack of trust. Memories of a period of being badly bullied as a child at school and her teacher's and mother's lack of support. Same sense of confusion in the last years of her first marriage where all actions seemed to be wrong – this leading perhaps to an over-sympathy for Simon's

behaviour and an unreasonable acceptance and tolerance, bearing in mind the needs of the other 31 children in the class.

Mrs Thrombosi
A fear of losing control, of being alone managing the control. Mrs Thrombosi accepted there was a deeper controlling side to her character which in part seemed to suit her for headship. As the youngest of four siblings and an apparent family planning miscalculation, Mrs Thrombosi had spent her childhood making sure her older siblings' needs did not overwhelm her. A judicious blend of bullying, charm, wit, humour, thoughtfulness, seduction, patience, short-term compromise and pathos all gave Mrs Thrombosi the edge when dealing with her siblings, her mother and, as the only girl, her father. However, her grip on the situation was as glorious and as precarious as a surfer on the crest of a wave. Mrs Thrombosi wanted to control Simon too much and too quickly.

Mrs Atkliss
Feelings of distrust and fear of losing control.

Mrs Tube
Feelings of vulnerability, great loss and hurt. Although at times she could be manipulative and seductive, there was an underlying willingness to give comfort and love, and an ability to express gratitude and affection. A great hunger for unconditional love, including control. She found Simon a likeable boy.

P3. Will this be a help or a hindrance in further developing your professional relationship with the child? Are there personal needs that may interfere with your judgements and actions?

Mrs Edwards
Some hindrances: over-protective. Transferred feelings from the past: I wish my mummy had protected me as much as I can look after you, Simon.

Mrs Thrombosi
Some hindrances. Over-reaction. Transferred feelings from the past: You are like my older brother during a difficult phase when I was 9 and he was 13. That was the last time anyone defeated me. It was very painful after nine solid years of precarious rule.

Mrs Atkliss
Some hindrances. Intimidated by the violence of the child's reactions.

Mrs Tube
Some help. As a welfare assistant with no class responsibilities and opportunity to give time to Simon that was reliable, firm and unconditionally loving. They could have a chat.

P4. What are the child's behaviours a defence against?
The consensus was fear – of further losses, of confronting loss (i.e. death of father), of taking responsibility for mother and the disorder she projects.

P5. Using emotional age as a model, at what level is the child functioning in class?
Two years old – maybe three, with a massive veneer of sophistication, having witnessed extreme adult emotions without being given contextualizing support and love. Arguably, in the same way, Mary Kelly behaves like a young, capricious adolescent. More of a sister to Simon than a mother. This too should be taken into account when dealing with her.

The strategy: What next?

St.1. Who else could be involved, co-opted, perturbed, etc. to assist in the process of positive change and who is best placed to make an intervention?
Examples are parents, peers, siblings, grandparents, other professional agencies, education welfare officer (EWO), school nurse, local police, social services, senior managers or governors.

Mrs Tube
Take time out to chat with Simon to gain further insights into his emotional state and his attitude to learning. Simon should be the best judge of what is of benefit for him.

Mrs Thrombosi
Try to provoke a dialogue with mother in the first instance and any other family member if this fails (Grandmother is local and looks a promising point of contact). The EWO to be contacted as soon as possible to bring the news of any possible or actual exclusion to the mother's notice.

Mrs Thrombosi to take a hard line, maybe even enforcing a temporary exclusion if Simon's behaviour becomes too anti-social – to focus the mother's mind on the reality of the problem. In contrast to Mrs Thrombosi, the EWO to try to form an alliance with the mother to work together to reduce Simon's difficulties. This can be described as a strategic one-down, whereby the professionals reframe their mandate as a problem to be shared. The EWO presents herself as the kind stranger (ensuring at all times to keep in contact with Mrs Thrombosi so as to check against taking sides with Mary Kelly against the school), whilst Mrs Thrombosi sets the firm boundaries.

Mrs Atkliss
To offer warm, non-judgemental contact with Mary Kelly. To try to form a supportive alliance in light of the institutional pressures Mrs Thrombosi is bringing to bear. Again a strategic one-down. Perhaps presenting herself as a kindly older sister with a mutual family concern.

Mrs Edwards
To implement a behaviour modification programme which keeps Simon in his seat and allows him short, specific excursions around the class to fulfil particular tasks.

To arrange with senior midday assistant to limit time in playground to five minutes' supervised play and the rest of the time walking around with Mrs Brickette, an experienced and motherly midday assistant. Simon's programme to encourage successful playtimes and lunchtimes.

The story continues

Mrs Tube talks to Simon
The day after the 'huddle' Mrs Tube casually offered Simon time out of class for a chat. He accepted gladly and spoke with a self-awareness and assurance which initially shocked her. He began to talk about the death of his father, expressing the unreconciled pain and devastation of a profound bereavement, which no adult in his life so far had taken time to acknowledge. His mother, having destroyed all material evidence of Nigel Kelly's existence (possibly preoccupied with her own loss and guilt, speculated Mrs Tube), studiously refused to talk about the subject, as did his maternal grandmother. In addition to being excluded from the funeral, Mrs Tube ascertained that Simon had never visited his father's grave.

Simon alluded to a life at home full of conflict, rage and chaos. Mrs Tube reflected to herself that this was possibly a strategy Mary Kelly had adopted for many years and now repeated to cope with her loss and guilt.

Simon spoke of his grandmother with some affection, although he was inclined to parrot his mother's criticisms about his grandfather, who had died before he was born. Mrs Tube wondered whether perhaps Mary had been abused in some way.

After the meeting, Mrs Tube made notes and fed back her ideas to a listening colleague in order to help her clarify her thoughts and feelings on the matter. Writing a short summary of the interaction also eased her own intellectual and emotional processes.

Mrs Tube's notion was to contact Mary Kelly to see if Simon could visit his father's grave, a suggestion from Simon himself. Mrs Thrombosi supported Mrs Tube's attempt to contact Mary Kelly, but things did not work out as she had hoped. Mrs Tube's opening gambit that Simon was not happy at school was met with a terse, 'If you think he is unhappy, what about me?' Thereafter the telephone hung up.

Mrs Thrombosi makes an authoritative clear 'one-up' posture with Mary Kelly
After the rebuttal of Mrs Tube, and in the light of Simon's continued disruptive behaviour, Mrs Thrombosi wrote a severe letter to Mary Kelly 'scolding' her for her lack of co-operation. She began with a blunt résumé of the main points of the class behaviour observation, and finished with a threat of exclusion and reports to the governing body.

Mrs Atkliss and Mrs Edwards try to ally themselves with Mary (strategic 'one-down')
Mrs Atkliss and Mrs Edwards continued to implement and modify Simon's behaviour programme. They also set themselves the target of making eye contact with Mary Kelly every day, and if possible engaging her in conversation.

Mrs Atkliss enjoyed some success at a perfunctory level, but the arrival of Mrs Thrombosi's letter seemed to provoke despair rather than the more usual retaliation. The next day when Mrs Edwards made eye contact with Mary Kelly she seemed poised to talk, but then in the confusion of the morning arrivals she appeared to become inhibited.

Mary's mother speaks to Mrs Thrombosi by telephone
Later that morning, a slightly agitated grandmother rang to ask Mrs Thrombosi why she had been sending letters to her daughter Mary – getting her all upset. Mrs Thrombosi suggested a meeting, with the grandmother, Mary Kelly, Mrs Edwards, Mrs Atkliss, Mrs Tube, Simon and herself. This seemed to relieve Mary's mother who quickly tried to form a coalition with Mrs Thrombosi against Mary, describing her as a wayward girl who deserved her unhappiness. Simon was evidently part of a very dysfunctional family web. Mrs Thrombosi also took the opportunity to tell the grandmother of Mrs Tube's findings relating to Simon's pain over his father's death. Mary's mother listened and sounded as if she was accepting the information – albeit like someone facing up to a much procrastinated and distasteful task. Mary's mother agreed to the meeting and said she would try to get Mary to attend.

Mrs Edwards talks to Simon and tells him of Mrs Thrombosi's arbitration with his grandmother
Mrs Edwards explained to Simon that he would also be invited to the meeting, so that his feelings could be made known to his mother and grandmother in a safe way. Simon seemed to realize that for once his emotions had been recognized and found empathy. In addition, his mother and grandmother were taking time out of their lives to come to school to discuss *him*.

In the week prior to the meeting, Simon's behaviour improved. He felt sufficiently confident to complete the demands of his behaviour programme with relative ease – a programme which at its inception had been quite challenging for him.

The meeting
In her usual way Mrs Thrombosi had a prepared formula to guide the meeting. Mrs Atkliss would meet Mary and her mother after keeping Simon behind at the close of school. In addition, Mrs Edwards, Mrs Tube and Mrs Atkliss would be present early in the meeting room to facilitate a friendly, relaxed atmosphere. Their role at this stage was to initiate some light conversation which did not include any of the problems of the moment. During this chat Mrs Edwards' role was to listen carefully for any remarks or behaviours which might be helpful to remember later in the official discussion with Mrs Thrombosi. In the meeting room Simon sat down calmly between his mother and grandmother with a slight look of adoration. Mrs Tube tried to guide the conversation towards the lives of those present and to Simon's life in particular. She tried to elicit points of commonality between Simon's family and those present, without being patronizing. The hidden agenda of the 'problem-free talk' was not just to get information, but also to set the tenor of the meeting which was to be non-judgemental, co-operative and problem-solving.

So that her presence would not interrupt the flow of conversation at the beginning of such meetings, Mrs Thrombosi always ensured that she had to complete some tasks before entering the room. She would also leave the meeting room door open so she might judge when to interrupt the conversation without undermining its purpose. She maintained a calm, warm, but authoritative demeanour as she entered the meeting place after the informal beginning.

The formal part of the meeting and setting the agenda

Mrs Thrombosi sat down and welcomed everyone thanking them for their presence. This gave Mrs Edwards her cue to cheerily give a résumé of any positive disclosures relating to Simon and his family from the 'problem-free talk'. Mrs Thrombosi then set out the agenda of the meeting clearly. It was to find solutions to answer the threat of Simon's exclusion. This meeting was not for critical argument or posturing.

Highlighting the abilities and strengths of character of those present, most particularly the child

Beginning by highlighting his strengths, together with giving examples of when he had successfully overcome problems, was important for Simon as well as for his mother and grandmother to hear. As both Mary Kelly and her mother also presented themselves as vulnerable and childlike, their strengths were also celebrated whenever possible. For example, Mrs Atkliss appreciated Simon's sense of humour and wondered whether perhaps this good side of his nature was inherited from Mary. Mary warmed to this suggestion, although her mother attempted to discredit it. Mrs Thrombosi continued by reflecting the various positive views back to Simon and asking him how he felt about them and if he had anything to add. Establishing Simon's own views and wishes was important, both in terms of valuing him as an individual and to set a supportive background to the more difficult task ahead relating to his behaviour. Mrs Thrombosi asked Mary and the others present to confirm his views. Again Mary's mother tried to be disparaging, but this time Mary bade her be quiet.

Triadic Questioning

The systemic approach of Triadic Questioning was much favoured by Mrs Thrombosi. It is in many ways like gossiping in the presence of the subject, or like an emotional version of reading a first draft of someone's ideas. Simon had only to confirm or add to the deluge of praise and sympathetic remarks going on around him. Mrs Thrombosi found that children responded well to having their feelings or ideas suggested to them in a coherent way – to which they only had to agree or disagree – and that fitting a structure to these reflections made a response more focused.

Another technique favoured by Mrs Thrombosi was that of the 'Miracle Question' (Rhodes and Ajmal 1995), which encourages reflection on an ideal outcome. Mrs Thrombosi directed the question at each of the adults present in a Triadic manner (in front of the others):

> If, after Simon goes to bed tonight a miracle happens, and the problems he has brought here today are all solved while he is asleep, when you woke up how would you know? What would be different? What would he be doing differently? How would you know that the miracle had happened?

O'Hanlon and Weiner Davies (1989) describe a similar Video Description Question:

> If Simon had solved his problems and a video was made of his problem-free life, what would we be seeing and what would he be doing?

Mrs Thrombosi asked the question of Mrs Edwards, Mrs Atkliss and Mrs Tube as well as asking Mary and her mother for their views. She constantly noted and fed back the suggestions, and asked for affirmation from the others – with comments such as 'So what you are saying is . . .' or 'This is very good. If I understand you correctly you are saying . . .'. She always ensured that Simon had listened and understood, and that he was given time to add to or correct the views of those around him. MrsThrombosi praised all positive remarks and insisted on clarity and consensus.

When it came to reviewing the details of the behaviour expectations and programme (in relation to the threat of exclusion) against this positive background, the experience was much more bearable and hopeful. Mrs Thrombosi had made a list of positive and hoped-for changes, and in many ways these reflected the findings of his behaviour management programme. Mary's mother would be meeting and taking Simon to school on a regular basis so that she and his teacher could monitor his progress at first hand, and so that he could feel the adults in his life supporting him together. Mrs Thrombosi recapped at the end of the meeting, and fed back to Simon the suggestions and the reflections on his recent improvements.

Just as at the start of the meeting so Mrs Thrombosi would arrange a 'buffer' at the end. She would ostensibly finish the meeting but not get up to leave immediately, allowing time for more informal and relaxed comments to arise. Mary stood up to go and put her arm on Simon's shoulder. At the door she addressed those present in a voice that was controlled and choked with emotion: 'I've got a miracle . . . that his dad would come back and tell him it wasn't Simon's fault for giving him the rope . . . or mine.' Mary Kelly and Simon fled the scene. Mary's mother gave Mrs Thrombosi a thunderous glance as if to say now look what you've stirred up. She too left with a flourish.

Subsequent events
Immediately afterwards
The following weekend Simon went with his mother and grandmother to lay flowers on his father's grave.

The next week he finished two pieces of work and hung his PE bag up. He played for 10 minutes with Elizabeth on one day that week, and sat quietly next to her when a story was being read. He was able to walk into the hall and sit down ready for gym. His mother had provided him with new plimsolls. Mary's mother had heard him read twice and wrote positive remarks in his home school contact book.

Mrs Thrombosi told Mary that the threat of immediate exclusion had been lifted. In addition, Mrs Thrombosi explored the availability of support from therapists at the local child guidance clinic and from bereavement counsellors.

Mrs Thrombosi gave the information to Mrs Edwards who shared it with Mary one day when she was in a good mood. Mary agreed in principle to the external support, although she clearly was not keen. Mrs Atkliss was delegated the task of gently extolling the virtues of therapy.

A few weeks later
Mary failed to turn up to all but the first meeting at the child guidance clinic. She claimed that the therapist was odd and that the other children met in passing there

were mad and frightening. The bereavement counsellors received no call from her at all.

Nevertheless, Simon was one spiral up on his journey of healing. The taboo subject of his father's death was now safely held by the school, enabling Mrs Tube to talk to Simon further about his father when she sensed he wanted to. This seemed to have the tacit approval of Mary's mother.

'You do what you can for the poor little thing. Mary doesn't mind,' she whispered to Mrs Atkliss. Fortunately, Mary did agree with her mother on this matter. Simon was never quite as badly behaved again. Mary Kelly had started to come to terms with his needs and generally attended his SEN review meetings. School had proven itself a safe place of learning, growing and healing, populated with trustworthy adults.

Two months later
The week Simon regressed was the week Mary Kelly's new boyfriend moved in – an attractive, muscular male divorcee some twenty years her senior. He stood proudly at the school gate with an immodestly dressed Mary Kelly, who was hanging on his arm and looking up at him in stupefied adoration.

'Father substitute?' wryly murmured Mrs Edwards as she strode out to meet the new beau.

'Where do you get your energy from?' smiled Mrs Atkliss.

'Two minutes' effort now saves two hours later,' replied Mrs Edwards, skipping out of the classroom and smiling broadly. 'I'm off to make eye contact. It is time to ally myself with "Mr Hunk" out there.'

ON USING A SYSTEMIC APPROACH IN SCHOOLS

It may be argued that a systemic approach has a number of attributes which, although not exclusive to this discipline, identify a particular way of dealing with relationships in schools. These are that:

1. Change is unavoidable, with humans struggling to achieve stability and homeostasis.
2. Behaviour is largely defensive and part of the process of trying to reach homeostasis. Behaviour should be read, contextualized and responded to in terms of change and relationships. For example, what are the emotional boundaries between individuals and what changes may have provoked particular behaviours?
3. Relationships can be seen in terms of alliances which are creative or coalitions which are arbitrary, unstructured, unfocused and usually to someone's detriment, e.g. a gang of bullies.
4. Systemics is a practice which borrows from many psychological disciplines. Counselling skills are of paramount importance with their emphasis on listening, empathy and feeding back information. These are defined by Jacobs (1982) as offering 'undivided attention'.
5. Consideration of transference (feelings and expectations transferred from a past ongoing relationship into a present relationship/situation), counter-transference (possibly unhelpful resonances with our own vulnerabilities/

expectations derived from our past relationships), and projection (unacknowledged/unbearable feelings/parts being located/criticized in others rather than in ourselves) are also important – as highlighted by Salzberger-Wittenberg, Henry and Osborne (1983). The use of behaviourist processes to encourage positive behaviour have also been mentioned.

6. The purpose of systemics is to facilitate affirming experiences for troubled children and to help those involved to see a purpose and pattern in a child's behaviour – hence viewing the child and behaviour in more positive and creative terms. For example, Rhodes and Ajmal (1995) suggest: 'In one case a boy's crying was seen as a possible sign of intelligence and sensitivity as opposed to disturbance and awkwardness.'

7. Practitioners should be clear about their actions, the purpose of their actions and the hoped-for outcomes – and whether indeed they have a mandate to proceed. Even coping and doing nothing are strategies if applied thoughtfully.

8. Decisions are seldom usefully made by one person, although one person may direct a dialogue. Systemics is against exclusivity. Teamwork is paramount. Roles and purposes may change depending on circumstances. In one intervention the headteacher may take a cold authoritative stance in order to police a situation. In another, this very authority may be the security a troubled child or parent needs to confront change. Each situation is unique with an ebb and flow of key workers carrying out clear tasks with a child in order to enable them to get the maximum benefit from their education.

9. In essence, systemic practice in schools is mindful of the needs of all those involved in the process of educating children. Systemics is a thoughtful discipline giving consideration to systems, sub-systems and the relationships which interact within and between them.

CONCLUSION

All children are entitled to a broad and balanced curriculum and to have an opportunity to fulfil their potential, but we forget that this is very much an emotional as well as an intellectual process. Where children are sorely troubled and where the systems and relationships surrounding children are chaotic, inconsistent, violent or insecure, they will not be able to hold their own emotions in check and make use of the broad and balanced curriculum to fulfil their potential. Salzberger-Wittenberg, Henry and Osborne (1983) describe the teacher–pupil relationship in these terms:

If the student is . . . realistic he may hope that the person in charge has enough authority to control violence, set limits on unreasonable behaviour, [and] treat destructiveness, negligence and sloth with benevolent firmness thereby allowing the more constructive elements of the personality and that of others in the group to come to the fore. It is the wish for the kindly but firm teacher who has enough belief in the good qualities of his pupils to set high standards, yet is not so stern as to intimidate them or show no forbearance at their inevitable mistakes and human failings.

I believe it is the constant striving to understand behaviour, in the context of the various and overlapping systems surrounding the child, coupled with forbearance and a belief in the underlying good qualities of children, which is at the core of systemic practice in schools.

REFERENCES

Ceccin, G. and Stratton, P. (1991) Extending systemic consultation from families to managing human systems. *Journal of Systemic Consultation and Management,* 2, 3–13.

Hayes, H. (1991) Re-introduction to family therapy: classification of three schools. *Journal of Family Therapy,* 12(1), 27–43.

Jacobs, M. (1982) *O Still Small Voice: An Introduction to Pastoral Counselling.* London: SPCK.

Mason, B. (1989) *Handing Over: Developing Consistency across Shifts in Residential and Health Settings.* London: DC Publishing.

O'Hanlon, W. and Weiner Davies, M. (1989) *In Search of Solutions.* London: Norton.

Papp, P. (1983) *The Process of Change.* New York: Guilford Press.

Rhodes, J. and Ajmal, Y. (1995) *Solution-Focused Thinking in Schools: Behaviour, Reading and Organisation.* London: BT Press.

Salzberger-Wittenberg, I., Henry, G. and Osborne, E. (1983) *The Emotional Experience of Learning and Teaching.* London: Routledge and Kegan Paul.

FURTHER READING

Dinkmeyer, D. and McKay, G. D. (1997) *The Parents Handbook: Systematic Training for Effective Parenting.* New York: Random House.

Herbert, C. (1995) *Bullying: A Quick Guide.* London: Daniels.

Peterson, L. (1995) Stop think do! Treating and preventing social behaviour in school. *Pastoral Care in Education,* 13(2), 17–22.

Wright, A., Hinton, S., Reason, R. and Fredrickson, N. (1991) *Developing Self-Discipline, Motivation, Self Esteem, Co-operation and Social Competence.* University College London Educational Psychology Publishing.

CHAPTER 14

Containing and modifying anxieties: on having an educational therapist in a primary school

Angela Greenwood

Some children have almost unbearable anxieties which are easily triggered into repeated and troublesome behaviour patterns or learning inhibitions, anxieties both within themselves and within the responses they evoke in others. It is only when these anxieties can be held and safely contained in someone else, and can begin to be thought about and understood, that children do not continually need to repeat the unhelpful patterns, or stay locked in their helplessness. Having a therapist in a primary school can provide opportunities for such containment through individual or group therapy for those who need it, and through fostering the growth of secure, understanding environments both in the school as a whole and in the classes. Thinking together about children's difficulties can increase teachers' capacities to bear, understand and respond helpfully to children's hurts, fears and problems. This chapter describes and discusses the benefits of having a Special Educational Needs Co-ordinator (SENCO) who is also an educational therapist in a primary school.

'Remember me?' came a voice from over the road.

'Tolston!' I said, 'My, you've grown. Yes, of course I remember you. It's good to see you. What are you up to?'

'Did you hear I ended up at St Francis?'

'Yes, I did actually.'

'I got really bad at the High School. I couldn't work. I ended up in lots of trouble.'

'It's strange. I was just thinking about you the other day. There was you and Grant. I remember that wonderful play you created with Grant on the tape recorder. Such imagination! I knew you should have been able to learn, but I just didn't have the skills then to help you in the way that you needed. I'm so sorry for the hard time you had at the High School. I can't change that now. But you know, it was your difficulties which prompted me to train as an educational therapist, a special training to help me work with young people like you . . . young people who have got good brains, but who have got something on their minds which gets in the way of their learning. So I would like to thank you. I wasn't much help to you; but you really set me thinking. It's good to see you again.'

He smiled, 'It's good to see you, miss.'

Where children have been abused, over-controlled or traumatized, their underlying feelings of being no good, hurt or angry will always be there in the background, inhibiting their ability to benefit from or even take in good experiences. In such cases, even very well-structured and interesting special needs support may be ineffective, despite a child's intelligence.

Educational therapy seeks to help these children by providing a space where they can begin to express their preoccupations and have them safely contained and gradually understood, at the same time as working on their learning inhibitions and difficulties. This 'containment' is not just about setting and enforcing boundaries. Paul Greenhalgh (1994) describes it as 'the holding or containment of disturbing feelings and anxieties' both in the child and in oneself, 'demonstrating that one can have a relationship with difficult feelings other than being possessed by them, by showing that a difficult feeling can be lived with, thought about and understood'. This experience gradually enables the child to internalize the 'container' for herself 'producing a mind that can hold thought'.

So educational therapy gives children an opportunity to grow into experiencing a relationship of love and trust which survives the bad times and which does not, after all, fulfil their worst fears. As well as the therapeutic relationship, educational therapy uses play, reading, writing, stories and the expressive arts, both as vehicles to help in understanding and as tools to help in resolving children's conflicts. Often a link can be made between the conflict or the fear in a child's mind and the learning or behaviour difficulty which can be slowly uncovered and worked through.

In educational therapy, indirect communication is the preferred method. That is, metaphor is used rather than direct questions. This makes it easier for children who can't remember, can't articulate, or can't face talking about their preoccupations to communicate them through stories and characters, and have a feeling that such difficulties are understandable.

In my role as SENCO and teacher in an urban primary school, I offer a variety of interventions and support as the needs of children require. Most of my time is spent support teaching with groups of children both in and out of classrooms and in supporting teachers, but because of my training I am also able to offer individual educational therapy to the few who need it. Sammy was such a child.

Sammy

Sammy was a helpless but very appealing little girl everyone tended to mother and wanted to help. She came up from the infants having had a high level of both individual and group support. However, she was still quite unable to manage anything by herself, apart from beautiful copywriting – although her careful detailed drawing seemed to indicate some hidden potential.

Her tolerance of frustration was very low, causing her teachers, helpers and peers to feel quite uncomfortable when she was left to struggle on her own. Being patient with her multitude of avoidance tactics, such as coughing, fidgeting and rubbing out, and getting her started without actually doing things for her was very difficult. We knew of course about her traumatic history of violence, loss and rejection as well as her very unsettled life and uncertain future but, as she was not disruptive and her work appeared neat, she was not prioritized at first for anything more than regular learning support.

After a long court case her mother went to prison, and Sammy went into long-term foster care. She began to seem a little more settled and to develop a few basic skills, but she continued to be reluctant to use them. She seemed to want her work, particularly her writing and her spellings, to be perfect. In class when we separated her from her peer supports, she would achieve very little – and sometimes nothing at all. Finally, in Year 5 we decided to change her weekly individual teaching time into educational therapy in order to see whether having the opportunity to play and 'work' through some of her anxieties might relieve her enough to have a go at difficult things.

As usual, the educational therapy sessions were arranged so that half the time was spent working on basic skills (reading, writing, learning games, etc.), and half was spent choosing – when she could choose from painting, making models, drama, making sand worlds with miniatures, playing board games etc. As well as the learning and choosing materials, she had her own special lidded box where everything she wrote and made, and any other items which became vested with particular meaning, could be kept safely from week to week.

Sammy was very preoccupied with the needs and hurts of babies at first. I remember a clay model and a sad story of a little elephant who wanted his mum, as well as stories of soldiers killing babies, and of babies needing to go away to safe houses. The story of poor hurt Pinocchio became quite important to her, enabling her reading to improve quite dramatically. Within the character roles we were safely able to express a lot of anger with each other as we read and acted out an argument between Pinocchio and the Puppet Master, in the very simple Ward Lock play version of the story.

Later, *The I Was So Mad I Could Split Book* (Frisen and Ekholm 1974) became a favourite. I read it to her and she read it to me several times, and she copied out a number of special pages:

Why are people daft?
Why are people rotten and nasty and daft?
Dad's daft.
Mum's daft.
Even Grandma's daft.
And the daft man next door's as daft as a brush.
Pat's very daft.
Everybody's daft.'

It seemed as if she were beginning to be able to reflect on some of her own feelings through the characters in the stories. This passively compliant and neat little girl was even able to admit: 'I get moody too. Sometimes I have tantrums. I get sent to my bedroom.'

For the first time she began to paint messy paintings. She enjoyed using clay, particularly cutting it up with a blunt knife. I remember one day she wanted me to do some clay cutting with her. She needed me to really experience what it was like to be her as we cut and slashed together, and to perhaps know what it felt like to see someone we care about holding a knife – as she had experienced so tragically in her own life. We began a time of reversing roles. She would be the teacher, and I would be the helpless child. She needed me to understand what it was like to be the child feeling useless and stuck, and to feel envious of the teacher's knowledge. In class her reading particularly was improving. Her peer relationships were much more equal and she became able to face and work on her mistakes a little more. But she was still quite blocked, and at times very blocked with her writing. Her classteacher and I both felt a strange difficulty getting close to her, and enabling her to get 'stuck into' what she was doing – perhaps not so strange when one considered the continuing uncertainty surrounding her future, while we were still concerned as to how she would manage at secondary school.

In her last 2 primary terms it became possible for her to have 2 short educational therapy sessions per week (in addition to her regular special needs support). Suddenly her maturity and involvement in her therapy and work seemed to grow. The improvement in her writing confidence and fluency was particularly marked, while in her educational therapy sessions we acted out long, ongoing dramas of babies and children, and sometimes an old lady, being wanted and then not wanted, badly treated and then welcomed back, as I pushed her around in an old typing chair. Clearly, she had found a relationship and a place where her worries and her ambivalences could be thought about and contained, leaving her much freer to learn and to remember. Her anxieties were no longer unthinkable. She was free to have a go at difficult words and spellings, and to risk making mistakes. She no longer needed to hide behind her beautiful, neat copywriting. The imperfect uncomfortable bits could be thought about and allowed to show.

The adoption came through just before she left, and she went off to mainstream secondary school. Two years later I met her in the library with her adoptive mother. Sammy looked very well cared for and happy. She talked of foreign travel and of history being her favourite subject.

METAPHOR

I am constantly amazed how children find and create metaphors which express their conflicts and anxieties so vividly and powerfully. I sometimes think they amaze themselves too. It seems as if the opportunity to doodle, daydream and be creative within a trusting facilitative relationship enables and inspires images and metaphors to arise, and become important and useable. Educational therapist Jenny Dover said in the *Young Minds Newsletter* in 1989 that 'the metaphor allows the creative process to unfold'. I would say also that the opportunity for the creative process allows the metaphor to unfold. I remember Daryl, who had probably been sexually abused but couldn't get anywhere near talking about it, struggling for many weeks with a Meccano truck. One day he picked up a pencil to poke some string through one of the holes at the back of the truck, and then suddenly it was as if something had taken over and he couldn't stop piercing the hole until it was badly damaged and broken. There was a long silence. He couldn't bear to talk about it, but we both knew we had experienced something painful.

I remember Simon, who buttonholed every adult who came into the room with an 'Are you going to help me?' and through whom love and attention just seemed to slip, discovering an old wool spool he could use to funnel sand into and out of endlessly, leaving both of us wondering if it was ever going to get full! . . . until one day he began to try and block the bottom up with plastic, paper towels, elastic bands and Sellotape – to make it into a 'proper container'. This struggle mirrored an improved ability to concentrate on his work in class without such desperate neediness, and an improved ability to 'hold on to' and 'contain' what he learnt. Waiting, and not helping him to secure the bottom of the spool until he was ready and able to discover it for himself, was an important part of the healing process.

Thus educational therapy is an option for the few seriously disturbed (usually statemented) children about whom there is a high level of anxiety and teacher frustration, and for whom other, less resourced options have not worked. It was originally developed for children like Sammy whose learning has become very blocked by their emotional problems. However, in my experience, it is also often requested for children whose emotional difficulties seriously affect their behaviour, and for children for whom behaviour programmes have not worked, because these are the children who cause most anxiety amongst staff. Over the years I have worked with many children in both categories.

Long-term educational therapy, like I have described with Sammy, takes time. It can be like travelling through a difficult, rocky path with someone you are growing to trust. Such work with children is fruitful to the extent that both the child and the therapist can develop a strong (and probably ambivalent on the part of the child) but time-limited attachment. If important relationships have been anxious attachments in the past, it will not be easy for children to believe 'that a transient attachment figure can be relied on' (Barrett and Trevitt 1991). They describe the educational therapist as an 'educational attachment figure', who creates a shared working and playing space for the child. In the educational therapy sessions children can find 'the right kind of space', where little by little they can communicate the uncomfortable anxieties and dilemmas which get in the way of their learning and affect their behaviour, and have them thought about and reflected back in a more palatable form, often in the context of their stories and images. Such an experience can be hard to lose in the holidays. Preparing children for breaks is crucial. Some children will have painful memories of difficult and hurtful separations which will easily transfer on to their educational therapist and will bring up resentment and anger, rejection, etc. Preparation for breaks can allow children 'to mourn their loss and hold the person in mind, freeing them to believe in their safe return' after the break (Barrett and Trevitt 1991), at the same time paving the way for a more secure attachment to their educational therapist, as they discover she can survive their destructive fantasies, and she is trustworthy after all. So gradually thinking becomes bearable and difficulties understandable. Relationships become rewarding and learning is freed. Children's vulnerabilities may still be triggered, but in my experience, as the months progress, they can grow stronger, become more relaxed, more likeable, more teachable and happier, and their learning improves – sometimes quite dramatically.

GROUPS

In addition to educational therapy with individual children, I have also run short-term therapeutic groups (for example art groups) for children who are very withdrawn, isolated, underconfident or over-anxious. The structure is very simple: a short talking time, followed by a longer art time when the children can choose between painting, drawing, plasticine modelling and chalking on a large shared board, ending with a time for sharing their work and talking, and recording stories.

The process is very unauthoritarian. The only boundaries enforced are those relating to safety, staying in the room, keeping everything in the group (the work goes in folders), and maintaining a consistent time and group membership. Everything made and said and done is thought about and taken seriously, paying particular emphasis to group themes, processes, feelings and difficulties. In the group, empathy and friendship are fostered naturally – as well as rivalry being able to be worked on in the 'here and now'. Individual and group metaphors arise and become important, develop and change, very much along the lines described in Chapter 9. One group, for example, became interested in grappling hooks! Clinging on was obviously an important theme for them – no doubt particularly so for Reece, whose older brother had been removed from school to be educated at home.

I sometimes find that the children in the therapeutic art groups change faster than those in individual educational therapy – maybe because the escalation into risk taking and the trying out of different roles and behaviours happen more quickly in a group, where peer relationships are as important as keeping the therapeutic relationship comfortable. However, it should also be acknowledged that the children we choose for the art groups are probably not as 'disturbed' as those seen individually.

We are careful about our choice of children for the groups. It is helpful to have a variety of problems, temperaments, ages and sexes in a group – so they can 'feed' off each other; but children who are very disturbed or needy would find sharing the adult in a group difficult, and could cause the group to become hard for one person to manage. However, even with careful selection, and with the understanding interpretations of their difficulties which go on as part of the group process, we have occasionally had a child in a group who has found the strength of feelings released too difficult to cope with on a particular day. This experience has highlighted the importance of setting secure and firm boundaries and support systems around the outside of the group, as well as thinking carefully about what goes on within it. Just occasionally it may be necessary to exclude a child from part of a session when the strong feelings coming up for them are not able to be contained within the metaphor of the art and the stories and the thinking which surrounds them. This can be a difficult experience for the group perhaps and one which needs to be supported with thinking and acknowledgement; but coming back into a welcoming and a more secure feeling group (where his difficulties had also been seen, acknowledged and survived) seemed to enable Martin to find ways to manage his particular very pressing and terrifying anxieties more by himself.

TAKING FEELINGS SERIOUSLY

Although educational therapy as such is only a small part of my job, I have found the insights and understandings invaluable in many ways in my work in school. In a talk to the Forum for the Advancement of Educational Therapy and Therapeutic Teaching (FAETT) in May 1989, child psychotherapist Valerie Sinason said, 'Having a therapist in the school fosters an atmosphere where feelings are taken seriously.' I have certainly found this to be the case. People can be very caring and supportive when a member of staff has problems, creating supportive systems and swapping children in extreme cases. Children's feelings are taken seriously too. They get us down at times of course. Sometimes we need to let off steam, but the idea that behaviour has meaning is increasingly a part of our philosophy. As well as needing effective and humane management, children's behaviour can often give clues to their needs and anxieties which teachers can think about and respond helpfully to. Taking these clues seriously and thinking with children about their difficulties, can foster understanding and free learning. For example, at the beginning of the school year a new boy in one of the classes was finding it hard to settle. He was beginning to disturb the other children, to irritate his teacher and produce very little work. His records showed a child with behaviour problems and poor concentration, but his classteacher noticed also a rather dark, preoccupied look in his eyes. In the context of talking about his several recent moves of home and school it came out that his parents had recently separated; and for many years he had felt 'stuck in the middle' of their arguments. This was something he had not been able to talk about before and you could visibly see his relief at being able to bring his worries and hurts out into the open. So his anxieties were let out a little, and he could experience them being contained safely in the teacher's mind; and from that day on he just looked different. He started to be able to work and to write stories he could be proud of and share. School seemed to become a haven where he knew we would understand when things were a bit difficult, and where he felt safe. A vicious circle was prevented and a virtuous circle begun before too many negative feelings had set in. Putting a little effort into developing a good and an understanding relationship with difficult children (as well as setting firm boundaries) is part of our philosophy – but it is not always easy! Deprived and disturbed children particularly need understanding and a sense of belonging. It is touching but a little sad when children say they wish they could stay in school all the time and not have to have holidays.

Children who are able to talk about their feelings can evoke sympathy and helpfulness. However, when feelings are too painful to acknowledge and just leak out in irritating behaviour, children can evoke the opposite response and end up feeling worse, like Sally.

Sally

Sally was continually claiming that others were disturbing her – calling her names and turning against her – whilst protesting her own innocence, causing the adults who worked with her to feel very irritated. Close observation revealed that little frustrations in her work – a crooked line or a word she couldn't spell – would be turned outwards into irritating remarks to others, e.g. 'What you doing *that* for?', which would escalate into a quarrel where she would end up getting hurt or offended. Escalation into coming to see me almost daily demanding that her problems with other children be 'sorted out' felt like problems 'spilling out'. Understanding her need to split off her troubling and disturbing feelings and push them into others, so she could feel better than the disturbing troublemakers and then seek to get *them* 'sorted out', rather than face her own inadequacies, was a helpful way for the classteacher and me to maintain sympathy and 'thinking space' for this unattractive, demanding 'only' child.

A meeting with her father revealed all sorts of good reasons why problems could feel quite unbearable for Sally, including a recent very violent family quarrel where she struggled to defend her father, highlighting her imagined need to control and push adults into 'sorting out' her problems. She obviously needs understanding and attention, but we need also to make sure that we are not manipulated into giving this inappropriately. She has requested help with her writing. We are now thinking that the opportunity of individual therapeutic teaching focusing particularly on writing, where she can also express her worries and anxieties within clear boundaries, might address both her needs.

BEGINNINGS AND ENDINGS

Increasingly in our school both beginnings and endings are taken seriously, as they are in therapy. The arrival of a new 'problem' child is seen as an important opportunity. The head will usually inform me as soon as the child arrives and I will see both the child and the parents as soon as possible, to look in some detail at both their learning and their emotional needs – in order to encourage everyone towards an attitude of hopefulness, and to set up a 'secure base' (Barrett and Trevitt 1991) and programmes. In extreme cases, decisions have been taken at this stage for a change to a more suitable class or teacher. For example, a very disturbed child was taken out of a newly qualified teacher's class and placed with an experienced teacher. Usually it is enough just to set up learning programmes and initiate good relationships and communication channels between all concerned, but occasionally more is needed. I remember when an expelled child from a school down the road was to be given a last chance at our school, we had a big family and professionals meeting to plan and prepare for her coming before she arrived. The child was shown round and spent a little time getting to know her teacher. Regular liaison channels were set up with parents and social services and some classroom strategies were prepared. It was decided that the child would receive regular educational therapy from the start. I had the feeling that she couldn't believe her luck when she came to her first session. She settled well, and the school became particularly supportive to her parents, who enjoyed coming in every week to help with crafts and chat to the teacher. Good liaison continued with the social worker, and the child used her educational therapy sessions well – particularly valuing and making use of model-making. Eighteen months later, after calm, secure classroom systems and educational therapy for the child were complemented by family therapy and social service support, the family no longer needs a social worker and the child no longer needs educational therapy. She is learning and working well, and growing stronger in herself.

In addition to the well thought-out beginning, several factors seem important here. One is the possibility in extreme cases that a child can begin therapy straight away, rather than having to join a queue at the Child and Family Consultation Service. Another is our belief in the value of developing good and ongoing relationships with social workers. Of course the material which comes up in the therapy is confidential, and the liaison person in the school would not necessarily be me, but as a school we actively foster and use such links. Occasionally, if the child requests it, joint family review meetings are arranged with the social worker and the child, when progress and problems at home and at school can be talked through. At such meetings my particular role would be to notice and acknowledge things from the child's point of view and to include them in the conversation.

Ends of terms and half terms, ends of years, leavings, losses and deaths are all thought about and taken seriously in educational therapy (see p. 233). In school too these difficult experiences can be real-life opportunities for growth and learning, although understandably some teachers prefer not to address them too much. However, where endings are ignored or denied, unresolved feelings of anger, for example, at being abandoned or rejected, or guilt that we might have been to blame in some way, can be projected back into the class or the teacher and spoil the good experience, particularly for children who have a history of 'bad' endings. This can prevent the good learning and memories from being internalized. On the contrary, a good ending, like a death properly grieved, can enable deep internalization of the relationship and the learning, and facilitate continuing opportunities to use and benefit from the work, as well as a chance to 'reprocess the experience of separation more successfully' (Geddes 1996).

Mrs M

Mrs M, a much loved teacher, was leaving at the end of term. It so happened that there was a little group of slow learners in her class that both of us had worked very closely with, and become very attached to. We knew they would miss her terribly. With her permission I read them the story of 'Janey' by Charlotte Zolotov (1973) about a little girl whose best friend had moved away. In the story, Janey nostalgically remembers her friend's qualities and idiosyncrasies as a way of coming to terms with her loss. After the story the 'little group' asked if they could make up a poem along similar lines for their teacher. They took turns to think of a line.

> *Mrs M*
> I remember when we first met last year.
> You were nice.
> I remember how you helped me when I got stuck with my sums.
> I remember how you helped me with my creative writing story.
> I remember when we first met, I was still shy
> And you introduced yourself to us.
> I remember when you had to wear glasses and you didn't mind,
> Because it helped you to see us better.
> I remember your white bead necklace, and the gold bracelets on your arm.
> I remember when you called us scallywags, and you made us laugh.
> I am going to miss you very much,
> From the ones who have help.

In class Mrs M was allowing the children (and herself) to come to terms with the ending slowly, by telling them in good time, and being available to think about it with them. The story of the two friends Amos and Boris, who had to say goodbye after a special journey together, was read to them (Steig 1989). They had their farewell party and were all ready for the last day when disaster struck. Mrs M received a phone call in the night to say that her father had been taken critically ill. She would have to go home immediately. She came into school briefly, for her presentation, and to say goodbye to the children, but had to go before the end of assembly. The teacher taking the assembly handled the situation very sensitively, and spoke of needing to allow feelings of sadness to come out, but that in the end we usually found, just as the friends of Jesus had found, that sadness and loss could turn into good and special memories, and could even turn into joy. I went back with the children into the classroom. Just about everyone was in tears. I asked them to sit in a circle on the carpet. I read 'Janey' to them and the poem the little group had made, and I asked if they would like to spend a few minutes remembering the things about Mrs M which were special to them. We passed a shell around the circle, giving them each a chance to say something if they wished to. A few offered poignant and moving memories.

Then we recalled the assembly where the teacher had described how sad feelings could later be turned into happy memories. I asked them if they would like to try out that process and cheer themselves up a little by telling jokes . . . and everyone told a joke! It was time for break. During the day at least four children came up to me at separate times and said how helpful our sharing time had been, and how they really did think that sad feelings could turn into joy in the end.

UNDERSTANDING PUZZLING DIFFICULTIES

'Emotional experience can directly affect a child's ability to think and learn in very specific ways' (Beaumont 1991). For example, 'difficulties may represent unprocessed experiences' (Geddes 1996). One of the primary tasks of an educational therapist is to think – to maintain a thinking space about children's difficulties and unprocessed experiences – and to observe carefully until glimpses of understanding indicate helpful responses to try or insights to explore. Sometimes briefer interventions or one-off observations combined with teacher consultations may be enough to set the ball rolling.

Carl, a child with unexpected maths difficulties

Carl, a very anxious 8-year-old, had been pressured by his anxiously involved grandparents into frozen failure – to the extent that his previous school felt he needed to go to a school for children with moderate learning difficulties. During his first year with us, we managed to ease his writing inhibition through several family meetings where, with the aid of various tests and assessments, we teased out his confidence difficulties and anxieties from his literacy needs, and through a therapeutic writing group where he could grow into writing confidence and risk taking in his own time. However, several months later, we noticed a puzzling failure to progress in basic maths. Although he had always had special needs maths support, suddenly there seemed to develop a great anxiety in the school about his maths difficulties. I hadn't remembered him having such acute difficulties the previous year and wondered whether we might have overlooked something.

I watched him try some simple addition with cubes. I could not believe the problems he was having bringing 6 and 4 together to add them up. He had been doing simple tens and units regularly at the end of the previous term, but here he was counting and checking, rechecking and counting the numbers again and again, but just not managing to bring them together. The same happened with other numbers. I tried subtraction – there was no problem. This seemed strange. I had seen children having unexpected difficulties with subtraction before – and learned on my training how this could relate to unworked through or unbearable losses – but never problems with addition. And then I realized that for Carl the experience of being taken away from the unbearable pressures of his grandparents and the failure situation of his previous school had been a good and a helpful experience. In many ways he was doing better. His writing and confidence had improved enormously. But his more recent experiences of difficulty and change were in the area of adding on. His mother had recently had a difficult pregnancy and given birth to twins, and he had a new dad, both of which would probably need some adjusting to.

'I'm just wondering,' I said. 'Do you think there could be a link between these new additions in your family and your present difficulty with adding up?'

'Mmm, yes, maybe,' he said. I was aware, of course, that he could have just been saying what he thought I wanted to hear, but I assured him that such difficulties and links could be quite understandable, particularly for a sensitive person. We remembered how he had suffered a lot in the past from learning anxieties in different ways. After our conversation I showed him how to do adding up sums and he could do them easily. He said he would like to have a family meeting to talk things through – which we duly arranged. His classteacher commented a few weeks later that he seemed to be managing much better, better in fact than some of the other children with special needs in the class, although he still needed maths support.

SUPPORTING AND CONSULTING WITH TEACHERS

Gerda Hanko calls the consultative process of teachers thinking together about children's difficulties 'joint problem solving', emphasizing the co-operative search for understanding which can yield helpful insights and responses (Hanko 1985). In my role as supporter of teachers, I often find that our discussions about children's difficulties will include emotional aspects and factors. Although it is crucial for teachers to maintain their roles as teachers, and not slip over into amateur social workers or counsellors at the expense of managing their classes and the children's learning, an understanding of some of the emotional aspects of learning and teaching, and of the ways children's learning and concentrating can be interfered with, can enhance teachers' skills and relationships (Hanko 1985). Developing reflective qualities akin to the reflective qualities in educational therapy can relieve stress, improve teacher–child relationships and enhance teacher effectiveness. (For a detailed discussion of the emotional factors which affect learning and teaching, see Saltzberger-Wittenberg, Henry and Osborne 1983.)

Reflections on Shaun

Mrs P was very concerned about Shaun, who could be extremely irritating with his constant interruptions. Teachers and children alike were beginning to find him the 'pain' of the class, raising their eyebrows every time he opened his mouth. We talked about how children can play roles for the class, releasing others from the need to act out their own irritating bits, and about the dangers of scapegoating and labelling. We talked of the need to change the vicious circle into a virtuous one – and of Shaun's need to feel valued and worthwhile. The next day Mrs P came up with a 'brilliant' plan. She had a very good relationship with Jonas and his mother, a mature, high-status child in the class whom she thought she could encourage to stand up for Shaun the next time the others sighed when he made a point or answered a question in class. Later that week she related how Jonas had said: 'No wait a minute – he might have something useful to say', when everyone had groaned as Shaun tried to answer a question one afternoon. So began a process of seeking opportunities to give Shaun's fragile self-esteem a real boost by valuing what he said and did in front of the class. Mrs P delighted to tell me of her little successes – although it was a slow process.

TRANSFERENCE

Educational therapy training includes developing an understanding of internal processes such as projection and transference. One of the ways therapy works is by the child unconsciously 'transferring' his or her anxieties and expectations on to (or into) the therapist, who, because of her training, is able to reflect on the feelings evoked in her and consciously decide how to respond helpfully. Of course this transference does not only happen in therapy. It happens all the time in significant relationships both at home and at school; but the way the transference is responded to in different situations can be helpful – or unhelpful, particularly if the feelings hook into our own vulnerabilities (see discussion in Chapter 13). In the regular contained situation of psychodynamic therapy, like longer-term educational therapy, a therapist may sometimes make interpretations of the transference, especially in relation to the therapeutic relationship and to breaks and endings, but it would not be helpful for a teacher to do that. Even as an educational therapist I would never make an interpretation outside a therapy session as this feels like stretching the boundaries, which are particularly important to respect in my position as SENCO. In this respect Sarah would push me to the limit when, as we approached the long summer holidays she would suddenly tell me when I bumped into her in the corridor or in the classroom that she was leaving, and I would feel fairly certain that this was much more to do with her anxiety related to my leaving her for the long break, but I knew it was not appropriate to interpret as such in that situation.

Mostly as school staff we experience helpful transferences causing us to like being with the children and enjoy teaching them, but with disturbed children they can sometimes be quite uncomfortable; and if we are not aware of what is happening we can collude with the problem by unconsciously repeating the damaging or confidence-sapping experience for the child. For example, Casey, who found the 'sudden' and conflict-ridden break-up of his family extremely difficult to cope with, identified his teacher assistant with his abandoning father (whom she had met several times the previous term) and refused to work with her at all, despite his extreme need for writing support. He said coming to see her reminded him of his dad, although she had hardly talked with him about his dad at all. We needed to wait a whole term for this unhelpful transference to be eased, and meanwhile support the teaching assistant in understanding and bearing this undeserved rejection; and we needed to find other ways to help Casey learn what he could, and hold on to a good enough relationship with his teacher. The high level of frustration Casey engendered made it tempting for adults to want to force him to have the help he so desperately needed, but that just precipitated irresolvable conflicts, uncomfortably like those at home perhaps.

As someone who is trained to understand these processes I can sometimes help teachers to appreciate them and think consciously about how to prevent collusions and repetitions, and how to distance themselves from the uncomfortable feelings children can project into them.

Gary

Gary came from a deeply divided and rivalrous family. He lived with his dad and partner during the week, and his mum and partner at the weekends. However, the competition and rivalry between the two sets of parents was so unbearable that most of the time they could not bear to talk to each other. Because of his extreme learning and behaviour difficulties there were several adults working with him in different ways in school. It was not easy trying to teach Gary. He could be very blocked and stubborn, and sometimes he went through phases of favouring one of us above another. We realized that differences of opinion and approach, along with a puzzling difficulty getting together to talk things through, was not helping his situation. Understanding our own difficulties working together as teachers as at least partly a transference of the almost unbearable splits and quarrels in his home situation enabled us to feel easier about our differences, and to acknowledge how vitally important it was for Gary to sense good communication and co-operation between us. Experiencing the school as a co-operating, well-functioning 'family' could be a valuable first-hand experience for him.

THINKING ABOUT INNER AND OUTER WORLDS

From the behaviourist viewpoint, children's learning inhibitions and behaviour problems are seen primarily as poor conditioning, which can be modified by using the external environment to encourage positive behaviours, and by managing the child's behaviour positively. In milder cases, where the child has just got into bad habits, or learnt that 'bad' behaviour brings easy attention, behaviour modification and good behaviour management may be enough to change a vicious circle into a virtuous one, enabling continuing rewards from good work to become a new motivator – although making an effort to develop a good caring relationship with the child is also crucial.

However, where children's pain, anger or anxieties are both acute and unthinkable they are bound to 'leak out' into their behaviour, their relationships or their learning in some way, causing them unconsciously to repeat problem behaviours, and preventing them from being able to benefit from normal rewards, support and encouragements. We have observed on a number of occasions disturbed children rubbishing their behaviour programmes, losing their 'home/school books', and even slipping into worse behaviours when they fail to reach their targets. Even praise and rewards can be hard for some children to take (throwing into *sharp* relief perhaps their own feelings of underlying 'badness').

In cases of more serious disturbance or neglect then, some therapeutic opportunity may be necessary for children to be able to work on and resolve some of their inner conflicts and anxieties, but paying attention to their outer environment is also important. As well as some (outside) family work perhaps, good consistent classroom management is crucial to enable such children to feel secure, so they do not continually need to test out the boundaries. Children who have good cause to be angry may also be terrified that their anger might be uncontrollable. They will need to feel the boundaries holding them securely and benignly like a 'good enough' mother or father – to use D. W. Winnicott's (1965) phrase (in addition perhaps to needing a safe place to work through the underlying causes of their anxieties) – in order to feel safe and relaxed enough to learn. I always remember my educational therapy supervisor saying children need to know that 'whatever happens their teacher can cope'. So effective behaviour management can be very much complementary to individual or group therapy. With very damaged children like Johnny, we find we need to think carefully about both aspects.

Johnny

Johnny's aggressive manipulative behaviour derived from a traumatic occurrence a few years previously when his brother was tragically killed. His desperate neediness was extremely hard to control and impossible to satisfy. He obviously required a regular therapeutic opportunity to work through his anxieties, but equally important were the totally consistent and firm classroom handling and routines to enable him to feel secure. His classteacher noticed that he could not cope with any extra or special attention from outside teachers in the classroom. His need was so great that he would just end up having a tantrum when they left him, or when they went to work with someone else. 'Come back. Why are you going away from me? I need you. You don't care about me', etc. So she just gave him appropriately differentiated work to do, and along with the other children it was signed off when he did it without any special allowances, support or rewards, which in previous schools (along with the lack of therapeutic opportunity) had been his undoing. Positive behaviour was encouraged by a 'rules, praise and ignore' approach (ignoring his non-disruptive bad behaviour and praising him and those around him when they obeyed the rules), and a whole class team point system, enabling him to gain attention only for good work and behaviour in a routine way. His teacher could certainly shout loudly when necessary, but most of the time she was interesting and enthusiastic, creating a perfect example of the 'whatever happens I can cope' atmosphere. So, as his anxieties began to be safely contained and thought about in his educational therapy sessions, he was freed a little to try out more healthy behaviours in the predictable and secure classroom environment, with his predictable secure classteacher who could be so much fun when things were going well. But it wasn't easy for her, especially at the beginning. Distancing herself from the almost unbearable feelings he would often put on to her, disciplining herself not to respond and allow him to manipulate her attention with such comments as 'I hate you. You don't like me. You want to kill me' was not easy. Many times we would discuss the meanings of his behaviours given his very pressing needs and disturbance. Think, plan, then act – rather than react – was the motto which enabled us all to feel stronger and more professional, and gradually to relax. Now, eight months later, working in the classroom is no longer any problem for him, or for his teacher!

By the same token to offer either individual educational therapy or even small group therapy to a child who is currently in a very rejecting, conflict-ridden or abusive environment either at home or at school (particularly if both environments are chaotic and rejecting) may be of limited use. It can feel mean to deny such a needy child the opportunity of therapy, but the priority for the child must be to develop safe and secure enough external environments both at home and at school. Certainly the two need to go along hand in hand, through liaison with external agencies perhaps, and as described above, for the child to be able to use the opportunity of educational therapy without fear of further hurt. It is also important to think carefully about the safety and reliability of the setting, and to consider the likely length of time available when thinking about what sort of involvement to have with a child in school. An uncertain foster placement, a chaotic class or temporary housing would all be factors influencing the type of work and relationship developed with a child. Even when all these aspects have been considered, however, things can sometimes change unexpectedly and unhelpfully, and we have to think creatively.

Veronica

Veronica, for example, became suddenly quite unable to use her educational therapy sessions when her apparently secure foster placement broke down unexpectedly, projecting her back into the unbearably rejecting relationship with her mother with its ins and outs of foster homes, and a parallel deterioration at school with exclusions both from the classroom and from the school. Continuing with a therapeutic relationship which could also turn bad was just unbearable, and we needed to respect her feelings. However, she was able later to find her own way to use the time helpfully – drawing joint pictures with a friend illustrating and talking together about the cruelty of grown-ups and her own 'unrequited love' for her mother. Interestingly, I was prohibited from talking during these sessions. I was the 'bad rejecting grown-up' who needed just to hear the awful ways children were treated without being permitted to 'reply'. It seemed as if the (unacknowledged) good attachment which the friend made with me enabled the very anxiously attached Veronica to use the time. In the end a relative agreed to adopt her and things gradually became better, and she was able to sustain a good enough relationship with her teaching assistant in her new school. Interestingly, although I no longer worked with the friend, our special relationship and concern for Veronica continued, and may have gone on being helpful, as we would meet in the corridor and have little concerned chats about how Veronica was getting on and send occasional letters to her.

FITTING INTO THE SCHOOL: ISSUES

Although there are many opportunities and benefits from having a SENCO who is also an educational therapist, I do acknowledge that there can be difficulties and issues which need to be thought through carefully.

Minimizing conflicting roles

We need to be aware of the possible conflict of roles in the minds of the children who receive educational therapy. In consideration of this, and because of the liaison demands of the SENCO role, I have been relieved of playground and assembly duties, although being seen as an authority figure and having to discipline children is bound to occur sometimes as I move around the school and work with the children. My different roles and behaviours in the different settings is something which is consciously thought about and addressed with the children, and I am amazed to find just how well they are often able to accept the different boundaries, expectations and opportunities. Sometimes this variety of roles can have unexpected benefits, as children who receive educational therapy from someone who also does many other things in a school do not stand out as the naughty or 'loopy' ones, contrary to my experience in some other schools where I worked solely as a therapist. When many children receive all kinds of help from the same person no particular label is attached nor is it feared. Some children are able to cope with and benefit from receiving both educational therapy and special needs group support from the same person, but we are aware that for others this would be unbearable and counter-productive. Of course the advantage of educational therapy is that learning and literacy needs can be addressed at the same time as emotional needs, but we are also fortunate in that statemented children in our area are often allocated 'county' SEN teaching support in addition to what the school provides. As nearly all the children who receive educational therapy are statemented children, any long-term conflicts of roles can therefore be minimized.

Jealousies and rivalries

Jealousies and rivalries between children who receive therapy or other sorts of support from the same person are always addressed and often usefully worked through in the therapy. It is obviously not ideal for children in the same class or family to receive therapy from the same person and it would probably be frowned upon in other institutions, but I have found that these are often issues which can be faced and worked through well enough. Children are often more resilient than we imagine.

Importance of setting

Finding a suitable undisturbed room has not always been easy, although it is very important. The relationship of trust, and the absolute security, reliability and confidentiality of the room, are quite crucial for some children (although here again I am discovering they are more resilient than I imagined, so as long as everything is acknowledged and thought about). It has sometimes been hard for staff to understand why interruptions are so unwelcome, even when the process has been explained and talked through. Consistency within each setting and careful separation of the settings are also important, and sometimes careful management of endings is needed. For example, we have arranged that some more disturbed children have their sessions at the end of the day, so that they can go home straight afterwards.

STAFF CONSIDERATIONS

One of the philosophies of educational therapy is that behaviour has meaning, although it has not always been easy for staff to hold this in mind, especially in relation to particularly troublesome children and to the more extreme incidents. I have always advocated understanding *and* firm boundaries, but there are certainly some times when I have found that to try to understand the offending behaviour is better left till later. I have learnt slowly that sometimes just to listen and to acknowledge the present stress is the first thing. Timing of supportive conversations is something which can need thinking about and planning for.

However, my being part of the staff means that we have ample opportunities to discuss the children, and teachers are always keen to share both the good and the bad news. Often it is possible to think helpfully together about what the child might be communicating (see Sally p. 235) or transferring into our relationships (see Gary p. 241), leading to more helpful ways to manage their learning or behaviour (see Casey p. 240).

Although staff relations and respect for each other's differing skills and attributes are generally good, it has not been easy over the years for some staff to accept having educational therapy in the school (albeit with only a few children). Sometimes the view has been expressed that such children should not be in the school when the inevitable bad patches occur. Certainly without their educational therapy it is likely that many would have ended up being 'passed on' – or causing extreme stress and resentment when this did not happen. As it is, when they can begin to trust the educational therapist, and to risk self-expression and attachment, the children have always improved – perhaps slowly at times but significantly and increasingly, and sometimes quite dramatically. Teachers are always delighted by the progress and we share the good news together – although the facilitating role of the educational therapy in freeing the child to relax, to think and to learn may be difficult to remember, as they experience the rewards of the child responding to their teaching.

Although educational therapy is only ever offered as an agreed and appropriate response to the particular special needs of a child, sometimes teachers may feel a conflict of priorities over which children should receive the time. Inevitably some of the children who receive educational therapy are those (certainly initially) teachers most resent, although they are also the ones they are the most desperate for help with. On a bad day such children can be felt not to deserve this 'special attention', unlike compliant responsive children who are felt to 'deserve it' so much more. It should be acknowledged that there may be all sorts of reasons why some staff might find it difficult to cope with selected children receiving such personal, individual and confidential support – support which they or members of their family were never able to have, or which brings to mind perhaps the sort of anxieties we can all have under our cool, coping exteriors. Unacknowledged jealousies of imagined special 'precious' relationships can perhaps be a factor with staff as well as children. When anxieties relating to the children are experienced in the classroom and the school generally, it can be tempting for staff to lay the blame at the doorway of the therapist. In my case it is not so much direct criticism or challenges but more implied blame or responsibility: 'Do you know what *your* child has done now . . . !'

Sometimes it is necessary to be a 'container' for the staff's anxieties as well as the children's (!) – by just quietly understanding the level of frustration and rage lying behind such a statement. Coping with these occasional bad patches can be one of the most difficult things in therapy. This is often the time when the child is really using the therapy well, trusting the therapeutic setting and relationship well enough to feel able to let the acute anxieties out to be thought about and slowly 'detoxified'. Of course, like therapists everywhere, I receive regular supervision on my work from a qualified and experienced child therapist, and this can be crucial to help maintain a thinking space when the child is really putting the awful and worrying dilemmas right into you, so that you feel them too. I find supervision (confidential consultation with another therapist) particularly crucial at these times – to aid understanding of what might be going on under the surface, and to reflect on possible helpful responses, to the child in the educational therapy, and perhaps in response to staff anxieties too, and in response to the child's behaviour in the school.

Talking about and demonstrating experientially how educational therapy works (including the realistic description of inner growth and change as being more like a wavy spiral, where old vulnerabilities can still be around at the same time as strength and confidence and learning capacity develop, rather than a straight upward slope), along with discussing pros and cons openly, are all important here, but not always easy. However, when teachers can understand and see the benefits, and see how we each have different, but equally valuable roles to play, co-operation and active support develops, and educational therapy can become part of the whole school process and policy, valued by children, staff, parents, Social Services and the Office for Standards in Education (OFSTED)!

In school the occasional periods of reluctance can be coped with more easily with therapy available on site. Although no child is ever forced to come to a session, occasionally when uncomfortable issues are being worked through, a child may be reluctant to come – often a sign that the child is very 'engaged' and the therapy is working well, rather than that it is going through an unhelpful patch. An encouraging teacher supporting a patient therapist can often help over these times. Children observing a good supportive relationship between their teacher and their educational therapist can experience a helpful triangular relationship like a good mother–father–child triangle, which they may not have experienced before. Sometimes it is important for children to know that the educational therapist will wait and not give up (like parents or teachers before may have done?), and to experience their teacher encouraging them when doubts and difficulties sap their confidence to come to sessions, although there may also be times when extreme circumstances get in the way of their using the time at all (see Veronica p. 243). At these times, being a regular member of staff with other roles enables me to use such 'empty times' productively with observations, assessments, monitoring work, etc.

SCHOOL BENEFITS

There are many advantages and gains to be had from having an educational therapist on the staff, and indeed from having someone who is both a special needs teacher and a therapist. Cross-fertilization of skills has already been mentioned, and is also discussed in Chapter 4 in relation to stories and writing. Assessments of children's difficulties, and approaches to their special needs can include acknowledgement and perhaps understanding of emotional factors, history and circumstances. For example, how do they feel about their difficulties; can they talk about/express their feelings appropriately; are they dependent on/resistant to help; are they generally chaotic and muddled/perfectionist/anxious; are they needy/switched off/distant; can they bear to take risks and have a go at/work on their mistakes; how do they manage frustration/rebuke/provocation; and what do they cause us to feel when we try to teach them? Talking with parents and children together about these questions can sometimes facilitate helpful links into understanding and relieving their difficulties and anxieties (see Carl p. 238, Andrew p. 248).

Having an educational therapist in the school enables classteachers and teaching assistants to be supported in thinking through difficulties as they arise, or in an ongoing way, focusing on understanding a behaviour perhaps, or on setting up containing systems. This thinking is more in the manner of joint problem-solving (Hanko 1985), reflection and sharing information than of giving advice, as we all have important contributions to make and complementary roles to play. I think that, in addition to consulting with teachers, the opportunity for consultations with and support for teaching and midday assistants is a particularly valuable benefit. These people are often very involved with the more 'difficult' children, and sometimes just a few words of understanding or encouragement can mean a lot. Longer, timetabled and more practical support for them can be enhanced by a consideration and allowance for emotional factors as they affect the children's learning and behaviour, as well as an opportunity for developing listening, relating and mediation skills.

Encouraging the development of helpful and supportive systems in the school is also a possibility, like arranging an indoor supervised 'playroom option' at lunchtimes for vulnerable children or those perceived by their teachers to be getting 'near the edge' – or for those who just choose it (depending on numbers).

As a therapist I also feel quite comfortable with the facilitative mode of working (in contrast to the more didactic style of much teaching today), and on several occasions I have been able to support teachers and teaching assistants in developing this more equal and reflective role – so vital in circle time and other sharing or experiential work. Increasingly, hard-pressed teachers are using my availability to offer one-off counselling or pastoral sessions to children who have experienced sudden traumas or difficulties – children such as David, whose concentration and behaviour had suddenly deteriorated, and who was found to be having nightmares after all his Christmas toys were stolen. He certainly valued being able to turn his nightmare into an exciting story on the computer. He also valued the practical opportunity of being able to think about how his parents had made his house very safe and burglar proof with another child who had also had her Christmas toys stolen some years ago. He tells me he no longer has nightmares now! Interestingly even brief, but significant, encounters like this can facilitate lasting good attachments with children, which can be helpfully triggered by a comment, or even an understanding look, at 'difficult' times. One very significant advantage is that some parents will agree to educational therapy with its educational as well as emotional connotations, whereas they would not like to think that their child needed psychotherapy. Also some parents may agree to educational therapy in school, whereas they wouldn't be organized or interested enough to sustain taking their child regularly to a clinic. This means that some children can have therapeutic help who would not otherwise be able to receive it.

Of course Child and Family Consultation Services and Social Services are often able to offer various therapies for children, and along with other schools we do refer to them children whose problems are severe but do not perhaps impinge so directly on their education, or those whose parents are willing and able to support and transport them to the clinic. But others without that support and commitment, or those whose emotional problems directly affect their learning, are certainly lucky to have the opportunity of educational therapy available on site. For children who receive educational therapy at school, there are of course no transport problems or costs, and no class time is wasted on journeys.

Although it is more expensive for children to be seen individually than in groups, in the long run even individual educational therapy, like other forms of therapy, saves money. Both social costs and educational costs later on are saved as the child grows stronger and ceases to be inhibited, muddled or disturbed and to need expensive interventions.

PARENT AND FAMILY BENEFITS

As mentioned briefly above, one-off or occasionally regular meetings with parents (usually mothers) and children can be very useful. I find it particularly helpful to be able to make links between learning and behaviour difficulties and a child's history, including early history, home situation and feelings. These meetings may touch on sensitive issues of course and it is important not to be intrusive with questions, and to respect confidentiality, but I have found that parents and children – as well as teachers – can find thinking about such links enlightening and helpful, and even quite a relief, if they are handled non-judgementally.

Andrew

Andrew had been very messy, and very irritating and annoying to classteachers and peers alike since he began school. The infant staff had been moving towards statementing, and after a short honeymoon he began to evoke similar feelings in the juniors. His teacher was seeing his mum or his older brother every day to talk about his behaviour, but things were not getting better. We decided to offer him a turn in the therapeutic art group and in preparation for that we had a family meeting. His mother told us that his younger handicapped sister, Rachael, had been born just as he was about to start school. She had severe problems at birth (many of which still continue), necessitating six weeks in intensive care. This resulted in Andrew being farmed out to foster parents just as he was beginning his schooling. Rachael continues to have periods of hospitalization and to be very fragile and delicate, needing careful handling and protection, and causing a lot of anxiety and practical problems in the family. It was immediately obvious that there were very good reasons why Andrew was so attention seeking. In front of everyone we could acknowledge to him how very understandable his difficulties were, and how very hard things must have felt for him, particularly when he couldn't express his anger to Rachael for taking his mum away from him just at the time when he needed her so much as he started school. I assured them that now we understood I was sure we would be able to help him; and from that day on he seemed to change. The next day he was showing the head his beautiful handwriting (a particular area of difficulty) and almost overnight it seemed as if his wild, resentful look had relaxed. Of course there were ups and downs, but he certainly never needed statementing. He is now off the Stages of Assessment altogether.

So it seems as if the difficulties of those early days when I felt I had nothing to offer the underachieving and disruptive children in my groups have borne rich fruit. Although we still have many difficulties and challenges, I never feel now that there are children that we can't help or begin to think helpfully about. To help them may take time and patience and much heartache. Often an orchestration of inputs from inside and sometimes from outside the school is needed, but there is a confidence and a belief that if we take time to listen carefully enough to them we will be able, little by little, to understand and respond in a more helpful way. For the few this may be through individual or small group therapy, and for the many through collectively developing an understanding approach to their management, their teaching and their learning, and to their difficulties. As I (and as we) spend time with the children and try to understand them, so we come to care about them, and despite the bad times it is those who are the most difficult and the most puzzling that we come to care about the most. Somehow I think they sense it – and they respond.

The confidence that we have something valuable to offer can give inner strength, which enables the setting of firm boundaries without wavering and without grudges, and the search for understanding brings compassion and love – even though we may not always like children's behaviour. Of course the best teachers have always had these qualities, but the rest of us can grow them too in our different ways, and through our struggles. It is surprising what we can do when we face our opportunities with courage and with creativity – and with sensitivity.

POSTSCRIPT

Unfortunately, since writing this chapter some two years ago, this confidence has been somewhat eroded by pressure in the school to concentrate on, and put substantially more resources into, academic standards, as a result of changes in the education system in Britain. My experience is that we have much less time to devote to special needs as a whole. Although I (and teachers generally) still try to address and include emotional needs in our approach, and although a very few children still manage to benefit from educational therapy, I am tragically aware these days that there are some children I (and we) could help much more effectively, but there is just not enough time.

REFERENCES

Barrett, M. and Trevitt, J. (1991) *Attachment Behaviour and the School Child*. London: Routledge.

Beaumont, M. (1991) Reading between the lines: the child's fear of meaning. *Journal of Analytic Psychology*, 5(3).

Frisen, G. and Ekholm, P. (1974) *The I Was So Mad I Could Split Book*. London: Black.

Geddes, H. (1996) Educational therapy and the classroom teacher. In Barrett, M. and Varma, V. *Educational Therapy in Clinic and Classroom*, London: Colin Whurr.

Greenhalgh, P. (1994) *Emotional Growth and Learning*. London: Routledge.

Hanko, G. (1985) *Special Needs in Ordinary Classrooms*. Oxford: Blackwell.

Saltzberger-Wittenberg, I., Henry, G. and Osborne, E. (1983) *The Emotional Experience of Learning and Teaching*. London: Routledge and Kegan Paul.

Steig, W. (1989) *Amos and Boris*. London: Picture Puffin.

Winnicott, D. W. (1965) *The Maturational Processes and the Facilitating Environment*. London: Hogarth.

Zolotov, C. (1973) *Janey*. New York: Harper and Row.

CHAPTER 15

Teachers thinking therapeutically
Gillian Salmon

This chapter relates some of the ideas and experiences explored by a group of teachers in a series of twilight sessions. They were teachers working in an Outer London borough who had responded to an invitation to join a 10-session course offering an 'Introduction to Educational Therapy'. Most of them were involved in special educational needs work, either in units attached to mainstream schools or as Special Educational Needs Co-ordinators (SENCOs). Three were mainstream classteachers, in infant, junior and secondary schools. The order and detail of some of the cases brought to the group have been altered to give confidentiality to the participants and greater coherence to the whole account. Each week, one of the participants was asked to closely observe an incident which had occurred as a normal part of the week's teaching. This was to be in class or elsewhere in the school, and to involve the teacher and either a single student or a group of any size. Innumerable incidents occur in the teaching day, but some may leave the teacher feeling puzzled, lacking in skill or having a concern about the way in which the incident developed. It was these which group members were invited to bring so that the rest of the group might reflect on what had happened in the interaction between teacher and child. As, in each case, it was the teacher involved who was bringing the observation, s/he had to trust the rest of the group to be supportive in considering incidents which had sometimes felt very uncomfortable to those involved.

Each discussion was preceded by an exposition of some aspect of psychoanalytic theory as developed by Sigmund Freud and others such as Anna Freud, Melanie Klein and Donald Winnicott, who further developed his ideas. These theories suggest that the unconscious deals with thoughts and feelings which are unacceptable to the conscious mind in ways which can affect emotions and behaviour. The term 'educational therapy' refers to a way of using the understanding derived from psychoanalytic theory to work with children who have learning difficulties. This approach was first developed in the UK by Irene Caspari when she worked at the Tavistock Clinic (Caspari 1976). The topic for a session did not necessarily relate directly to the subsequent presentation, but was intended to offer a basis for relating these ideas to the teaching and learning experiences in education. In the examples which follow, the presentation and the following discussion are the only aspects of the sessions described, and are summarized. The differing typefaces are intended to allow the reader to think about his/her reactions to the presentation before reading about the thoughts of the group.

PRESENTATION 1

In the second session, Penny looked despondent and out of touch with what was being discussed. She was a very experienced teacher who had been working for the previous two and a half years in a unit for children with emotional and behavioural difficulties (EBD). The unit took children in at any time of the year when there was a vacancy, when the authority had completed an assessment of the child's needs and when the teacher in charge of the unit had met the child and the parents. A new child, Matthew, had been admitted two days previously. Penny had carefully prepared work for him which she felt was interesting and within his capacity, and had hoped to settle him to do it. He had apparently accepted the task but, when she moved away from him, she had been astonished to find him talking loudly about what rubbish it was. He was critical of the worksheet she had prepared, of the topic she had chosen and of her as a teacher. As she gave this account, Penny felt quite puzzled at the depth of feeling the incident evoked in her. She did not expect the children to be grateful to her for her efforts, but she was very angry at this unprovoked attack. As the group thought with her about what had happened, it became clear that she had been left feeling that there was some truth in Matthew's words. Despite her wealth of teaching experience and the care she gave to her work, on this occasion she felt incompetent, useless and disliked. The fact that the group of teachers took her feelings seriously, and that most of them had at some time had a similar experience, seemed to enable her to think further about what had been happening between her and the pupil.

Discussion

We discussed the notion that the way a teacher feels in relation to a pupil can often give important clues about the child's feelings about itself. In psychoanalytic thinking, the practice of externalizing our feelings, and then attributing them to someone else, is known as 'projection'. The idea that we can locate in others some of the more uncomfortable feelings we find in ourselves has commonly been recognized in such terms as 'that's the pot calling the kettle black'. That this is a way in which we may deal with the unconscious wishes or feelings which seem likely to disrupt the balance between the ego or conscious mind and external reality is part of a system of thinking which accepts the idea of unconscious processes. A number of other 'defence mechanisms' have been recognized as strategies by which aspects of the self are dealt with in manageable ways when they might otherwise create intolerable anxiety (Brown and Pedder 1985). While this can contribute to healthy functioning, it is also possible for these defences to inhibit the development of the self. For the teacher, a recognition of the unconscious processes affecting both the child and the teacher can be very helpful as it may enable him/her to consider interactions between teacher and pupil at something other than 'face' value. It does not make the experience of disparagement any more comfortable, but it allows it to be thought about in a constructive way.

We considered Matthew's case and the reasons why he might be feeling 'incompetent, useless and disliked'. His arrival at an EBD Unit was a consequence of many instances of unacceptable behaviour in his mainstream school. He had some learning difficulties and had found school neither an interesting nor an enjoyable place to be. He had frequently been in trouble for his behaviour and it was likely that he understood his removal to the unit as the most recent evidence of teachers' rejection of him. Penny suggested that this way of thinking about Matthew made it easier for her to respond to his attack upon her with patience and understanding rather than the angry reproval he had initially evoked.

PRESENTATION 2

The experience of beginning something new is frequently anticipated with optimism but also with anxiety. It puts us in touch with some of our earliest feelings of vulnerability and we re-experience much of the pleasure or pain we have felt on other similar occasions. Kate was part of a learning support team and she had just started work with a small group of girls in a school for children with moderate learning difficulties. The headteacher had suggested that these children were making slower progress than any others in the school and had grouped them together for enhanced support. Kate was new to the team and it was her first experience of working as a visiting teacher in an unfamiliar school. She had made careful preparation for the work and had asked the school to ensure that there was a room available for her to work in regularly throughout the life of the group. She planned that, in her first meeting with the group as a whole, they would talk about themselves and their interests and think about why they had been chosen to be in the group. She hoped that this would give the girls a good basis for future work together.

Kate was, therefore, rather concerned to find that one of the group members was absent from school and that the room assigned to them was still in use as the regular classroom for the girls' own form. Their planned return to a newly decorated classroom had been postponed and they were to work in a specialist room for this period. She had set about beginning the group work, but found that six different children from the form came in at separate times, ostensibly looking for the classteacher. Another child came in to get a book from his tray, but took the opportunity to walk around the room in an apparently leisurely fashion. By the end of the lesson, Kate was feeling very annoyed at the children's invasion of the space she was trying to preserve for her work with the group and resentful that the teachers did not appear to have them under better control. It was clear that she was quite in touch with her own feelings, but she remained very puzzled about why she and the pupils selected for her group should have been treated so badly when there was apparently a warm welcome for the work she was there to do.

Discussion

It appeared that envy and jealousy might have played important roles in the behaviour of the children and the staff at the school. Envy is an angry feeling that there is something good available which is being denied. Although the concept had been a part of psychoanalytic thinking from the time of Freud, Melanie Klein developed a different understanding of it. She considered that this experience derives from earliest infancy when the baby seeks to maintain an idea of a continuing sustaining presence (Klein 1977). This is later integrated with the notion of a painful and denying presence so that the infant no longer feels persecuted by the absence of nourishment and is able to function without wanting to attack the provider for its absence. In some people this integration never takes place and they are left unable to enjoy what is good and able only to attack what they most wish for. In most, this does not happen, but a feeling that there is some good thing which is being withheld can put both the child, and the child within the adult, in touch with the primitive wish to destroy what they cannot have.

The support teacher who goes in to a school in a visiting capacity to work with a small group of children can excite the envy of the other children and also the jealousy of the teachers, who may feel that the visitor is in a very privileged position because she does not have to cope with the larger numbers and the administrative minutiae of the usual school situation. The other pupils wonder why they have not been chosen for the special treatment, what it is that the special group is receiving, and what will happen to them as a result of their deprivation. The teachers, rivals for the response of the children in a triangular relationship with the visiting teacher, feel that this response, which is theirs by right, is in danger of being taken away. Kate managed to carry out some useful work with her group of children, but she reflected that, in setting up further work of this kind, she would attempt to engage the classteacher more fully in the planning for it and would acknowledge the problems she faced. She would also set out very clearly the aspects of the work which required the co-operation of the school, to give the staff a sense of being involved in and of contributing to the success of the work.

PRESENTATION 3

Ray worked for another support service and was asked to give some in-service training to the staff of one of the schools he routinely visited. He had thought about the topic he had been asked to talk about and considered he had some useful things to say. He had been talking to the assembled staff group for a while when the door opened and in came a man dressed as though he was a PE teacher. He carried a bag which he put down noisily and Ray was disconcerted by this inconsiderate behaviour. When the teacher opened his bag and took out a magazine which he then started to read, Ray's patience ran out and he said, 'If you don't want to be here, you don't have to stay.' The teacher picked up his holdall and walked out.

Discussion

As the group thought about Ray's experience and the discomfort it was still causing him a few days later, they reflected that this is the kind of thing which can easily happen in school and particularly with adolescent pupils. At a stage when the pupil is striving to become adult and to decide for himself what he will do and how he will do it, he is struggling with the fact that he is actually still a child, and subject to the rules and conditions laid down by the adults around him. This urge for independence is a healthy one and can lead to the ability to take responsibility for the self, but it sometimes involves a certain amount of conflict with adults in the interim. In the school where Ray had been presenting his training, it appeared that some of the staff, at least the one in question, might have been ordered into the session without any sense of its possible interest or relevance to him. This seemed to have left him feeling and acting like a disgruntled adolescent.

This was not the only aspect of the incident which interested the group of teachers. They wondered what had caused Ray to react in a hasty and irritated manner. It was becoming clear to the group that, in thinking about the times when they faced difficult situations in their work, they had to think not only of the emotional experience of the children, but also of that of the teacher. It has been well recognized that, in therapeutic situations, the patient, whether adult or child, transfers some of the feelings associated with earlier relationships to the person of the therapist in a process known as the transference (Freud 1976). It is also the case that, in many other situations, particularly when our expected reaction is not clearly laid down, we transfer feelings and attitudes from earlier experiences to a new situation. Many teachers (both male and female) have found themselves inadvertently addressed as 'Mum' by a child wishing to ask for help.

It is generally recognized that, in the therapeutic relationship, counter-transference is also an important factor. This is considered to have two aspects and to include both the feelings which the therapist brings from his own experience and his emotional response to what the patient brings. While the relationship of teacher to pupil should not be thought of as having the intensity of a therapeutic experience, it is helpful to recognize that emotional experiences similar to those described as 'counter-transference' can be a part of the experience of the teacher. In Ray's case, it was likely that there were two aspects to his reaction. He may have sensed the challenge in the PE teacher's manner and responded to it challengingly, rather than allowing it to inform his judgement about how he should deal with the man. He may also have been put in touch with feelings of his own associated with the experience of wanting to offer something of value to someone he wished to please, and finding his offering rejected. This can be a very uncomfortable experience and one which leaves a sense of vulnerability and a readiness to react with confusion and apparent petulance.

In discussing this episode, the teacher group suggested that a greater awareness of his vulnerability to this kind of situation would allow any teacher to be more objective in his reaction. They also felt that the challenging behaviour of pupil or trainee could perhaps be acknowledged as indicating his reluctance to take part and accepted as such without offering a rejection in turn. They felt that, as with Penny above, having your feelings (particularly the less 'worthy' ones) accepted, can allow pupil or trainee to feel that s/he has a place in the group and perhaps something to learn from it.

PRESENTATION 4

The following week's case was brought by Susan. She was a newly qualified teacher working in the reception class of a small primary school. She was very concerned about the behaviour of a 5-year-old who did not seem to be settling into school. Jack spoke very little and what he did say was very unclear. Susan found it difficult to give him tasks which he could do, except for using the computer. He seemed to like this, to be able to manage it competently and to be able to respond to some of the teaching activities on it. She could not, however, let him use it all the time because the other children needed to have a turn and it would be unfair if Jack was always using it. One of the times she described as finding most difficult was when she had to take the class to assembly. Jack would stand near the door instead of getting into line properly and would push at the other children, making sometimes quite aggressive attacks on them. Susan was worried that one day he would hurt someone and she was also concerned that parents, who often brought their children into the classroom at the start of the day, were beginning to complain about Jack. The class had to be conducted across a small, open area before they reached the assembly hall in another building. Here, instead of listening attentively to the assembly, Jack would spend the time rolling around the floor, distracting other children and being a severe embarrassment to his teacher.

The last comment was not one which Susan initially volunteered, but it became clear that Jack's behaviour was particularly painful to her as a new teacher. She felt open to possible criticism by the children in her class, by their parents, by her colleagues and by the headteacher. She felt apprehensive about what Jack might do next and fearful that his aggressive attacks would escalate. Despite being able to manage and teach the rest of the class quite effectively, she felt that her work was being undermined by Jack's behaviour and that he was almost making a personal attack on her. She felt so exposed by this that it was difficult for her to think about Jack's needs and the ways in which she might be able to meet them.

Discussion

As the teacher group thought about Jack and gained more information from Susan about him, it became clear that he had arrived at school quite unready for this difficult new experience. His language was delayed, especially when compared with that of his peer group, and he might have special educational needs. Nevertheless, as Susan's task was to develop his abilities from where he now was, it was important to think about whether there were ways in which she could help him. Jack had previously been at home most of the time. His language was at an immature level, but it was likely that within the home situation his needs could be understood and he could be helped to know what was required of him by a mixture of repetition, demonstration and signs. Much of this was still available, but it was confused by the large numbers of children and adults now surrounding him. He may have been very fearful of what was likely to happen to him, aroused by the apparent lack of structure, apprehensive about the rapidly changing environment and extremely frustrated by his failure to communicate his own needs and responses to the situation. In this context he had little opportunity to master in play any of the experiences which he was now being asked to face.

In some respects this mirrored Susan's own experience of being new, of having only a tenuous control over what was happening and of being uncertain about who to turn to for support. She began to think about ways in which she could give him a greater sense of being in touch with her, could ensure that he had a clearer idea of what was required of him, and could make some of the most frightening experiences, such as sitting in the vast space of the assembly hall, seem less overwhelming. The comparison with her own predicament surprised her at first, but helped her to think about how angry she felt when she thought about him. It seemed likely that Susan's anger was related to the feeling of smallness and vulnerability which she was experiencing and finding very uncomfortable. As a new teacher, she felt she ought to be able to manage her class well and Jack's behaviour reminded her of how fragile her feeling of competence might be. Instead of being aware of this, and acknowledging it, she had sought to rid herself of these feelings and had hoped that, by Jack's removal from her class, she would restore herself to full mastery of the situation. His apparently aggressive behaviours towards his peers could be seen as acting out similar angry feelings to those Susan had in relation to her situation as a newly qualified teacher. Finding this anger unacceptable in herself could, by a process referred to as 'projective identification' by Melanie Klein (1977), lead her to identify this part of herself in him, and feel that, in doing so, she was relieved of the need to bear it herself.

PRESENTATION 5

The balance between encouraging the healthy assertion necessary for learning and yet maintaining a mutual respect and concern is one which teachers often have to consider. Maxine taught in a unit for children with emotional and behavioural difficulties which was attached to a mainstream school. She brought an observation of two 9-year-old boys who had been playing a simple board game at the end of a morning session of basic skills work. She had become aware that of the two boys, Terry and John, only Terry seemed to be able to play consistently by the rules. They were playing snakes and ladders, and Maxine noticed that John's throw of the dice would frequently leave it on the floor where it was easier for him to 'read' the number he wanted without his opponent being aware of what he was doing. His counter was also liable to move to the bottom of a ladder or away from the top of a snake and, when he seemed in danger of losing the game despite these manoeuvres, he insisted that it was now time to pack up for lunch. Maxine was concerned that John would not always find himself playing with such an amenable character as Terry and that his inability to play by the rules would greatly affect both social and life skills.

Discussion

Bruno Bettelheim (1987) gives an absorbing account of the meaning which play has for the growing child. He speaks of the opportunity which play gives to the young child to gain mastery over the feelings which threaten to overwhelm him and over the difficult events with which he is faced in reality. He also talks of the 'magical' quality which the ability to win at a game may seem to have and the way in which games of chance are often those which give the child an opportunity to learn that there are rules of the game which, when followed, make it more satisfying.

Maxine knew that, at other times, John had been able to play a game of chance by the rules and that he had sometimes been able to lose without throwing a tantrum. She began to consider that other events in his life might have put him into the emotional state where he could not bear to lose and needed to cheat in order not to have to suffer this humiliation. She reflected that he had found the morning's work more than usually difficult and had seemed to find it hard to settle, wandering around the room in a distracted way and touching objects as though to reassure himself that they were real. She had an idea that his life at home might be particularly unsettled as, after a long period of angry scenes, John's parents had decided to part. Maxine recognized that he might especially need to feel the presence of a dependable adult who would be interested in his company since his sense of security had been undermined. At a time like this, it seemed that a game of chance could only exacerbate John's feeling of impotence and of the arbitrary nature of what he had to cope with. Maxine decided that offering him the chance to help her with a task at the end of the morning might be a more suitable activity than inviting him to compete with one of his peers as it would offer a period of undivided adult company.

PRESENTATION 6

The following week, Linda brought in a piece of written work done by 8-year-old Luke. She was rather puzzled because Luke did not usually take much part in class discussion and she did not regard him as a very able pupil, but on this occasion he had written a relatively long diary which was the children's activity first thing on Monday morning. It read:

> I went to my Dad. We go to see Pete and Jennie. I asked can you ake Pete and Jennie. Yes. Thank you Dad. We must be on our way. Where are we going to? The seaside. Good I like the seaside. We wont be there for long because we have to take you back to home. Bye Luke, bye Pete. We have to go home now.
>
> Are we home now Dad? Yes. Can I press the button Dad, please? Yes Sandra. Its me Luke. We were in the flat. I jumped on my bed. My Dad said are you tired Luke. Yes Dad I am tired today. Have a good sleep.
>
> In the morning I said to Dad are we going home. I am going to miss you dad. Then I went home. I didnt want to leave you dad. I couldnt go to sleep. Im missing my dad I love my dad. I want to live with my dad, mum and you. I love you and my dad. Why did you pack up, Mum.
>
> I want to know. Go to sleep Luke. We will cum back together one day. We might be back to make a family.

There was very little punctuation in the writing and several of the words had been spelt with the help of the teacher. She had written on it, 'What a long diary, Luke', but as she brought it to the teachers' group it was clear that she had been unsettled by the pain and longing which he had expressed.

Discussion

Such raw emotion is not frequently written about in what is often a rather sterile exercise and some of the most difficult experiences can be more manageable if they are read about or written about in the third person. But the opportunity to put his feelings into words was an important opportunity for Luke. The group of teachers was very moved by his writing and this allowed Linda to think about the sadness she had felt when she first read it and her wish, at the time, to distance herself from the pain. Her colleagues' willingness to talk about occasions when they had felt quite overwhelmed by loss made it possible for Linda to acknowledge how difficult these feelings can be, rather than having to deny them. On reflection, Linda felt that she could have received and acknowledged quite simply what he had to say in a way that gave validity to his experience and allowed him to feel to a greater extent 'contained' or understood.

The group had had a relatively short life, but the teachers who made up the membership felt that they had begun to understand more fully some of the ways in which their own feelings and those of the children they taught had an impact on the work they were able to do in school. This understanding clearly had implications for the way in which they would think about the children, for the way in which they developed management strategies and for the curriculum choices they made. In this sense, they were developing skills in therapeutic teaching because they would enhance the opportunity for emotional growth in their pupils and consequently their ability to learn. These thoughts were considered as they reviewed the life of the group and acknowledged some sense of the loss which they felt at the end of it. The group had in no way set out to be a therapeutic group for the teachers, but they had feelings about it and a wish that it might have continued. There was also an understanding that, in order to take children seriously, the teachers' own feelings needed to be taken seriously.

REFERENCES

Bettelheim, B. (1987) *A Good Enough Parent*. London: Thames and Hudson.

Brown, D. and Pedder, J. (1985) *Introduction to Psychotherapy*. London: Tavistock.

Caspari, I. (1976) *Learning and Teaching: The Collected Papers of Irene Caspari*. London: FAETT.

Freud, S. (1976) *Introductory Lectures on Psychoanalysis*. Harmondsworth: Penguin.

Klein, M. (1977) *Envy and Gratitude and Other Works 1946–1963*. New York: Dell.

Afterword

Steve Decker, Sandy Kirby, Angela Greenwood and Dudley Moore

The contributors to this book provide mostly anecdotal, qualitative evidence that taking children's emotional needs seriously yields worthwhile benefits. Its benefits are very apparent to those who work at the individual human level, but it would be naive to imagine that this area of work could attract finance on a large scale without evidence provided by a stringent analysis of results. Potential funders are most unlikely to be persuaded to invest in the kind of therapeutic work described unless the claims made for its value are justified by thorough research. In order to gain investment in the emotional health of our young people, a strong case needs to be made through a rigorous evaluation of a range of therapeutic approaches. Peter Hindley and Helen Reed in Chapter 7 show that it is possible to provide hard quantitative evidence to demonstrate the value of their work.

Roth and Fonagy (1996) have produced an extensive review of research into therapeutic work and its efficacy; they cite much evidence relating to adults, but far less relating to young people. Here is an area which desperately needs the attention of more researchers who can combine an appreciation of the qualitative aspects of the essential work of therapy with the rigour of investigative methods which will convince the more sceptical holders of the purse strings.

It is worth reminding readers that the valuable therapeutic resources described in this book are provided in only a few fortunate schools. The vast majority of educational institutions not only lack such resources, but also have little hope of gaining such help. It is imperative that the powers that be encourage and facilitate the availability of such resources as a right for all children.

As part of the development of resources, there is a clear need for a new specialist qualification in counselling children and adolescents. In recent years there has been a rapid growth in training courses for counselling adults. The time is ripe for the development of post-diploma courses in specialized areas such as counselling young people. The existing training in child psychotherapy, educational therapy, art therapy and play therapy is designed to meet the emotional needs of young people, although it is not nearly widely enough available. While a great deal of useful work follows from this training (as described in several chapters of this book), there remains a need for more accessible training for therapeutic work with children. If more workers are needed in this field, and this seems indisputable, then appropriate training is also needed for them.

Both research and training are at least medium-term issues, but it is clear from the examples within the pages of this book that more could be done in the short-term to meet the emotional needs of children in school, and there is enough experience and expertise to make a start on improving the quantity and quality of work being done in this area. There is no reason why preventative measures such as circle time (Chapter 10) and PATHS (Chapter 7) should not be much more widely used in education, while the apparently increasing number of children who have become emotional casualties in the system surely deserve the kind of therapeutic approaches described in other chapters.

From the evidence of our contributors it follows that taking the emotional needs of children seriously will involve:

1. Research programmes put in place to further test the efficacy of a range of therapeutic approaches with children in school, linked to realistic funding proposals.
2. Training courses developed to prepare experienced counsellors to work with children and adolescents.
3. Counselling and therapy made available on site for children and adolescents in all schools in order to enable early intervention in cases of emotional difficulties. This needs to be a real, additional resource, and not drawn from what already exists.
4. Emotional health/literacy being promoted positively in all schools. There needs to be specific training for teachers to facilitate this.

Such developments would demonstrate that there is a willingness to acknowledge the importance of taking children seriously.

REFERENCE

Roth, A. and Fonagy, P. (1996) *What Works for Whom?: A Critical Review of Psychotherapy Research*. New York: Guilford.

Trust in yourself. Your perceptions are often far more accurate than you are willing to believe.

Claudia Black

Name Index

Subject Index